Economics of Services

A Story of Transformation of Cinderella into the Queen of Hearts

Economics of Services

A Story of Transformation of Cinderella into the Queen of Hearts

Vijay K. Seth (Ph.D)
Faculty of Management Studies,
University of Delhi

Ane Books Pvt. Ltd.
New Delhi ♦ Chennai

Economics of Services - A Story of Transformation of Cinderella into the Queen of Hearts

Vijay K. Seth

Published by

Ane Books Pvt. Ltd.

4821, Parwana Bhawan, 1st Floor, 24 Ansari Road, Darya Ganj,
New Delhi - 110 002, Tel.: +91(011) 23276843-44, Fax: +91(011) 23276863
e-mail: kapoor@anebooks.com, Website: www.anebooks.com

Branch Office:

- Avantika Niwas, 1st Floor, 19 Doraiswamy Road, T. Nagar,
  Chennai - 600 017, Tel.: +91(044) 28141554, 28141209
  e-mail: anebookschennai@gmail.com, rathinam@anebooks.com

ISBN : 978-81-8052-205-5

Printed at R.K. Offset Process, New Delhi

For

Two Ocean Like Souls of Delhi School of Economics, overflowing with knowledge, compassion and humility.

***Prof.* K.L. Krishna**
***Prof.* V.N. Pandit**

The conceptualization of services by Adam Smith, the father of *economics* but *step-father* of *economics of services*, which transformed services into the *Cinderella* of economic activities in economic analysis (for more than two centuries).

> **"The labour of some of the most respectable orders in the society is like that of menial servants, unproductive of any value, and does not fix or realize itself in any permanent subject, or vendible commodity, which endures after that labour is past, and for which an equal quantity of labour could afterwards be procured.... In the same class must be ranked, some of the gravest and most important, and some of the most frivolous professions: churchmen, lawyers, physicians, men of letters of all kinds; players, buffoons, musicians, opera signers, opera dancers.... Like the declamation of the actor, the harangue of the orator, or the tune of the musician, the work of all of them perishes in the very instant of its production..."**
>
> **Smith [1776 (1961) pp. 351–352].**

The emerging significance of the *service economy* as explained in Thomas Friedman's, *The World is Flat*

> **"I had come to Bangalore, India's Silicon Valley, on my own Columbus-like journey of exploration. Columbus sailed.... to discover.... route to India.... India and the Magical Spice Islands of the East were famed at the time for gold, pearls, gems and silk—a source of untold riches.... I set out for India by going due east via Frankfurt.... Columbus was searching for hardware—precious metals, silk and spices—the source of wealth in his days. I was searching for software, brainpower, complex algorithms, knowledge workers, call centres, transmission protocols, break-through in optical engineering—the source of wealth in our days."**

Thomas L. Friedman (2005); *The World is Flat—Brief History of Globalized World in the Twenty-first Century*; Penguin Books p. 4.

PREFACE

As an individual who has been exposed to the ideas evolved by different schools of philosophical thought that originated in the fertile soil of India, I have come to accept one core principle of our existence—that there exists, in a strange and complex way, a unique relationship between the *microcosm* (i.e. individual or biography) and *macrocosm* (i.e. universe or history). This relationship between biography and history is quite obvious from my own transformation from a student of industrial economics to a student of economics of services. In this transformation of my biography, history has played a pivotal role.

In the mid 1960s and early 1970s, when I was being initiated and groomed as a student of economics, at the Delhi School of Economics, most of the developed economies had almost completed their transformation from an agricultural economy to being an industrialized economy. Since most developed economies had attained their development through industrialization, it was generally accepted that the road to development is through industrialization. This belief also received support from the writings on economic development, which were growing at an exponential rate after World War II. These writings established that industrialization and development are coterminus. Development economists at that time were also laying emphasis on the notion of *market failure*. Therefore, for developing economies, this period symbolized itself as a period of deliberately attempted transition from colonial pre-capitalist agrarianism to rapid industrialization. Therefore, as a student of that era, I got attracted to the study of industrial economics and development economics. This was quite an obvious choice because the study of industrial economics would provide knowledge regarding the functioning of industrial organizations, and development economics would equip me to identify appropriate policy instruments which will provide pace, direction and structure to the process of industrialization.

However, the study of development economics exposed me to the economics of education and human capital—thanks to the lectures given by Prof. A.K. Sen, who initiated a course on 'Economics of Education and

Manpower Planning' to make us aware about developments in the understanding of economists of developed economies, regarding the important role that education has played in the process of economic development. Prof. A.K. Sen happened to be one of the leading economists, alongwith Professors T.W. Shultz, Mark Blaug and Tinbergen, who were exploring the relationship between development and education. This understanding remained with me always, in my subconscious mind, and proved to be of great significance when I needed this understanding the most.

Despite this influence, I remained focused on these areas for a considerable period of my life. During this period of my love for industrial economics and development economics, I made attempts to study different aspects of industrial economy of India, and also did some work in the area of economics of education. I would have continued to study other related aspects of the industrial economy of India but an important historical event changed my choice.

In 1991, the Government of India experienced a payment crisis which necessitated borrowing from IMF for structural adjustment. The adoption of the structural adjustment programme required the initiation of the processes of liberalization and globalization. These changes in the policy regime led to several debates among Indian economists regarding its various consequences on the Indian economy. One such debatable issue, which divided Indian economists into two rival camps, was whether employment potential of Indian industries will increase or decrease after reforms. Accepting that the debate on the issue is quite relevant for the Indian economy, I adjusted my biography in response to the structural adjustment programme to seek answers to questions regarding the consequence of economic reforms on employment in Indian industry.

It is while pursuing my studies to get an answer to this question that I started exploring the experience of developed economies with regard to consequences of flexible labour markets on employment. My explorations were quite an eye opener because I realized that all the developed market economies have entered the stage of *post-industrialization* where they are experiencing job-less growth in their industries. There, the scholars were discussing *de-industrialization*. These developments have transformed these industrialized economies into service economies in which most of the new employment was emerging in the services sector whose contribution to national income and employment has become larger than the industrial sector. Moreover, the emerging integration of the service economy with new technological advances in the fields of information and communication has radically changed the mode in which services are being delivered in these economies. These new changes are manifest in the increasing global trade in services and emergence of several service-oriented multinational enterprises.

Similar trends are being observed in the case of some of the developing economies in general and India in particular; where services are growing much faster than the rest of the economy; both in terms of their contribution to national income and employment. It is now being increasingly realized that some developing economies are experiencing a transition from the primary sector directly towards services, without being fully industrialized. Similar is the experience of the Indian economy, which is emerging as an important global player in provisioning of services like software and BPOs. India is also emerging as a potential destination for outsourcing R&D in medicine and health care. Realizing the increasing importance of services in the Indian economy, Faculty of Management Studies, University of Delhi, where I am teaching, planned to launch a new programme on management of services (MBA (MS)). These new global, national and local-level changes impacted my biography. This is how I got transformed through the powerful forces of history—from a student of industrial economics to a student of services.

My experience as a participant in designing the course on MBA (MS), and my quest to understand the economics of services, led me to realize that there is paucity of literature which can be used to provide an understanding on economics of services to new inquisitive minds. It is not that economics of services is an underdeveloped area of economics but its literature is scattered in various academic journals and periodicals. Some of the literature is also lying unattended by the economists, in the writings of scholars belonging to other disciplines like Sociology and Geography. The present book is my modest attempt to fill this void—I have collected informations, ideas, concepts and theories from diverse sources at one place in this book with a certain amount of complementary research to make students and researchers realize that economics of services is a rich field to explore and cultivate.

Looking at the nature of my efforts, I am not claiming to make any original contribution to the subject; my originality lies in the explorations and collection of material from diverse and scattered sources and exhibiting them at a single place, so that readers can see for themselves the variety and richness of ideas on economics of services, and admire the beauty of the subject. In this sense, my role has been like that of an art collector who identifies valuable ideas, concepts and theories concerning the subject; having collected them, who has woven them to fit into their right places in the overall framework. Hence, my contribution is in the collection of precious stones (ideas) from different mines, spread across different mine fields located at diverse locations. After collecting these precious ideas, I have arranged them in a logical sequence at their right positions; with very little touching to maintain their originality while designing a necklace. However, while joining them I have had to bridge certain significant as well as insignificant gaps. If this necklace appears beautiful to the readers, I will feel that my objective has been achieved. Even if there is a single economist in this entire world who accepts that the necklace that I have prepared has an original design, it will give me immense happiness.

In the present book I have focussed on various macro-economic aspects of the service economy. I am planning to write another companion book which will address various micro-economic issues concerning the economics of services. In the course of writing this book, I have learnt a lot from the works of several scholars whose works have inspired me and have significantly influenced my thoughts on the subject. These scholars are V.R. Fuchs, W.J. Baumol, Jean Claude Delauney, Jean Gadrey, Daniel Bell, T.P. Hill, Joachin Singlemann, Ian Miles, Jonathan Gershuny, Manuel Castells and P.W. Daniels.

Apart from the scholars who have made a contribution to my understanding of the subject, there have been some other scholars who have rendered help either through their comments on earlier drafts of different chapters or by being a constant source of encouragement. These scholars are Professors Arup Mitra and B.N. Goldar of the Institute of Economic Growth, Delhi; Professors G.K. Chadha and Ashok Mathur of the Jawaharlal Nehru University, New Delhi; Professors C.P. Thakur and Raghav Gaiha, Vivek Suneja and Dr Harsh Vardhan Verma, Dr Tanuja Aggarwal, Dr Simrit Kaur, Dr Mala Sinha and Dr Sunil Sharma of the Faculty of Management Studies, University of Delhi.

I am equally grateful to the first two batches of the students of MBA (MS) programme of the Faculty of Management Studies, University of Delhi, on whom I experimented most of the ideas contained in this book. It was their encouraging feedback which gave me the courage to present these contents in the form of a book for larger readership.

I am dedicating the book to two great souls of the Delhi School of Economics, who have touched the lives of several scholars in different ways, including mine. These great souls are Professors K.L. Krishna and V.N. Pandit.

I will fail in my duty if I do not mention the quiet contribution made by my wife Meera Seth and daughter Arpita Seth in the writing of this book. It was their support, which I took for granted, that has been a constant source of inspiration and encouragement. I also want to place on record the continuous support and encouragement that I received from my bother-in-law, Shri B.B.L. Sharma.

Vijay K. Seth

CONTENTS

List of Figures

List of Tables

INTRODUCTION

In the contemporary economic analysis, it is accepted that contribution to national output can be made by adding value to natural resources through processing and transforming them, and also by transforming intermediate inputs and components into finished products. These material objects are described as *goods* in common usage. Along with these material goods, contribution to national output can also be made by improving the state of products and persons through a variety of intangibles like marketing, sales distribution, research and development, education, health and entertainment. These intangibles are referred to as *services* in the common parlance. Therefore, the aggregate output of an economy, during a particular period of time, consists of goods as well as services. However, for around two centuries, economic analysis recognized that only persons engaged in the production of goods perform productive work and that only their contribution should be accounted for while estimating national output. Earlier, economists undermined the importance of services because for them services were represented by 'domestic servants'.

In the 1930s and 1940s two economists, Collin Clark and A.G.B. Fisher, added a third sector, the *tertiary sector*, in the two sector model (consisting of only primary and secondary sectors) of economic analysis. This third sector provided the beginning for separately accounting for the contribution made by services to national income and employment. The collection of data on income and employment, categorized in terms of three sectors by development economists, led to the evolution, almost like a stylized fact, that with economic development, contribution of services to national income and employment increases. As a consequence of this fact, our generation is witness to a *quiet revolution* in the composition of economic activities in most of the developed market economies and also in the case of some of the developing economies. In their case, the provisioning of services have replaced manufacturing as predominant economic activities. This transformation has occurred quiet silently, therefore, there has not been any formal announcement of the historical event. This happening is quite unlike the declaration of the industrial revolution in 1770—very early and premature as the industrial economy emerged only in 1821 when the proportion of workers employed in the manufacturing sector in

England exceeded the employment in the primary sector i.e. 38 per cent and 28 per cent respectively [Neff (1943), Ashton (1948), and Dean and Cole (1969)]. It is interesting to note that even now economists are debating about the exact timing of the industrial revolution [Acemoglu and Zilibatti (1997), Galov and Weil (2000) and Lucas (2002)].

The emerging service economy has drastically altered the structure and functioning of the economy. The economic landscape, which was once monopolized by factories, has now been replaced by big malls and stores; cinema halls, branches of banks and insurance companies; chambers of lawyers, doctors and accountants; educational institutions, hospitals and nursing homes. The landscape has changed so much that industrial cities have been transformed into service cities. The grim history of deindustrialization and spatial restructuring that emerged thereafter left the cities of developed market economies with less options, except to compete with each other mainly as financial, consumption and entertainment centres [Harvey (1989) and (1989a) p.92]. The doomsday thinkers have started talking about *de-industrialization*; whereas optimists are talking about the *service revolution*. This transformation can be understood with the help of the fact that by "1990's the level of employment in the secondary sector of U.S.A. was 3 per cent (i.e. one million workers) less than its level in 1980s, meanwhile, service employment increased by 30 per cent (i.e. by 20 million workers)" [Daniel (1991) p.37]. Services are now contributing the largest share in national output and are also providing employment to a major proportion of the working population in most of the developed market economies of the world and also in the case of some of the developing economies.

The emerging symbiotic relationship between services, knowledge economy and information technology has created new forms of services, described as Information Technology Enabled Services (ITES). The emergence of ITES has made the transformation of industrialized economies into service economies almost complete. These new developments have made services the *Queen of Hearts* [Fuchs (1968), Bells (1974), Boden and Miles (2000) and Adrey and Gallonz (2002)]. In altered circumstances, the key determinants for creating wealth no longer seem to be land or material objects; instead, it is technology driven by knowledge and services which have emerged as the leading determinants of economic growth. It is now being increasingly realized that only those economies have the potential to grow faster which have efficient and better quality of services.

Services have always existed, in one form or the other, in almost all kinds of social and economic formations. Like all other economic activities, services also emerged as a consequence of the emerging complexities in social and economic division of labour. Despite this fact, it is quite revealing to note that until the beginning of the twentieth century, a dominant part of mainstream economic analysis considered the service sector an unproductive sector of the economy, and the persons who performed service occupations were considered parasites, serile and unproductive, i.e. the *Cinderella Sector* of the economy [Boden and Miles (2000)]. This bias against services in economic analysis emerged through the writings of physiocratic economists and it continued to dominate the thinking of classical economists; it became almost like an orthodoxy or dogma in the writings of Marx and Marxist economists. Until recently, this view remained dominant amongst the economists of socialist planned economies of Eastern Europe and U.S.S.R. It was based on the premise that services have certain characteristics which make them incapable of contributing to accumulation—intangibility, non-storability, non-transportability and non-tradability due to non-separability between services and their producer, and also due to simultaneity between their production and consumption.

This suggests that the writing of a biography of the economics of services amounts to retelling the story of Cinderella. The character of Cinderella was initially, perhaps, created by the French intellectual, Charles Perroult. In this story, Cinderella is a beautiful girl who is left at the mercy of her malicious stepmother and two step-sisters upon the death of her father. Enters a fairy godmother in her life who magically transforms her into Claudia Schiffer in a Valentino dress and glass shoes. This transformation helps Cinderella in drawing the attention of the crown prince who, subsequently, crowns her as the queen of hearts. Only variation between the biography of Cinderella and the biography of economics of services is that unlike Cinderella, services had been left to live the life of Cinderella at the mercy of their stepfather (Adam Smith, the father of economics) and stepbrothers (other classical and Marxian economists).

Even in modern economic analysis, conceptualization and theoretical analysis of services and debates regarding their role in the process of economic growth emerged only after World War II. This is because in mainstream economic analysis, economists do not draw distinction between goods and services. Instead, it is based on the premise that the ultimate object of production of goods and services is to provide satisfaction to the consumers. Therefore, economists never felt a need for evolving a separate theoretical framework for analysing services. Adam Smith's views were a product of his time; he wrote his book, *Wealth of Nations*, when factories were gradually covering the landscape of England and had begun to produce large quantities of goods. Production of services reduced the availability of workers for factories. Therefore, the obvious choice was to state that services were unproductive.

After World War II, a new discipline emerged in economics, described as development economics. Theories of development were evolved in response to the need of post-war reconstruction of developed economies and to provide guidance for policy interventions in the developmental efforts of new independent economies, which were given a common category—underdeveloped economies or developing economies. Development theories established that industrialization and development are coterminus. They evolved a development ideology which propagated the idea that industrialization is an important instrument for achieving not only higher rates of growth but also to achieve socio-economic transformation. In this development ideology only those services received attention which were either part of preconditions for achieving industrialization or were considered as complementary to the process of industrialization [Meir (1970), Leibenstein (1975), and Seth (1987)]. Services could not draw the attention of economists because, for a considerable period, they were highly regulated and some of them were supplied by state monopolies. Moreover, economists did not attempt the economic analysis of services because they found it quite difficult to measure output and prices of services more accurately.

Though mainstream economics appears to have ignored the analysis of services, there were some scholars who explored various aspects of services. Their explorations led to the birth of economics of education, health economics, transport economics etc. It is because of the efforts of these economists, that the rise of service economics does not seem like a sudden dropping from the heavens. It is, in fact, the culmination of a long drawn-out process of human society. Each stage of human evolution created new services which helped in sustaining that stage of development; some of them were remnants of earlier stages and some which lost their relevance in new circumstances got destroyed. The progress of society and economy has been described in terms of three revolutionary changes (i) neolithic revolution (ii) industrial revolution and (iii) information revolution. Neolithic revolution is being described by anthropologists as cultures that included the knowledge of cultivation of crops and rearing of animals which together form part of the agrarian economy [Daniels (1943)].

Once man learnt about the domestication of animals and plants, he created a system of social organization in which he developed capabilities to control, increase and improve the supply of food. This form of organization increased the attachment of man with a defined geographical space. The increasing agricultural surplus, along with advantages of a settled life, helped in the emergence of social and economic division of labour. The specialization of socio-economic functions led to the birth of royalty, nobility, clergy, army, judiciary, craftsmen and various kinds of artists. This organization also created certain low-end services of barbers and also a large group of services which were performed by domestic servants. At this stage of evolution of human society, the persons who were engaged in agriculture were considered productive. This view was quite consistent with the historical social reality of the time because people engaged in other economic activities restricted the availability of workers for cultivation. This view was articulated by physiocrats in France. The crafts provided a pre-condition for the emergence of a stage in the process of economic development which has been variously described by scholars as the *protean-stage of industrialization* [Hobsbawn (1954)]; *Proto-industrialization* [Mendels (1972)] and *proto-factory* [Frendenberger and Redleak (1986)]. These terms are self-explanatory in nature, because they are describing a particular stage in the evolution of human societies which contained the seeds for the emergence of the industrial revolution [Seth (2003)].

At the apex of this process came the age of discovery: it refers to that period of history when attempts were made to discover new ocean routes to reach the countries of Asia, Africa, America and Australia. The discovery of ocean routes connected various centres of trade and crafts to one another and created conditions for the emergence of services like shipping, shipping insurance, banks, finance and international trade and commerce. Thus, for the first time, there emerged a rudimentary global economy of which Western Europe became the core region or centre. Within this European core region, in Great Britain, there simultaneously sprang a series of inventions regarding processing of cotton. These inventions, alongwith the invention of steam engine, transformed the proto-industry into the industrial revolution. The beginning of industrial revolution is dated in 1760 [Neff (1943) and Ashton (1948)] but the industrial economy actually emerged only in 1821 when, in Great Britain, the percentage share of working population employed in the industry exceeded the percentage share of working population employed in agriculture [Dean and Cole (1969) and Hoppit and Wrigley (1994)].

Improvements in services like transportation and communications are an integral part of the process of industrialization. As the size of the market expands, it increases the distance between location of inputs and the place of production, as well as the distance between the place of production and markets. The increasing distances enhance the turn-over-time of capital which is equal to production time plus the circulation time of the product of capital [Marx (1958) p. 248]. In industrial economies, the role of means of transportation and communication is to reduce the turn-over-time of capital. Therefore, the growth in services related to transportation and communication and the process of industrialization are intertwined processes.

As markets expanded, it led to increases in the size of the representative industrial firm, due to economies of scale. Integration of economies of scale and technological change created necessary conditions for the emergence of service related activities and occupations within the manufacturing enterprises. The culmination of this process was the rise of mass-production processes based on the use of assembly-line and extreme use of vertical integration to make products for mass markets, known as Fordism [Kenny and Florida (1993), Amin (1995) and Seth (2001)]. The process of vertical integration, to internalize the economies within the industrial enterprise to maximize the economies of scale, also facilitated the integration of different service related activities within the manufacturing organizations. The service occupation and activities, that got integrated within manufacturing, consisted of large armies of technocrats and administrators which were required to coordinate activities, provide specialized services and manage the enterprises, once the separation between ownership and control occurred [Berle and Means (1932)]. These categories of workers belong to those occupations which can neither be described as workers nor as owners of capital. The workers form the bulk of factory managers, belonging to different functional areas like accounts and finance, sales, marketing and distribution, personnel administration and human resource management, specialized engineers, scientists engaged in designing and industrial R&D. The stratum of workers consisting of these service occupations has been variously described by scholars as *managerial revolution* [Burnham (1941)]; *pecuniary class* [Veblen (1961)]; *new industrial middle class* [Drucker (1956) and Deherendorf (1957)]; *technostructure* [Galbraith (1967)] and *industrial bureaucracy* [Bendix (1956)]. These workers are also described as *non-production workers* [Delhanty (1968), Seth and Bhasin (1978) and Seth and Aggarwal (2004)].

Services grow in industrial economies as a consequence of the transformation occurring in the mode of organization of production and consumption which happens as a result of the emerging strong symbiotic relationship between economic activities and markets. It was the mode of organization of production at the stage of mass-production (or the supply side of the industrial economy) which provided the necessary conditions for the growth of services. Mass-production necessitated the need for complementary *producer services* or intermediate services [Daniel (1982)]. The complementerity between manufacturing and producer services facilitated the growth in several services like accountancy, marketing and distribution, legal services and consulting services [Daniel and Moularet (1991)]. Expansion in the methods of mass-production led to increases in other complementary services also because mass-production cannot be sustained unless and until there is concurrent expansion in wholesale and retail trade, financial services, insurance and real estate (FIRE) [Bell (1973)]. The process of industrialization and mass-production also increased the level of economic development which was manifested in the increasing level of income and employment. The increasing level of income, through its influence on demand side, led to the expansion in the demand for several income-elastic advanced social and personal services like health, education and entertainment.

By the 1960s, economists had realized the importance of education in economic development [Harbinson and Myers (1963)]. Various improvements in the growth theory had made it apparent to economists that the accelerations in the rate of growth of the economy cannot be explained solely in terms of traditional factors of production; a large part of growth in output remained unexplained. This unexplained residual was termed as *coefficient of ignorance* [Blaugh and Streeten (1963)]. Scholars tried to explain this unexplained residual, and some of them established that the unexplained changes in output can be attributed to the hetrogeneity that exists among various units of labour in terms of education experience and skills embodied in them [Abranovitz (1956) and Solow (1957)]. This realization amongst economists led to the emergence of a new branch of economics, known as economics of education, which makes the core of the economics of *human capital.* The term human capital includes the sum total of all acquired and useful capabilities of the population like education, skills, learning by doing and health. All these capabilities are forms of capital because they create productive stock embodied in man that provides returns, services and satisfaction over a future period [Schultz (1961)]. In the case of the American economy, it was estimated by economists that increases in the level of education between 1929–1957, per-person of labour force, explains 36–70 per cent of unexplained increases in the earnings per head [Schultz (1961) and Danison (1963)].

The concept of human capital created, amongst economists, the acceptability that educational services make permanent and durable changes in persons which can be accumulated in the form of capital. It is the human capital which not only develops the capacity to create new products and processes through R&D but also leads to technological changes and innovations. Moreover, efforts of human capital in R&D get transformed into patents which can be freely traded in the market. Companies like IBM, Intel, DuPont, Pfizer, Microsoft, Dell, Compaq, Sun Micro Systems developed unique benefits from their consumer-brand-awareness to reinforce their patent brands and strengthen their corporate bond [Berman (2002)]. Expansion in educational services also directly contributes to the process of capital formation through its impact on improvements in productivity, efficiency, profitability and higher levels of income and savings.

In a similar vain, economists also realized that improvements in health can also affect changes in the level of national output by providing availability of more healthy days of work to each person and also by prolonging the life of each individual so that each individual can contribute to national output for a longer time [Anderson (1990) and Fuchs (1972)]. In this way one can visualize that education increases the *quality* of human capital and health increases its *durability*. According to the human capital concept, individual's invest in themselves through expenditure on health to increase their income. It is not only health care *per se* that consumers demand, but also inputs of health to produce health. A consumer does not purchase health passively, instead, actively produces it by spending time as well as money. Health lasts for a longer time period and it does not get exhausted at the instance of its consumption. Therefore, it can also be treated like capital or as capital investment because it increases the number of healthy days available for work and thus helps in increasing income [Grossman (1972) and (1972a)]. This suggests that *health capital* differs from other forms of human capital because, while education and skills influence market and non-market performance of an individual, stock of health capital determines the total amount of time that an individual can spend producing money income and commodities [Grossman (2003) p. 350].

Economists have also realized the significance of media and information services in adding value to the image of organizations and goods. These services add value through advertisement expenditure which helps in developing the image, brand and brand equity of the organization and goods. Brand equity becomes an important component of intangible assets of the organization which can be accumulated and also provides returns. This brand equity can be encashed in the form of goodwill by trading it in the market.

The economic significance of all three processes which facilitate the rise of the service economy, as an economy travels along the path of economic development, was made obvious by two economists, A.G.B. Fisher and Colin Clark, with close Australian association. They are attributed with being the first to explore the possible relationship between economic growth and structural changes. Their works were published in the 1930s and 1940s, when developed market economies were experiencing recession. Their contribution is now knowns as *Fisher–Clark hypothesis*. This hypothesis suggests that high-level of growth in real income will be accompanied by a higher proportion of work force engaged in tertiary or service sector [Fisher (1933), Fisher (1939), Fisher (1949) and Fisher (1954); Clark (1938), Clark (1940) and Clark (1947)]. Their empirical work led to a debate amongst economists during the 1950s and 1960s [Baur and Yamey (1951), Triantis (1953), Mink (1955), Kuznets (1957), Chenery and Taylor (1968); Katouzian (1970) and Haig (1973)]. In the 1960s Fisher-Clark hypothesis was further extended by Baumol (1967) who stressed the distinction between *progressive* and *non-progressive* services [Baumol (1967)].

It was perhaps Fuchs who officially declared the arrival of the first service economy in U.S.A. by giving the title of his book, *The Service Economy* [Fuchs (1968)]. The same kind of empirical work was conducted by Singleman (1979) to explain the process of transformation which transforms an agricultural economy into a service economy. This conceptualization was further extended by Bell (1974), who envisaged that the emergence of the service economy is inevitable as a consequence of economic growth in most economies of the world. In fact, the increasing dominance of services in developed economies has been described by him as the emergence of *Post-Industrial Society* [Bell (1974)].

According to Bell (1974) "Post-industrial society is based on services. Hence, it is a game between persons and the game is poised in favour of the person who has more information and knowledge" [Bell (1974) pp. 126-127]. Post-industrial society emerges at a stage when services have begun to dominate in the contribution to income and employment in an economy and manufacturing sector experiences a relative decline (de-industrialization). Bell's work received empirical support from the study of Porat (1977) and Naisbitt (1983). The decline in manufacturing activities does not mean that manufacturing activities disappear; it simply means that the relative contribution of manufacturing to income and employment declines [Castells (1996)]. Even in his futurological work, Toffler (1980), who evolves future scenarios of societies in terms of *waves*, projects that the *Third Wave* (first wave being stage of agriculture and second wave being industrial economies) includes a combination of information revolution, high technology and services. Several scholars have analyzed the structure of the emerging service economies and factors that are influencing the perception of economists regarding services [Stanback (1981) and Inman (1985)]. The evolution of service economies began in 1960s in the North America (i.e. U.S.A. and Canada). After two decades, it crossed the Atlantic and reached Europe. It has already moved to Asia in Japan and the Indian economy is also waiting in the wings.

The conceptualization of the service economy was based on the development experience of Western developed economies. The basic premise of this conceptualization was that increasing incomes of households, as a consequence of economic growth, has made shifts in the tastes of consumers from inferior (material goods) to superior goods (i.e. services), because demand for material goods gets satiated very fast. The shifts in demand for the consumption of services leads to the emergence of service economy—this was perceived as the process of de-industrialization. This theme created a counter movement amongst economists who started advocating that the excessive growth of service economy was putting additional burden on the industrial economy. The apprehension of some of the economists can at best be represented by their fear that in future most people will be employed in barbershops, laundaries and serving fast food [Feketebuty (1988) p. 62]. Therefore, they started advocating for initiating policy interventions to achieve re-industrialization. Some of these economists went to the extent of stating that "if consumer demand is shifting to services, this is a symptom of cultural decadence, the growth of the domestic consumer culture, welfare dependency, rather than a creative and production oriented society" [Boden and Miles (2000) p. 4].

The possibilities that in future economies will be dominated by services led to different kinds of reactions from different economists. One set of response was led by Gershuny (1978), which has been described as *Neo-Industrial Theory of Self-services* by some economists [Delauney and Gadrey (1992)]. The economists adhering to this strand of thought believe that in future relatively larger share of services will be produced in the household by combining the purchases of consumer capital goods and unpaid inputs of self-service. Some of the scholars belonging to this strand of thought are trying to rehabilitate the importance of the industrial sector. These scholars believe that even now 'manufacturing matters' [Dornbusch *et al* (1988) and Schmid (1988)]. The other set of responses came from economists who have been contributing to the theory of *Neo-industrial Society*. These economists accept the increasing contribution of services to production and also accept that there are possibilities of technological changes and innovations in services [Machlup (1962) and Parker (1975)]. However, it should be mentioned that the post-industrialization view, which visualizes growth in services as a consequence of shifts in consumer demand, and the other view contained in the idea of de-industrialization, which still believes that services are an unproductive sector of the economy, are extreme views. The fact remains that services have now got integrated with the rest of the economy through complicated linkages; therefore, they reinforce the growth of each other.

The spread of the service economy has increased since the advent of revolution in information technology which has significantly altered the meaning of several conventional concepts in economics. Information has now become a fourth factor of production alongwith the traditional factors like land, labour and capital. Information revolution has revolutionized activities relating to generating, processing, transmitting, dissemination, storing, archiving and retrieving of information. Information revolution has diffused quite rapidly across all the sectors of the economy, alongwith services like finance, banking, insurance, hospitality, health care, education and entertainment. The symbiotic relationship between services and information technology has led to the emergence of the knowledge economy in which the most important factor is knowledge. The knowledge economy has transformed the character of the service economy beyond recognition [Law (2000)].

The integration of information and communication with services has made services relatively more *footloose* in comparison to manufacturing. Digital communication with light beams through fibre optics has become immensely fast, accurate and efficient. Therefore, it no longer matters where the service enterprise is located. Fax machines, photocopiers, telex, telephone and filing of documents have converged into a single box, the personal work station. Hence, one can carry one's office anywhere in the world which is connected with the power of communication. For example, until recently, bookkeeping meant classification of transactions into account books in essentially the same way that an accountant did during the days of the industrial revolution. Today, with the help of computer software, an accountant can store entire accounts in a floppy disk or a C.D. This possibility has revolutionized accountancy and has transformed it into a globally traded service. The world's largest accountancy firm, Peat Marwick, now operates in each of the continents.

Until recently, if a person intended to use the services of a library or intended to book an airline ticket, he had to visit the booking office of the airline and library personally during office hours. The integration of libraries and airline offices with the Internet and availability of a personal computer now equips the person to use the library and book an airline ticket at any time, without going personally, from anywhere in the world. Adam Smith described services as an unproductive activity because "it perished in the very instant of its production"—this argument is no longer valid. The symbiosis that has occurred between services and information and communication technology has made many services storable, transportable and separable from their producers, and hence tradable. Services also require specialized infrastructural facilities—comparable to the kind of infrastructure that was needed to facilitate the process of industrialization. Manufacturing needed well developed infrastructure in the form of means of transportation like railways, highways, power stations, canals, harbours, suitable locations, silos etc.; modern services also require data highways, VANS, LANS, ISDNS, computer workstations, optical fibre cables, teleports, intelligent buildings, communication satellites and data banks for their proper growth. Information revolution has affected services in the same proportion as assembly-line had affected manufacturing in the twentieth century. With the help of information technology, it is now possible to produce services in assembly-line like format. Now services can be assembled from different components, packed, stored and shipped with very low costs [Karmakon (2004)].

Before the emergence of revolution in information technology, most services were consumed at the same location where they were being produced. Therefore, foreign direct investment (i.e. establishment of service enterprise) or movement of natural persons as consumers or as producers of services were necessary for their trade. However, this scenario has altered in recent times. The altered scenario has facilitated the magnitude of global trade in services. The evidence of increasing magnitude of trade in services can be understood with the help of the fact that international trade in services has been growing at the same rate as trade in goods had grown in the 1990s i.e. about 6.5 per cent per year. During the period 1990–2003, trade in commercial services grew by six per cent per year on an average, and the share of service trade to total trade remained at about 20 per cent. Despite the fact that the share of services sector in national income has reached around 72 per cent in the case of developed economies and around 52 per cent in the case of developing economies, the global trade in services accounted for merely 20 per cent of total trade in 2002 [IMF (2003)]. This is largely due to the fact that trade in services is not yet liberalized to the extent that trade in goods has been liberalized or due to the fact that some of the services are not yet tradable. Therefore, an alternative way to trade in services is by setting of local operations through FDI mode. This shows that there exists a great potential for trade in services. This is because international business is not possible without globalized trade in services [Blouin (2000) and Chanda (2003)].

The significance of trade in services has been recognized in the international arena; this recognition gets reflected in its inclusion in the multilateral trade regime in the Uruguay Round of WTO. However, commitments taken by WTO members at the Uruguay Round with respect to services were targeted at specified services. The General Agreement on Trade in Services (GATS) includes all the services provided by service providers of one country to another country. These services might be supplied in the territory of one country to the consumers of another country (e.g. tourism and education); or services supplied through the presence of establishments of one country in the territory of another country (e.g. banking, finance and insurance); or services provided by the natural persons of one country in the territory of another country (e.g. consultant, software experts); and construction workers [Nayyar (1988)]. Despite the fact that the importance of services is increasing in international trade, economists have not paid proportionate attention to different issues related to trade in services. This neglect can be attributed to two extreme positions held by economists. There are some economists who believe that there is no need to evolve a separate theoretical framework to explain the issues related to trade in services, because they assume that theoretical contributions made by economists to enrich the international trade theories are also appropriate for analysing trade in services. On the other hand, there are also some economists who take extreme and opposing view; they believe that services cannot be traded therefore there exits no urgency in evolving an elaborate framework to explain the trade in services [Sampson and Snape (1985) and Bhagwati (1984)].

If one agrees with the premise that services are essentially non-tradable because they need proximity between producer and consumer, it is not acceptable because even then there is a way to serve foreign markets—by setting up local global operations through Foreign Direct Investment (FDI) mode. This view is supported by the fact that in FDI mode, share of trade in services is growing quite rapidly. This is supported by the title given to the World Investment Report of 2004 prepared by UNCTAD: *World Investment Report—Shift Towards Services* [UNCAD (2004)]. FDI has grown, over time, in all the three sectors but its sectoral composition has shifted in favour of services. FDI in services has been growing in capital intensive as well as human capital intensive services. In the service sector, global FDI stock more than quadrupled during 1990–2002. As a result of faster growth of FDI in services, as compared to other sectors of the economy, the share of inward FDI was around 60 per cent of global stock in 2002 [UNCTAD (2004) annex Table A.1.18 and A.1.19]. One of the reasons for the growing volume of FDI in services is that slowly liberalization of trade in services is occurring. Until recently, many service industries were closed for foreign investment, for various national, strategic, social and political reasons. However, the process of liberalization and globalization that began after the 1980s also facilitated the growth of FDI in services. The impetus to FDI in service received dramatic turn after the Uruguay Round of WTO which has helped in reducing the barriers to FDI in services.

Service multinational firms have immensely benefited from the new developments which have helped in reducing barriers to FDI in services. These new developments have provided preconditions for the emergence of services-specific theories of FDI and multinational operations. Much of the literature on the subject is concerned with the explanation of FDI through the factors that motivate a national service firm to control foreign operations through equity participation. The theories that explain FDI in goods producing firms have finally come to terms with the *eclectic paradigm*, which explains the increasing incidence in FDI mode arising due to ownership advantages, locational advantages and internationalization advantages [Dunning (1981) and Dunning (1988)]. However, it has now been increasingly accepted that service firms usually use a wide range of arrangements, other than the equity arrangement, to control their foreign operations [Sauvant and Mallampally (1993)]. Such forms include franchising, management control, concessions, partnerships, turn key, build operate and transfer (BOT), and build transfer and operate (BTO) projects. For example, in the hotel industry, partially owned foreign affilitates accounted for only 36 per cent of overseas operations in the 1990s; the rest of the arrangements took non-equity mode [Contractor and Kundu (2000) p.300]. Similarly, amongst the multinational airline companies, *code sharing* arrangements constituted 75 per cent of agreements and joint ventures consisted of only four per cent of their global operations [UNCTAD (2004) p.108]. The provisioning of services involves greater human element, which results in quality variability in the supply of services. Due to this distinguishing feature of services, ownership related advantages of the service provider are far more crucial than in the supply of goods. Moreover, some of the services require face to face contact between producer and consumer of service. Therefore, these services can be traded only where buyers and sellers are located at the same place. These two important characteristics of services compel the service enterprises, which want to trade their services, to become multinational firms.

The present study deals with all the macro-economic issues related to services that have been discussed above. The main objective of the study is to provide to the reader a sort of biography of economics of services. The study begins with analysing the process which led to categorizing them as the Cinderella sector of the economy and how the services achieved the status of queen of hearts. For this purpose, the study traces the treatment given to services in economic analysis in historical perspective. This is the subject matter of chapter I of the present study. In chapter II, an attempt has been made to evaluate different premises that have been used by economists to conceptualize services. This is also, in fact, an exercise to the biography of economics of services in terms of different bases that have been used to evolve the concept of services. The different bases of conceptualization of services implicitly bring out the attitude of economists towards services. Chapter III extends the analysis of conceptualization of services to the understanding on different premises that are being used to categorize services. In chapter IV, an attempt has been made to understand the experience of developed and developing economies regarding inter-sectoral shifts in employment. It also narrates different empirical methods which have been used for analysing these shifts. Chapter V deals with shifts in the composition of employment among different services. This exercise has been done because it is being felt by economists that different services are rooted in different socio-economic formations, therefore, different services have varying kind of relationship with the process of development: some experience a decline, while others become important as the economy grows. To evaluate this aspect of employment in services, we have also analyzed the changing composition of employment in services. Chapter VI deals with the issues related to treatment given to services in the national accounting framework. This chapter analyses how the attitude of economists has changed, over time, to account for contribution of services to national income. In this chapter, the problems regarding comparison of contribution of services over time and over space (i.e. international comparisons) have also been dealt with.

In chapter VII, we are focusing our attention on issues related to global trade in services. The issues discussed in this chapter are—how far trade in services is different from trade in goods and whether theories on international trade evolved by economists can be used to explain trade in services or not. This chapter also deals with the understanding to barriers to trade in services and how the magnitude of these barriers can be estimated.

Chapter 1

Services in Economic Analysis

In common usage, the term services refers to activities that are engaged in the production of intangibles. This interpretation of the term encompasses a wide spectrum of economic activities like trade and commerce, transport and communication, banking insurance and financial intermediaries, hospitals and hospitality, research and consultancy, education and training, arts, sports entertainment and mass-media. It also includes the activities of state institutions, voluntary organizations and activities of liberal professions. Personal services rendered by service enterprises like repair and maintenance, malls and departmental stores, beauty parlours, restaurants, fast food outlets, call centres, or in the household by domestic servants are also included in the term services.

Since the origin of the social and economic division of labour, services have continued to exist, in one form or another. Even in tribal societies tribal chiefs, *shamans*, faith healers, traditional medicine men provided services to the members of their tribes. Each stage of social and economic transformation created some new services and, in the process, destroyed some other services. Therefore, services have also been victims of the ongoing process of *creative destruction* because of which their composition, at different stages of socio-economic development, also keeps changing. These changes in the composition of services have influenced the attitude of economists and policy makers towards services.

In contemporary economies, the composition of services includes some services that are remnants of past distinct socio-economic structures, some others are having complementarity with the existing socio-economic structure and some have originated as a manifestation of the changes which are likely to emerge in the socio-economic structure in the future. This suggests why most economies have quite a heterogeneous group of services co-existing contemporaneously. The existing diversity in the composition of services, and the fact that they have roots in distinct stages of evolution of societies, makes it difficult to conceptualize services in a manner which can be all encompassing. In the present chapter, an attempt has been made to study how services have been treated by economists in economic analysis at different stages of evoluation of the subject. The purpose of this exercise is to understand the process of transformation of services from the status of Cinderella sector of the economy to being the queen of hearts. For the purpose of this exercise, this chapter has been divided into four different sections and each section deals with how a specific paradigm of economics has incorporated services in the economic analysis. Therefore, section I deals with how services were treated in the early writings of the economists. Section II deals with the treatment given to services in the economic analysis evolved by classical economists, section III deals with the treatment of services in the writings of Marx and Marxian economists and, finally, in Section IV, we are describing the treatment given to services in contemporary economic analysis.

I. Services in the Writings of Early Economists

For a considerable period of economic history, services were a marginal phenomenon. A dominant part of services existed in the form of personal services of domestic servants employed by the middle and upper classes. In pre-industrial societies, because of low productivity, there existed a very high percentage of under-employed masses. These under-employed workers were available in abundance and at very low costs. Therefore, they were usually distributed in low end agricultural activities and were hired for several domestic services. The British Census Report of as late as 1851 shows Britain as an economy in which agriculture and domestic services were the main occupation of labour force [Landes (1969)]. The dominance of domestic services in the economy is also revealed in *Vanity Fair* where the author mentions about Bekley Sharp and captain Crawlay who are penniless, yet, they have a domestic servant. Karl Marx, with his large family, lived in Soho in 1850. Even though he was sometimes evicted for failing to pay rent, he had a faithful servant, Lenchen [Bell (1974) p. 126].

In India, two distinct institutions were created to provide services to communities at the local level which were apparently devoid of any market relationship. These systems were *baluta* and *jajmani* systems. In *baluta* system, hereditary functionaries supplied services of barbers, laundrymen, watchmen, folk artists, priests and domestic servants to all the members of the village community in exchange of equally specific payments, generally in kind but sometimes accompanied by certain amount of cash. These payments were made at the time of the harvest, occasions like birth, marriage and death and on festivals. *Jajmani* system, on the other hand, can be described as an organization evolved for symbiotic existence between patron households and service providing households, in lieu of customary payments on occassions as mentioned above. These two systems have been described and discussed in detail in different writings in sociology and economic history [Wilson (1936), Fukajawa (1972) Commander (1983), Fuller (1989) and Mayer (1993)]. A reference to this system also exists in the writing of Max Weber, who termed this system as *demiurgic* [Weber (1950)]. According to Weber, villages used to allot common land to village craftsmen, temple priests, barbers, laundrymen etc belonging to the village. They were not paid for their services on a job basis but in the form of a share of land or a share at the time of harvest [Weber (1950, p 22, Fukajawa (1972), Guha (2004)].

The dominance of personal services and domestic services in the agrarian economies, and also during the early phases of industrialization, explains why, for considerable period, economists ignored the inclusion of services in economic analysis. According to the thinking of economists, these services were not of great significance for the economy and existed as a consequence of wasteful expenditure of the landed gentry. Therefore, they thought that growth of national output solely consists of growth in material production (i.e. production of goods). This also suggests that, while economics was emerging as a distinct discipline, services did not draw the attention of economists.

The mercantilist school, which dominated the thinking of economists during the 16th and 17th century, had a very narrow view of the functioning of an economy. The views of this school are spread in the writings of Thomas Mun (1571-1641) and Josiah Child (1630-1699) in England, and Antoine de Mantchretien (1576-1621) and Jean Bodin (1530-1596) in France. The followers of this school believed that it is the stock of gold, that is in the possession of an economy, which is its real wealth. Gold has been the obsession of the Europeans during this period of history, also known as the *period of discovery,* during which the commercial horizons of Europe were vastly extended and pushed thousands of miles across the oceans of North and South America, Australia and Africa. It is a well known historical fact that their discovery of new lands were primarily motivated by stories of large volume of gold, silver and other precious stones in the possession of people inhabiting these lands. Chritospher Columbus, who opened the gates of America for Europeans, writes "Gold is a wonderful thing. Whoever owns it, is the lord of all he wants. With gold it is even possible to open the soul of the way to paradise" [Wright (2000) p.11]. There also exists the story of Atawallpa, the ruler of Peru, who was made hostage by Spaniard Castilian Francises Pizarrow and was killed despite paying the ransom of a roomful of gold and two roomfuls of silver for his freedom [Prescott (1847) and Wright (2000)]. The lust for gold among Europeans, at that time, was quite surprising to the people of other civilizations where gold had only ritualistic or iconic value, e.g. for Peruvians 'Gold was Sweat of Sun and Silver the moon's tears' [Wright (2000) p. 81].

The glitter of gold was so overbearing for the mercantilist economists that they not only undermined the importance of services, they also undermined the contribution made by other economic activities which did not help in increasing the stock of gold. However, they attached overriding importance to services such as trade and shipping, which helped in increasing the stock of gold. They accepted the importance of the services of State which also helped in increasing the stock of gold by manipulating terms of trade, for example, imposing protective tariffs.

Unlike the mainstream mercantilist economists, some of their contemporary economists like William Petty (1623-1687) of England and Pierrele Peasant de Boisguillbert (1646-1714) of France evolved a comprehensive framework of economic analysis which considered production of goods as well as services of equal importance for an economy [Delauney and Gadrey (1992)]. In his book, *Political Arithmetic,* published in 1676, William Petty included the civil services, defence services and services of professionals as a part of national income. He also anticipated the increasing dominance of services with economic development. However, amongst these two, Boisguillbert was a more consistent thinker about the role of services.

Boisguillbert explained his ideas in two important books, *Detail De France* published in 1697 and *Factum de France* published in 1707. He believed that the ultimate object of creation of wealth is *consumption* not *accumulation* as advocated by physiocrats, classical and Marxian economists. He viewed "that all riches of the world, whether belonging to the sovereign or to his subjects, are useless if they are not consumed" and "that the growth of a nation is in proportion to the growth in consumption" [Studenski (1958) p.14]. In his world view, he thought that a comfortable life includes the consumption of not only material objects (i.e. goods), but also of non-material objects (i.e. services). He writes, "comfortable life consists of complete enjoyment not only of necessities of life but also superfluities, including all things catering to the pleasure of senses which the continued corruption of human heart invites and refines from date to date" [Studenski (1958) p.15].

He also approached services from the perspective of service occupations and clearly mentions that their growth in an economy is associated with rising income levels. He describes this process in an interesting way. According to him, in a primitive economy, there will be four occupations but in a developed economy there will exist a multitude of them; beginning with occupations of baker and tailor who provide necessities and ending with that of an actor who symbolizes the last word in luxury and superfluity. In a way, he considers the work of performing artists as superfluous because an actor's work is to flatter the ears and satisfy the spirit often by fanciful tales which everybody knows is far from reality. Therefore, their services can be enjoyed only by those people who feel perfectly secure in their necessities and can afford to buy pleasant lies. Thus, he accepts that consumption of services of an actor are manifestation of higher income levels and prosperity. Boisguillbert also accepted a basic principle that "all occupations in a given country, whatever may be their nature... work for each other and maintain themselves reciprocally" and that "once having become part of a social body in the course of historical evolution, they can no longer be disjoined or separated without causing a fundamental alteration in a social body". This suggests that he never considered any occupation less productive, less socially useful, than the other occupation.

The ideas of Boisguillbert were turned upside down by French phyisocrats. Physiocratic tradition took roots in France in the 17th and 18th centuries with the writings of Francois Quesney (1694-1774), Mercier de la Riveire (1720-1793) and Dupont de Nemours (1739-1817). The economic doctrine of physiocrats emerged in response to historical conditions prevalent in France during this period.

French economy had lost in the race of industrialization and had also lost significant share in overseas trade and commerce due to a series of unsuccessful wars. However, it emerged as the richest agricultural nation of Europe. The landowners of France considered themselves as the most productive class of French society. Therefore, French economists evolved a world view which put farmers in the centre stage and undervalued the importance of industry, trade and commerce in which England was emerging as a leader in Europe.

In order to establish the supremacy of landowners, physiocrats treated agriculture as the only productive economic activity because it had the capacity to produce *economic surplus* over and above the cost of capital and labour. This surplus *produit net* emerges only in the agricultural sector due to the contribution of nature. This is shown in Quesney's *Tableau Economique*. In this economic table, the flow of income generation begins with the contribution of farmers and workers engaged in farming (i.e. productive classes), and reaches the hands of owners of land (i.e. the class which controlled the distribution of surplus) and, finally, the flow terminates after reaching the hands of non-agricultural classes. These non-agricultural classes have been described as *strile classes* by the physiocrats [Meek (1962) and Rubin (1979)]. Strile class consists of artisans, merchants, manufacturers, professionals and artists etc. These occupations and economic activities were considered unproductive because they were capable of producing value equal to only their labour and, therefore, were incapable of creating economic surplus. It is because of their stress on capability to produce economic surplus as a criterion to consider whether an economic activity is productive or not that they have not included services in their famous zig-zag graph, Tableau Economique [Baumol (2002)].

This concept of defining productive activities led to a dramatic shift in the understanding of services. This view, which adopted the criterion of generation of economic surplus to consider whether an economic activity is economically useful or not, put services in a state where economists did not consider them worth economic analysis. This view also created a bias in the minds of not only contemporary scholars, but also in the minds of most economists, now collectively known as classical economists, who evolved the criterion of *accumulation* for deciding whether an economic activity is *productive* or *unproductive*. Their notion of accumulation broadened the concept of economic surplus. This conception of productive and unproductive economic activities also influenced the thinking of Marx and Marxian economists who evolved the concept of *surplus value* from the term economic surplus. However, the criterion of *accumulation* of classical economists or *surplus value* of Marx made the physiocrats' concept of economic surplus much broader and made the entire material *production* of *goods* as productive activity while leaving only services as unproductive activities. This suggests that the process of converting services into the Cinderella sector of the economy began with the writings of physiocrats.

II. Services in the Writings of Classical Economists

Adam Smith, the father of classical economics, was highly influenced by the physiocratic writings; however, he extended the meaning of the terms productive and strile classes used by them by redefining their meaning. He included, in the category of productive workers, all the workers who are engaged in the production of material goods (i.e. both agricultural and industrial). This is because only workers engaged in the production of material goods were capable of returning a net income to the producer: in the case of agriculture it is economic surplus and in the case of industry it is profit. Therefore, workers who are not earning surplus for their employers are unproductive according to Smith. For Smith "there is one sort of labour which adds to the value of the object upon which it is bestowed. There is another which has not such effects. The former, as it produces a value, may be called productive, the latter unproductive labour" [Smith (1961)]. In his concept, productive work was limited to that kind of worker who (a) produces material goods for the market (b) produces a good which commands market price equal to the amount of labour required to produce it and (c) which adds value to the product equal to its maintenance cost and generates profit for the employer. All other kinds of workers who do not satisfy these conditions are described as unproductive.

While elaborating the nature of unproductive labour, he writes that "the labour of a menial servant adds to value nothing; the labour of some of the most respected orders in society is like that of menial servants, unproductive of any value and does not fix or realize itself in any permanent subject or vendible commodity which endures after that labour is past.... Their services, how honourable, how useful, or how necessary so ever, produce nothing for which an equal quantity of service can afterwards be produced.... In the same class be ranked... churches, lawyers, physicians, men of letters of all kind, players, buffoons, musicians, opera singers, opera dancers etc." [Smith 1776 (1961) pp.331-352].

Thus, by adopting accumulation as a criterion for classification of economic activities into productive and unproductive categories, Smith accepted that only primary and secondary economic activities were productive activities and grouped all the services into the category of unproductive economic activities. Therefore, in his overall economic framework, a nation is richer to the extent that it spends more of its income on durable commodities (i.e. goods) and less and less on intangibles i.e. services [Smith 1776 (1961), Book II, chapter III]. By shifting the basis of classifying economic activities from consumption to accumulation, following the logic inherent in the physiocratic tradition, Smith turned upside down the views held by Boisguillbert who described services of an actor to be a manifestation of prosperity, when he wrote that "Just as in times of opulence one reaches for the services of actors as the highest mark of luxury, so when misery strikes a people, their services are the first to be dispensed with in an effort at retrenchment of expenditure". Adam Smith, who was more influenced by Scottish philosophy of thrift and austerity and had political hostility towards aristocracy's wasteful expenditure on their own upkeep declared, after 100 years of Boisguillbert, that actors were unproductive.

Smith provides an exhaustive list of unproductive services. If we take the numerical strength of the persons involved in supplying these services, a significant part of the economy remains unproductive. For instance, these services constituted 22 per cent of the working population in Britain in 1700 and 30 per cent in 1820 [Madisson (2003) p.95]. In India, during the Moghul reign, 18 per cent of the total working population consisted of non-village economy which was primarily engaged in services, and out of the remaining 72 per cent of working population occupied in the village economy, a significant proportion also consisted of workers engaged in service occupations [Madisson (1971) p. 33]. The numerical representation of service activities and occupations in the total working population of France, of 10 million, towards the end of the eighteenth century is worth analysis. There were 1.8 million domestic servants, 0.2 to 0.3 million priests and nobility, 0.15 million lawyers, 0.2 to 0.25 million soldiers and naval persons. Therefore, these unproductive workers, according to the categorization of Smith's definition, consisted of about a quarter of the total working population [Delauney and Gadrey (1992) p.13-14]. This occupational pattern, according to Smith, has emerged due to wasteful consumption expenditure of the *ancient regime*. Their employment, according to Smith, was a loss to national wealth because it was competing with capital accumulation.

Hence, in the framework of Smith, all intangible products (i.e. services) become unproductive because "they perish in the very instance of their production". It is worth mentioning here that the concept of material production evolved by Smith, based on the criteria of accumulation to classify economic activities, facilitated the emergence of a particular mindset of economists which converted services into the *Cinderella Sector* of the economy [Boden and Miles (2000)]. His criteria ignored several services which were being supplied on the capitalist line, even at that time, with the use of hired labour and significant amount of capital, viz, the "service of innkeepers, stage coach operators, ship owners, bankers, owners of boarding schools and the like" [Studenski (1958)].

If one follows his categorization of economic activities, it becomes quite evident that classroom furniture and equipment, including chalk and blackboard, would be part of productive economic activities but the instructions of the teacher through which these goods acquire meaning will be unproductive. The set, costume, cameras, lights, musical instruments, all are products of productive activities, but actors, musicians, director of the motion picture are all unproductive, despite the fact that these artifacts are meaningless and useless without their services. Not only this, the absurdity of the argument makes us believe that the person who prints tickets for the performance of Ravishankar and Zubin Mehta is productive, while Ravishankar and Zubin Mehta are unproductive.

It is interesting to note that Smith accepted the inclusion of services like trade, transportation and storage in the estimates of national income because these services facilitated the completion of utility of material goods. According to Smith, these services play an important role in helping the utilization of material goods and without them the very meaning of their production will be lost. However, he did not extend the same logic to other services—after all, the very usefulness of the theatre building and musical instruments disappears without they being used by performing artists and musicians.

Despite its several logical inadequacies, the conceptualization of Smith remained very dear to most classical economists. Mill (1852) seems to have been in the process of evolving an alternative approach to that of Smith when he identified three distinct types of utilities, viz. (a) embodied in outward objects (i.e. goods) (b) embodied in human beings like education and knowledge in teacher, physician, clergymen etc. (c) direct services of performing artists, public services like those of the army, navy, judiciary and legislation [Mill (1832) p. 57]. Despite going so far, he could not overcome the habit of thinking in terms of productive and unproductive economic activities, and ended up being entrapped in the thinking of Adam smith. For example, according to Mill "all labour is, in the language of political economy, unproductive which ends in immediate employment without any increasing of accumulated stock of permanent means of enjoyment" [Mills (1852) p. 60]. He further elaborates this view by stating that "what is gained by an actor is a mere transfer from spectators funds to his, leaving no article of wealth for spectators identification. Thus the community collectively gains nothing" [Mills (1852) p. 64].

Precisely at that moment in history, when economists began to doubt the appropriateness of the materialist view of production evolved by Smith, his conceptualization of production received remarkable resurrection from the writings of Karl Marx (1818-1883), the father of scientific socialism. His ideas regarding the services sector are contained in his books, *capital Vol. II* and *Theories of Surplus Value*. Marx observed that the concept of Smith regarding productive and unproductive economic activities implicitly contains two different conceptualizations—one of the concept accepts labour in terms of the creator of *surplus-value* and accumulation of capital, and the other views labour in terms of producer of useful products or *use-value* for consumption. Marx believed that earlier scholars had emphasized the distinction between productive and unproductive labour only on the basis of creation of surplus value. Therefore, they lay stress on material production—that is—that labour "must fix itself in a more or less durable product" [Marx (1954)]. However, if we view labour in terms of creation of use-value for consumption then materiality or immateriality of the product ceases to be of great importance.

Hence, the fact that goods are more tangible than immaterial services does not make the labour engaged in manufacturing goods more productive. He describes that the concrete character of the labour and, therefore, its products do not, as such, play any part in the division of labour into productive or unproductive. Labour which helps in the accumulation of capital is productive. The use-value of the commodity, in which labour of productive labour is realized, may be of trifling nature. The material result has no relation at all with the quality of materialization of productive labour [Marx (1956)]. Hence, Marx was convinced that the contribution of services to accumulation depends on their locations in the capitalist division of labour. In his analysis, presented in the *Theories* of *Surplus Value*, Marx gives full credit to Smith for moving the idea that, under capitalism, only that labour is productive which creates surplus value for the capitalist. His analysis regarding materiality and immateriality of product suggests that Marx recognized that goods and services can be reproduced along the capitalistic line to earn profit and for the purposes of accumulation. However, he ignored the role of services in the process of accumulation and evolved his main thesis on the basis of materialization of surplus value through the production of only goods. He, therefore, ignored lots of services which were organized within the framework of the capitalist system of production even during his lifetime, like passenger services, railways, shipping and the services of telegraph agencies.

The undermining of services and acceptance of materialistic concept of production was essential to provide a strong basis for his political ideology. It was the materiality of the products which provided the logical justification to establish that surplus value which was created by the working classes was inappropriately appropriated by capitalists. The withheld portion of surplus value amounts to exploitation of workers. Hence, like physiocrats who elevated the status of French peasants, Marx helped in elevating the status of workers engaged in the production of *goods* (material) and also arming them with a theoretical construct which provided them the basis for organizing against capitalists. It was this conception of Marx which got embedded in the socialist thinking and, later on, became the basis of national income accounting in socialist economies.

The Marxist understanding of socialist economies like U.S.S.R. on services is ingrained on the premise that only production of material goods is productive. The official textbook on political economy published by U.S.S.R. states that "Political economy studies the laws of social production and distribution of material wealth. The basis of social life is material production [S.S.S.R. Institute of Economics (1962) p. 7 and Thalherm (1973) pp. 324-328]. In this way, the contribution of Marx helped in the continuation of bias of economists against incorporation of services in economic analysis. For classical economists, services were a remnant of feudalism and were products of wasteful expenditure of feudal lords: the expenditure on services could be saved and converted into capital stock. For Marx, since services could not be produced along the capitalist line, they were not worth considering for economic analysis.

Thus, for almost three centuries, the understanding of economists regarding services remained enshrined in the dichotomy between tangible (goods) and intangible (services) products; they considered only the production of tangible products worth economic analysis. One of the important consequences of this distinction created by classical economists, and adopted by Marxian economists, resulted in the formulation of national accounting framework known as *System of Balances of the National Economy,* popularly known as *Material Production System*, used by U.S.S.R. and other centrally planned economies of Eastern Europe until the 1990s. The philosophy underlying this framework of national accounting is that "all the multiplicity of form of economic activities in the national economy may be reduced to two main spheres: the sphere of material production and the non-material sphere of services... application of labour in each of these spheres differs substantially" [U.N.O. (1971) Para 11.4] and that "productive labour is considered to be the labour expanded on the production of goods" [U.N.O. (1971) Para 1.5].

III. Services in Contemporary Economic Analysis

The dichotomy between different determinants of value of a product can also be observed in the writings of classical Greek scholars. This dichotomy arose from an epistemological problem associated with the puzzle i.e. whether value of a product is based on its intrinsic quality or depends on subjective evaluation by the user of the product. This epistemological problem initially emerged in the writings of Aristotle which contains the seeds of alternative ways of looking at the product [Ethica Nicomanchea (1132a-1133b)] Aristotle [(345 B.C. (2004) pp. 120–127]. This dichotomy is essential to know the differences between the understanding of classical and Marxian economists on the one hand and contemporary economists on services, on the other. This is because, if one believes that value of product depends on its intrinsic quality, then it becomes quite obvious that material content of the product, like labour embodied in the product, determines its value (i.e. labour theory of value). On the other hand, if one accepted that value of the product depends on subjective valuation of the user of the product, then you start associating usefulness with utility (i.e. utility as the basis of value).

This dichotomy received importance in the writing of Aristotle when he realized that products must possess, in same degree, a measurable common quality to facilitate the process of exchange. This necessitated the creation of a *unit* which could as be used a measure of the common quality. Aristotle identified two units to measure these qualities (a) needs of the consumer that render all commodities commensurable, and (b) the exchange value in proportion to the work necessary to produce it [Georgescu-Roegen (1968) p.238]. Classical and Marxian economists followed the second proposition of Aristotle and evolved the materialist conception of production. This bias towards materialist approach is now described as *commodity fetishism* and is based on the proposition that value of a product lies in itself. This idea remained close to the minds of economists for a considerable period.

Despite the fact that the materialist conception of product remained dominant in economic thinking, there always existed an undercurrent view which did not accept the validity of this strand of thought. The strong reactions against commodity fetishism led the scholars to evolve alternative views based on the first proposition of Aristotle i.e. things do not have value because it is assumed it costs, but costs because it has value (in use). The use value concept facilitated the evolution of the utilitarian approach.

The term utility initially appeared in 1750, in the writings of Galiani, but received academic acceptance after being used in a much wider context in the work of Bentham for whom utility stood for "that property of any object, whereby it tends to produce advantage, pleasure, good or happiness [Bentham 1789 (1948)]. The same definition can be observed in the writings of Gessen (1884), Mills (1861) and Edgeworth (1881) [Georgescu-Roegen (1968)]. One of the important contributors to the utilitarian approach, Jevons (1871), states that "utility was strongly associated with the pleasure felt during the act of consumption" and he expressed that value in use total utility [Jevons 1871 (1965)].

The utilitarian approach led to the birth of *comprehensive concept of production* which accepts that production means creation of utility. Since utility can be created through material as well as immaterial ways, all acts of human endeavour which help in increasing the usefulness of an object assumed the same status in economic analysis. This is because utility can be created not only by increasing the tangible content of the product but also by changing its shape (i.e. converting wood into furniture), its space (i.e. by transportation) and its time (i.e. storage). This approach was strongly advocated by Marshall (1879)—it made the distinction between tangibility and intangibility of a product totally irrelevant. Marshall (1879) mentions that "everything that is produced in the course of a year, every service rendered, every fresh utility brought about is part of national income. Thus it includes the benefits derived from the advise of a physician, the pleasure got from hearing a professional singer, and enjoyment of other services for which one person may be hired to perform for another... it includes the services of the domestic servant who makes or mends or cleans carpet or a dress" [Marshall 1879 (1959) pp.52-53].

Marshall also did not differentiate goods from services on the basis of materiality and immateriality, instead, he believed that even goods can be material or immaterial. In his words, "material goods consist of useful material things, and all rights to hold, or use, or derive benefit from, or to receive them at a future time... non-material goods fall in two classes. One consists of his own qualities and faculties for action and for enjoyment... All these lie within himself and are called *internal*. The second class is called *external* because they consist of relations beneficial to him with other people" [Marshall, 1879 (1959) pp.45-46]. It is worth emphasizing here that Marshall is not using the term immaterial to refer to services, but for a class of goods. Marshall (1879) also wrote that if we have to make a fresh start, it would be best to regard all labour as productive, except that which failed to promote the aim at which it was directed and produced no utility [Marshall, 1879 (1959) Book II chapter III].

The emergence of the utilitarian approach has shifted emphasis from *accumulation* to *consumption*. It has now been largely accepted that the best definition of national income is "the largest permanently maintainable value of consumption" i.e. "economic activity has as its ultimate end consumption, not capital formation... investment must be treated as an intermediate good in a multiperiod system, whose final products are consumption of different years" [Weitzman (1976) p. 1159]. These developments made the division of labour and economic activities into productive and unproductive totally irrelevant and it completely disappeared from economic analysis. Instead, in the new understanding on the issue, most economic activities in market economies are described as service relationships. Accepting this view amounts to saying, like Bastiat, that "If tangible objects are the essence of value, than there is no value without objects... Smith should have rejected that notion because he explains the value on the basis of work done. Do not services in their pure form consist solely of work done, hence should they not imply value" [Delauney and Gadrey (1992)].

The above analysis suggests that it took nearly two centuries for the services rendered by domestic servants to be recognized as an important economic activity. Smith believed that the effect of work done by a domestic servant leaves behind no visible and tangible results which are easy to spot, but it is now being realized that "the effect of the domestic servant who attends to cleanliness and tideness of the premises does appear immediately after the act. The utility of his effects lasts for certain period and increases the well being of his employer" [Gadrey (2000) p. 371]. Thus, it was the utilitarian approach which provided recognition to services and made them a part of mainstream economic analysis. This also helped in the evolution of a framework of national accounting in which contribution of services has become an important part of national income. The attitude of economists changed dramatically during the inter-war period when most economies of Western Europe and America were experiencing the Great Depression of the 1930s. This view received further strength from the spread of neo-classical and Keynesian economics which ignored the distinction between goods and services.

The interest in services, clubbed together as *tertiary sector*, emerged during the period of Greate Depression, when Fisher and Clark drew the attention of economists. They felt that by directing investments towards the services sector (i.e. tertiary sector) economies affected by depression can solve their problem of mass unemployment. The emerging new field of economic analysis, better known as development economics, accepted the split of the economy into three distinct sectors, depending upon the nature of their product. The term tertiary sector was evolved to describe all service industries [Fisher (1930) (1933) (1946) and (1952); Clark (1940) and (1984)]. The division of economic activities into the three sector framework, *primary* (extractive), *secondary* (manufacturing) and *tertiary* (services), was based on the characteristics of their product. Creation of utility becomes the basis for distinguishing the tertiary sector from other sectors of the economy. However, in earlier studies, the tertiary sector was essentially a residual sector. Therefore, all those economic activities which failed to satisfy the criteria of being extractive and manufacturing, were included in the tertiary sector. This approach did not require any well defined concept of services, but defined it indirectly through negation i.e. an economic activity that *neither* belongs to the primary sector *nor* belongs to the secondary sector belongs to the tertiary sector.

Fisher, while describing how he got interested in the tertiary sector, writes that "the original purpose in mind in inventing the term tertiary production was to suggest some kind of framework, the consideration of which might give a lead in answering the highly important question—in what direction is it desirable at this state of history to accelerate the rate of economic development?" and also correct the understanding of "equally unsatisfactory position based on implicit assumption that classification of economic activities into primary and secondary industries exhausted all possibilities of employment" and he further adds that "everybody knew that many people had employment which did not fit easily into the primary-secondary grouping [Fisher (1939) p. 30]. Hence, he invented the term tertiary sector in order to correct the mindset of economists and policy makers who were accustomed to thinking in terms of primary and secondary production alone. He finally states that invention of "tertiary production was intended as a signpost for this purpose" [Fisher (1939) p. 31].

Colin clark (1940) adopted the concept of tertiary production as "all forms of economic activities not included under primary and secondary sector". Fisher, instead, tried to evolve a definition of tertiary production because he believed that "it would be a cowardly evasion of the issue to ask the reader to be content with the conclusion that tertiary production is everything left over after all types of primary and secondary production have been enumerated" [Fisher (1939) p. 31]. Therefore, he made an attempt to define tertiary production as something that concerneds with very new or relatively new types of consumer's demand, the production and consumption of which releases resources hitherto required for primary and secondary production". A more concrete form of definition might suggest the word luxury" [Fisher (1939) p.32]. However, while elaborating his definition, he points out that the word luxury cannot be used universally for all services, "the service of medical practitioners, and perhaps of other professional-men, the supply of which in a rationally ordered progressive economy would be considerably greater than it is at present and demand for which would than be 'relatively new' over a wide range of income [Fisher (1939) p.33]. He finally describes that "everybody who produces a service, as distinguished from material goods, which affords direct satisfaction to the consumer, must be regarded as a tertiary producer" [Fisher (1939) p.33].

Clark (1940) and Fisher [(1935) and (1939)] accepted that tertiary production was growing as a consequence of structural changes experienced by the economy, caused by an ongoing process of economic growth. However, they had divergent explanations regarding the nature of structural breaks. In the analysis developed by Fisher (1935), economic growth resulted in a decline in primary sector employment because of the high *income elasticity of demand* for services. On the contrary, Clark explained that structural changes in the economy occur because of reswitching of resources between sectors, which can be explained with the help of *inter-sectoral differences in productivity*. In this way, he is looking at the growth of services from the *supply side*. He explains the shifts in inter-sectoral employment structure in favour of the tertiary sector because of low productivity in services which necessitates a shift of large proportion of labour force towards the service sector [Hartwell (1973)].

It is interesting to note that both scholars developed their analysis based on an exclusivist view of different sectors of the economy, ignoring interlinkages between sectors which results in overlapping of occupations. This happens especially when there emerges integration between some service industries with manufacturing industries. The integration necessitates rethinking on distinction between service occupations and service industries. This occured as a consequence of integration of retail trade, transportation and distribution with large scale manufacturing enterprises. The emergence of large scale manufacturing and integration of services with manufacturing is necessitated by the emergence of methods of mass production. It was also the emergence of managerial revolution and managerial hierarchies which gave birth to several service occupations within the manufacturing sector. This process was further facilitated by integration of research and development activities within manufacturing enterprises.

The distinction between service occupations and service industries, and the interdependence of sectors, remained not of vital importance so long as the tertiary sector remained insignificant in comparison to other sectors of the economy. As the services sector grew larger and began to contribute a substantial share to national output and employment, the complexity and heterogeneity of services became more apparent [Bair and Yamey (1951), Trientis (1953), and Mink (1955)]. Despite this simple yet important weakness of the Fisher-Clark approach, their study encouraged several such studies to evaluate the validity of structural changes in the inter-sector composition of employment identified by them. These studies were able to collect evidence from time-series as well as cross-section data regarding these structural changes and also evidence regarding reversal in the tendency of productivity and labour share among different sectors. They recorded variety of experiences shown by different economies. Their empirical work suggests that there is a need for developing models which are capable of integrating both supply and demand side factors while explaining the growth of the service sector [Kuznets (1957) and (1966), Chenery and Taylor (1968), Dowie (1966), Fuchs (1968) and Haig (1973)]. It is interesting to note that the dominance of the tertiary sector in terms of its contribution to national income and employment emerged initially in the U.S.A. that where both supply side as well as demand side factors, that increase the services, worked in tandem. It was also due to the increasing importance of the tertiary sector in U.S.A., it began to be referred to as the service sector.

Economics of services, as a specialized field of economic enquiry, perhaps began with the writings of Fuchs [(1964) (1965) and (1968)]. He uses the term *service economy* in his writing not to refer to a sector or a segment of an economy but as an economy which has been transformed into a service economy, where services have occupied commanding heights of the economy [Fuchs (1965)]. Fuchs's detailed analysis of the services in the U.S.A. evolved three testable hypotheses regarding growth in services (a) services generally have an income elasticity of demand greater than unity. Therefore, as real per capita income increases, demand for services grows faster than a proportionate growth in income (b) the increasing economic specialization and technological change, resulting from economic development, will make efficient provisioning of services which were earlier provided within the household or a firm. Therefore, it will become economical to outsource these services from specialized service providers. This hypothesis has already become a reality with the increasing use of business processes outsourcing (BPO) and of market provided services as a substitute for services earlier produced within the household. The first alternative, that is BPO, may not significantly increase the overall employment in the economy because the volume of services provided by BPO firms may not be much larger than services provided earlier inside the manufacturing enterprises. However, the second alternative, where marketed services are purchased in place of household production of services, does increase additional income and employment in the services (c) finally, employment in service sector grows faster because of relatively slower growth of labour productivity in the services. Therefore, as an economy expands, the share of employment in services increases faster. Moreover, the sluggish growth in labour productivity also establishes that costs in services will increase faster than the average costs in the economy.

In order to further elaborate the work of Fuchs (1965), Baumol (1967) evolved a two sector growth model to explain the reasons for the emerging significance of employment in services. In this model, an economy consists of two sectors with varying rates of productivity growth. Here, one of the sectors (i.e. secondary sector) is technologically *progressive* in which innovations, capital accumulation and economies of scale result in cumulative gains in productivity. In the other sector (i.e. services), sporadic gains in productivity can be achieved. In his two sector model, the services sector is considered to be the *stagnant* sector of the economy, in terms of productivity growth. He provides an interesting example to substantiate the basis of his conceptualization—"between 1670 and 1970, the output per-watch maker in Geneva is estimated to have risen from 12 watches to over 1200 watches per day. Purcell wrote *Dido* and *Aneas* in 1680s and today it takes as many person-hours and instruments to perform live as it did then" [Baumol et al (1985) p.807]. The model establishes that relative costs and prices of the output of stagnant sector (i.e. services) would increase continuously and cumulatively, therefore, the share's of the inputs used by the stagnant sector and share of consumer expenditure devoted to the output of the stagnant sector must rise. The net result of this tendency of the stagnant sector will *cetris paribus* reduce the overall productivity growth of the economy. The two sector model of Baumol (1967) throws light on Fuch's hypothesis regarding the role of inter-sectoral differences in the productivity and growth of employment in the services sector.

Fuchs (1968) also identified certain differentiating characteristics of the services sector. He said that the growth of employment in services is accompanied by their feminization, meaning that it increases the rate of participation of women in the labour market [Fuchs (1965)]. He also studied the relationship between inter-temporal variations in employment in services and business cycles. He observed that employment in the services sector does not significantly change with business cycles [Fuchs (1988) pp.158-182]. Fuchs was perhaps the first economist who highlighted that the consumer is an important factor of production in the production of services. He stated that "this unmeasured input can significantly influence productivity in services like retailing, health and education" [Fuchs (1968) p. 12]. Now it is being increasingly realized that the quality of health service depends on the quality of information given by the patient regarding his illness; the quality of complaint prepared by the lawyer depends on the quality of brief given by his client; and quality of teaching depends on the quality of participation of students in the class. Fuchs also identified that, unlike in the production of goods, the production and delivery of services might create *labour embodied technological change* [Fuchs (1968) p. 195].

However, understanding of economists changed significantly by the 1970s and especially by 1980s. This change occured (a) because by this time most developed market economies had been transformed into 'service economies' as defined by Fuchs. This happened when the linkages of the services became quite strong with different elements of the economy and got extended to all the sectors of the economy, and (b) because of the emergence of knowledge economy and revolutions in information technology which gave birth to new knowledge based services and information technology enabled services. These developments forced the economists to take a new look at services.

The increasing role of services in contemporary developed market economies facilitated the development of the phenomenon called *post-industrial society* [Bell (1974)]. According to Bell (1974), in pre-industrial societies, i.e. in agricultural societies, life was primarily a game against nature and the nature of work was conditioned by the vagaries of seasons and geographical elements. The industrial society was a goods producing society where life was a game against fabricated nature. The post-industrial society is based on services. Hence, it is a game between persons, and this game is poised in favour of those persons who have more information and knowledge [Bell (1974) pp. 126-127]. Following the logic embodied in the framework of analysis evolved by Fisher-Clark and Fuchs-Baumol, Bell, in fact, talks about the pre-eminance of 'true services' i.e. services which enter into the direct consumption of households rather than those which are intermediate in nature.

His ideas regarding the primacy of knowledge in post-industrial society are quite similar to the ideas of Richta (1969). However, in contempary writings, post-industrialism is used as a blanket term to represent those groups or economic activities that play significant roles in service societies.

In reaction to the conceptualization of post-industrial society, some scholars evolved an alternative conceptualization of *new industrial society*. This approach also accepted the increasing importance of services in modern economies, but emphasized only that segment of the service economy which emerged as a consequence of increasing organization changes in industrial enterprises [Galbraith (1967)]. Galbraith (1967), in fact, focused on the emergence of new changes occuring in the organization of industrial enterprises in terms of complexity and power structure. However, he emphasizes those services which have evolved strong linkages with modern corporate business. Through analysis of changes that are occuring in industrial enterprises, he evolved concepts like *advance business services* and their relevance in the new industrial order, and *techno-structure* as a new power elite in modern enterprises. However, he ignores all those services which do not have linkages with the new industrial organizational structure despite the fact that these services constitute a significant part of employment in developed economies [Fuchs (1968), Singlemann (1974)].

The important effects of these developments were that Baumol revised his two sector model [Baumol *et al* (1985)]. In his revised model he incorporated the new reality of services i.e. the integration of services with new information technology. Therefore, in his revised paper, he accepts that the services sector consists of quite heterogeneous economic activities—some of them are most progressive economic activities of the economy whereas some others are most stagnant economic activities. To accomodate this heterogeneity of the services sector, he added a third sector of the economy which was not a part of his earlier paper [Baumal (1967)] which he describes as *asymptotically stagnant activities* like T.V. broadcasting and data processing. These services are outstandingly productive but carry the seeds of their own stagnation because they use a fixed proportion of one set of inputs produced by the progressive sector (i.e. secondary sector) and matching inputs from stagnant sector (services). For example T.V. broadcasting, with one hour of its progressive component (i.e. electronic transmission infrastructure), requires one hour of inputs from the stagnant sector i.e. services of performing artists, actors or newsreaders. Therefore, progressive component may experience innovations and economies of scale but the other component cannot experience any change. Hence, in these services, productivity increases as and when technological changes occur in the progressive component of the services, which subsequently also stagnate till new technology is conceived. This characteristic makes them asymptotically stagnant services. However, his new model helps in separating the effects of (a) lagging productivity of service sector (b) income elasticity of demand for services (c) exogenous changes that cause shifts in the demand for services and how these changes affect the rate growth of employment in services.

These developments have given rise to alternative views regarding services. The rise of services sector in developed market economies coincided with substantial reduction in employment in the manufacturing sector. This phenomenon was described as *de-industrialization* and this hypothesis is based on the implicit assumption that production of goods constitutes productive works and services are unproductive. Therefore, it amounts to a re-emergence of the mindset of economists which is based on the premises of classical and Marxian economists. On the contrary, scholars who evolved the idea of post-industrial society, visualized the growth in services as a consequence of shifts in consumers demand and preferences due to growing prosperity. They also thought that service products are superior products because their demand increases after the consumers are satiated with the consumption of material goods.

Scholars adhering to the industrialization thesis explained the shift of consumer demand towards services as "a symptom of cultural decadence, the growth of a hedonistic consumer culture, or welfare dependency, rather than a creative and production-oriented society" [Boden and Miles (2000) p.4]. These divergent views held by different strands of thought amongst economists arise due to complexity and heterogeniety that exists in the composition of services which makes it difficult to evolve any approach which is all encompassing. Therefore, the realistic contemporary understanding about services in the economic analysis is that in a post-industrial society the relationship and linkages between different sectors of the economy have become quite complex. In this complex relationship, the goods producing sector and services producing sector have evolved *symbiotic* relations, where none of them is important in *isolation*, but *together* they are the backbone of the economy.

Contemporarily, the phenomenon of service economy has spread to several economies of the world. There have emerged thousands of service enterprises that have global operations [Clairmonte and Cavangh (1984) and Dunning (1989)]. Economists, till recently, believed that services are not tradable because service products cannot be separated from their service providers. The emergence of new technologies has facilitated trade in services, which is growing at a much faster pace than trade in goods [Hindly and Smith (1984). A symbiotic relationship has also emerged between services and new technology which has changed the characteristics of services, as conceived by the economists in the past [Warf (1989) and Howell (1990)]. These developments have paved the way for rethinking in the status of services in economic analysis. The rest of the book will provide knowledge about the treatment given to services in contemporary economic analysis.

The description given above regarding changes in the treatment given to services in economic analysis, with a historical perspective, narrates a long drawn out process of transformation of Cinderella sector of the economy into the queen of hearts. In this historical analysis, it becomes quite apparent that Adam Smith, the father of economics, emerges as a step-father of services, classical and Marxian economists appear as step-brothers of services who compelled services to live the life of Cinderella. In the process of transformation of Cinderella, Fisher and Clark receive the honour of drawing attention of economists and policy makers towards services. The contribution of Fuchs and Baumol has been to provide the new attractive dress and Bell provided the magical glass shoes to the Cinderella. These changes helped her to walk on her own feet with confidence, and participate in the competitive dance of economic activities to emerge as the queen of hearts.

CHAPTER 2

CONCEPTUALIZATION OF SERVICES

We have discussed, in the earlier chapter, different shifts that have occured in the treatment of services in economic analysis. The analysis gave us knowledge regarding the long historical process which transformed the status of services from the Cinderella sector of the economy to being the queen of hearts. This process of changes also narrated the shifts in the attitude of economists towards services which also led to changes in the way they were conceptualized in economics. Since the story of services is quite akin to the story of transformation of Cinderella, the conceptualization of services also followed the same process of transformation—from being narrow to broader and finally comprehensive.

In the previous chapter, we also highlighted the fact that at any given point in time there exist services that have roots in different stage of socio-economic formations. This fact leads to the existence of heterogeneity in the composition of services. Therefore, the concept of services has to be all encompassing which can account for this heterogeneity which is so enormous and unmanageable. On the one side of this extreme diversity are modern services like telecommunication and information services and on the other extreme are traditional services like domestic services. The services also differ in terms of technology being used to deliver them. Again, on one side of this spectrum of technological complexity, we have services like haircut and beauty salons which are labour intensive while on the other end are information technology enabled services that are capital intensive. Some of the services are distinguished from goods merely on the basis of their contextuality. For instance, if a landlord rents out a fully furnished apartment to a tenant, then all fittings, furniture and fixtures become *services* provided by the landlord. On the contrary, if all these items are purchased by the tenant, they are classified as *goods*. Therefore, *owning* or *hiring* of a product determines the context in which that product is being categorized as a good or a service. Moreover, if one purchases a hamburger from a retail outlet, it is classified as a good while the same hamburger when purchased from a restaurant is being described as a service. Despite these complexities, scholars have made attempts to conceptualize services.

Nomen est numen—to name is to know—is an ancient maxim. In the cotemporary understanding of knowledge, *nomen* are not merely names of objects, but concepts or paradigms or prisms. A conceptualization refers to the evolving of a *schema*, which helps in selecting attributes or characteristics from a complex reality in order to identify similarities and differentiations. This suggests that the process of conceptualization is just the evolution of logical ordering aparatus; it is never judged as *true* or *false*, but in terms of being *useful* or *not useful*.

Scholars have attempted to conceptualize services from four distinct perspectives (a) as *service industries* (b) as *service occupations* (c) as *service products* and (d) as *service situations*.

Hence, in the present chapter, an attempt has been made to study the changes that have occurred over time in the conceptualization of services with a historical perspective. This exercise will provide knowledge regarding consistent and continuous efforts made by economists to arrive at an appropriate concept of services. As has been mentioned above, there are four distinct perspectives to conceptualize services and the rest of the chapter has been organized into four sections, where each section deals with a specific perspective on services. Therefore, Section I deals with conceptualization of services which views services in terms of service products; Section II analyses the conceptual basis of analysing services as service industries; Section III provides understanding regarding the perspective which views services a service occupations. Finally, in Section IV we provide the approach which conceptualizes services as service situations.

I. Conceptualization of Services as Service Products

Conceptualization of services in terms of service products is as old as economic analysis. In certain ways, it can be accepted as an approach which came much earlier than the birth of economics as a separate discipline. It seems that the original distinction between goods and services arose from an epistemological problem associated with the puzzle i.e. whether value of a product is determined by its intrinsic quality or depends on subjective evaluation by the users of the product. The puzzle originated in the writings of Aristotle [*Ethica Nicomachea* 1132a-1133b]. This epistemological problem contained the seeds of alternative ways of looking at the product. The dichotomy is essential to understand the difference between the views held by classical and Marxian economists on the one hand and the neoclassical economists on the other: if one accepts that the value of a product depends on its intrinsic characteristic, than it is quite obvious that the content of the product, like labour embodied in the product, determines its value (i.e. labour theory of value). On the other hand, if one believes in premises that the value of the product depends on subjective valuation of the user of the product, then you start associating usefulness of the product with utility (i.e. the utilitarian approach). Aristotle writes that "there must, therefore, be one standard by which all commodities are measured. This standard is in fact demand which holds every thing together for if people had no needs or needs on different scales, there could be no exchange" [Aristotle, 345 B.C (2004) p. 125]. The classical and marxian economists followed the first proposition of Aristotle and evolved the materialistic conception of production.

In the writings of classical economists, the distinction between goods and services revolves around the concept of productive and unproductive labour. Adam Smith [1776 (1961)] indirectly distinguishes between the two by defining productive and unproductive labour. According to him, only workers who are engaged in the production of material goods are productive because only these workers are capable of returning a net income to the producer in the form of economic surplus. While elaborating the characteristics of an unproductive labour he writes "that it does not fix or realize itself in any permanent subject or *vendible* commodity which endures after that labour is past...." [Smith, 1776 (1961) p. 351].

Thus, in the approach of Smith, the criteria of contribution to accumulation is essential to draw a distinction between goods and services. Since goods are vendible they can contribute to accumulation; services are not vendible they cannot contribute to accumulation. However, this term, vendible, evolved by Smith, in the writings of subsequent classical economists became *tangible*. Therefore, initial dichotomy between goods and services rests on the proposition that goods are tangible, services are intangible; or goods are *material* and services are *immaterial* [Hill (1999)].

The materialist concept of production evolved by Smith and other classical economists received remarkable resurrection from the writings of Marx. His ideas regarding services are contained in his books, *Capital Vol. II* and *Theories of Surplus Value*. He also indirectly defines the distinction between goods and services in terms of his notions about use value and surplus value. In his framework, it becomes quite obvious that all those economic activities that only create use value are services, whereas those economic activities which are capable of producing, in addition to use value, certain amount of surplus value are producing goods.

Therefore, the premise which believed in the view that the value of the product rests in the product itself leads to conceptualization of goods and services based on their intrinsic qualities. Hence, goods are tangible, services are intangible; goods are storable, services are non-storable; goods can be transported because they can be separated from their producer, services cannot be transported because they cannot be separated from their provider; production and consumption of goods can be separated in time whereas, in the case of services, production and consumption is instantaneous; ownership of goods can be changed because they can be separated from their producer, but ownership of services cannot be altered because they cannot be separated from their providers. Despite this exhaustive list of distinct characteristics identified by this conceptualization of goods and services, it is still not all encompassing. The acceptance of these characteristics of services suggests that services are "impermanent, made by people for people... and consumable only at the instant of production." They are also viewed as "a state, activity or sensation, rather than a thing" [Gershuny (1978) p. 363]. To present the essence of this conceptualization of services in a humorous way the *Economist* defined services as "those fruits of economic activity that you cannot drop on your toes" [quoted in Paulin (1987) p. 33].

A strict adherence to the intangibility criterion presents problems. A dentist who makes a false tooth and places it in the mouth of a patient is a tangible product, but the activities of the dentist are classified as services [Fuchs (1968) p. 15]. Similarly, when one is buying a car, it is not clear whether one is buying a good or buying the service of transportation. Therefore, intangibility may be a necessary and sufficient condition to define some services, but not all the services. This is also true in the case of certain services where, at the instance of final delivery of the service, some thing tangible is delivered by the service provider. For instance, photograph as an end result of photographic services, project report, study or brief as an end product in the case of consultancy services. On the other hand, tangibility of some of the goods can be doubted (e.g. electricity).

If one accepts that services cannot be stored because they are produced and consumed instantaneously, this characteristic is again true for some services but not for all. There could be considerable amount of time-lag between production of consultancy services and their final consumption. The acceptance of non-transportability characteristic of services assumes that their consumption must occur at the same location where they are being produced. This might again be true for some services but not necessarily for all of them. This is especially not true for information technology enabled services some of whom can be stored into electronic or magnetic devices and consumed anywhere in the world, for example, music stored in cassettes, VCD and DVDs and information stored in CD Rom. Similarly, artistic performances, sporting events etc can be viewed, simultaneously, throughout the world, away from the places where they are being performed live through satellite T.V. networks.

The distinguishing characteristics of services, mentioned above, might appear very simple but, in real life situations, these distinctions are no more valid. In the contemporary world while the intangible component in goods is increasing, in the case of some services the tangible component is increasing over time. This has emerged because most purchases of goods are accompanied by facilitating services; and purchases of some services are accompanied by facilitating goods. For example, pharmaceutical industry is included in goods producing sector, despite the fact that a significant share of costs in this industry consist of research & development, clinical trials, patent fees, regulatory clearances, drug marketing and distribution [Reich (1991)]. Television set is a good but what is the usefulness of this good without the services of television channel operators and enterprises that are supplying software and contents to channel operations [Russel and Murdick (2003)], Similarly, a computer as a good is useless without the availability of complementary software to make it useful. Therefore, it is now being increasingly realized that neither are goods completely tangible nor services completely intangible, but are in fact two poles on a continuum.

The debate on tangibility of goods and intangibility of services is also becoming misplaced as the knowledge base of the economies is increasing. The knowledge economy is making continuous effort to *dematerialize goods*. This process has been made possible by altering the cost structure of goods where a significant part of the costs are incurred on intangibles. Here, by dematerialization of goods, we do not mean that there has occured absolute fall in materials required to produce a product [Bernardi and Galli (1993)] but that a situation has emerged where costs on intangibles have increased substantially causing a fall in the relative costs on materials being used in the production of goods [Hertog et al (1997) p. 35]. The process of dematerialization of goods has given rise to new characters to the production process where material content constitutes either limited or decreasing share of total value creation. It has been estimated that within American manufacturing, 75-80 per cent of value-added can be attributed to intangibles [Quinn (1988) and Quinn et al (1990)]. The dematerialization of goods also means that in the production process a large part of value-added originates from improvements in brand equity, quality, design and delivery of goods and other complementary services employed by manufacturing units. The increasing importance of intangibles in the process of production becomes more obvious when visualized at the macro-level i.e. at the level of the aggregate economy. Its importance is manifest in an increasing dominance of service sector in most developed marked economies. In these economies, a majority of the working population is employed in service industries and service occupations; and a significant share of value-addition in their national income also originates in the service sector.

A similar trend has been observed in the case of services also, where complementary material content is increasing significantly. It has been noticed, in the case of services, that to make improvement in their quality and delivery, and to make them more efficient, the tangible component is increasing over time: this increasing role has been aptly described as the process of industrialization of services [Levitt (1976)]. This process is based on improvements in the production and delivery of services through large scale investments in land, technology, equipments and other tangibles. These factors are used in the same way, in the services sector, as they are used in manufacturing enterprises to make improvements in efficiency in the production of good and also to improve their quality. This process is also described as *McDonaldization of Services* [Levitt (1972)] derived from the McDonald's production and operation system which has become an important symbol of industrialization of services. To improve the quality of its products, improve efficiency of its operations, and to make its products global, McDonald's has standardized not only tangible but also intangible service components. This process of standardization has reduced the relative relevance of intangibles in its operations.

Similarly, supermarkets can be visualized as an example of industrialization of services; they are a unique combination of more space, more capital intensity and use of better technology to reduce the importance of intangibles from the delivery of service. This combination has been able to replace the traditional retailing based on labour intensive personalized service to an efficient, low cost system, which is highly impersonalized and has replaced service by self-service. This system not only enhances the efficiency of the system but also improves customer's satisfaction. In this sense, the supermarket model of retailing represents a case of technological changes in retailing. This process of technological change in services has the same technological consequences which were ascribed to the use of assembly-line in the manufacturing of goods which helped in the industrialization of the craft-based primitive method of production [Seth (2002) and (2003)]. Hence, as the assembly-line brought about revolutionary changes in manufacturing in terms of mass-production and economies of scale, the supermarket mode helped in the transformation of traditional retailing. Modern supermarket mode provides advantages to retailing in terms of economies of scale, improved efficiency and better quality of service [Levitt (1972)].

These days the tangible component in the production of services (intangibles) is increasing in innumerable ways. The symbioses between tangibles and intangibles is giving rise to new possibilities. Services are now being industrialized with the help of the same technologies which are being used in the manufacturing industries, i.e. by using hardware, softwares and hybrid of both hardware and softwares. The use of hardware is making it possible to make people-intensive services into capital-intensive and technology-intensive services. For instance, the electrocardiogram, which can be operated with the help of a semi-skilled technician, replaces and saves the services of a skilled doctor. The airport X-ray machine substitutes manual work of checking each baggage personally by security guards. A.T.M. machines have made it possible to make available cash to customers of the bank twenty-four hours of the day by replacing the services of cashiers [Levitt (1976)]. Similar is the role of vending machines.

Even soft technologies are replacing organised preplanned systems of individual service deliveries. Fast-food restaurants like McDonalds, Pizza-Hut, Domino's, Kentuky Fried Chicken provide their services with speed, accuracy and quality, by combining standardization of their products with rational systems of labour. Since the first mass-marketing campaign organized by Ford Motor Company, tele-marketing has come a long way. With the availability of Wide Area Telephony, FX cells and use of satellite communication, the costs of long distance calls are continuously declining. These new possibilities have created the opportunity for Business Process Outsourcing (BPO), resulting in the emergence of call centres and global data storing and processing centres [Murray (1978)].

Innovations in the new information technology have made the traditional basis of conceptualization of goods and services totally irrelevant; they now cannot be defined in terms of binary oppositions like tangible–intangible, storable–non-storable, transportable–non-transportable. This is because new technology has made the output of some services tangible, permanent and storable. New service products, stored on the magnetic tape, belie the old characteristics of services [Marshall et al (1988) and Castells (1996)].

In the context of contemporary reality, considering evanescence of all the services is quite erroneous. For example, education and health help in creating human capital which produces everlasting, tangible accumulable changes. This realization led to the emergence of two new branches of economics, economics of education and economics of health care. The term human capital includes the sum total of all acquired and useful capabilities embodied in human population like education, skills, learning-by-doing and health. All these capabilities are a form of capital because they create productive stock embodied in persons that provides returns, services and satisfaction over future periods [Schutz (1961) and Denison (1963)]. This concept created, amongst economists, the acceptability that educational and health services make permanent and durable changes in workers which can be accumulated in the form of capital. In this formulation, education improves the *quality* of human capital and health care increases its *durability* because it increases the number of healthy days available for work, which help in increasing income [Grossman (1972) (1972a) and (2003)].

Economists have realized the importance of investment in R & D services which gets translated in the form of patents, which can help in either changing processes or in introducing new products. Moreover, knowledge accumulated in the form of a patent can also be traded. Even media and information services add tangible gains to organizations as well as to goods produced by organizations. These services add value through expenditure on advertisement— a service which helps in developing the image of the organization and brand-equity of brands of products. Brand equity becomes an important source of intangible assets of the enterprises. This can be accumulated, over time, and can be traded in the market place in the form of goodwill.

II. Conceptualization of Services as Service Industries

When product based classification of services appeared quite difficult and not all inclusive, economists tried to view services in a new perspective. This new perspective was to view services not in terms of products but in terms of service industries. This conception grew out of the identification of a new sector, the *tertiary sector*, in the three sectoral classification of economic activities. Tertiary sector was evolved as a residual sector of the economy, consisting of left-over economic activities which can neither be included in primary economic activities nor in secondary economic activities: a tradition that originated with the work of Fisher and clark [Fisher (1933) (1939) and (1946); Clark (1940)]; [Gershuny and Miles (1983)]. This approach leaves scope of subjectivity while making decisions regarding exclusion and inclusion of certain industries into service industries. One noted economist expressed this dilemma by saying that "there exists no authoritative consensus on either boundaries or classification of service industries" [Stigler (1956) p. 47].

Since its earlier use, there has emerged a vast literature dealing with various aspects of service industries, but careful assessment of these studies shows that there does not exist any unanimity amongst economists to provide any theoretical basis for defining services industries. Some studies include transportation and communication and exclude public utilities while defining service industries [Kuznets (1958) and (1966), Lengell (1966), Guir Ofer (1967) and Worton (1969)]. Some scholar advocate for a separate treatment for these industries because they are capital intensive, requiring huge investment, unlike the typical service industries [Stigler (1956) p. 47].

To minimise the element of ambiguity in identifying industries that belong to a set of service industries, some scholars have tried to identify certain criterias (a) whether there exists a closeness between consumers and producers, (b) whether product of industry is intangible or not [Fisher (1935), Clark (1940) and Fuchs (1968) p. 15]. On the contrary, economists like Marshall (1929) have taken an extreme view when he describes that in one sense all industries provide services because he believes that "man cannot create material things and in both goods and services he produces only utilities" [Marshall (1929) p. 63]. Despite all the problems associated with the identification of industries which can be conclusively described as service industries, United Nations have evolved the International Standards Classification of Industries (ISIC) which also identifies service industries. This classification is now being used for the purposes of preparation of national accounts as well as for distribution of working population in different service industries by most economies.

The industry based conceptualization of services becomes quite complex when used for the purposes of inter-temporal comparisons. The existence of service industries as separate entities depends on the level of integration and disintegration practised in manufacturing enterprises. Since the birth of methods of mass-production, popularly known as *Fordist Methods* of *Production*, several service activities got integrated in manufacturing enterprises. The necessity for increasing the volume of output to achieve economies of scale forced manufacturing enterprises to integrate transportation, distribution, marketing, designing, retailing, research and development within manufacturing industries [Kenny and Florida (1993), Amin (1999) and Seth (2001)]. This process of integration of services with manufacturing emerged after 1911 with the birth of Ford's *assembly-line* method of production. This new way of organization of production in manufacturing enterprises led to the integration of various services with manufacturing. Due to this process of integration, some services lost their independence, and their contributions to employment and income were recorded in the data on manufacturing sector.

Since the 1980s, methods of flexible manufacturing or *flexible accumulation* have become the driving force underlying the restructuring of the manufacturing sector, after the experience of stagflation, in most developed economies [Piore and Sable (1984), Harvey (1989), Womack and Jones (1996), Seth (2001) and (2004)]. The restructuring of manufacturing enterprises to achieve flexibility had strong implications for service industries [Christopher (1989), Beyer (1990) and Wood (1991)]. A flexible production system is totally at variance with rigities that are inherent in the Fordist system of mass-production. The main differentiating characteristic between flexible method of production and method of mass-production is *vertical disintegration* in place of vertical integration of production process. Here, instead of complete internalization of the entire production process, the main enterprise controls only final production and key technology, whereas activities that are not strategic, together with the production of parts, components and ancilliary services, are *outsourced* or *contracted* out. The functioning of this type of production system results in a kind of social division of labour which existed among enterprises in a primitive form at the stage of *proto-industrialization* [Seth (2003)].

The flexible manufacturing system of production evolves its competitive advantage from maximizing *external economies*, *economies of scope* and *economies of agglomeration*, rather than from internal economies of scale. Therefore flexible system of production provides options to manufacturing firms to obtain the supply of certain services *externally*. This process of externalization of services results in outsourcing, also known as Business Process Outsourcing (BPO). The practice of BPO creates free standing service firms. In this way a flexible manufacturing system helps in creating a separation between services and manufacturing. This happens when some of the service functions, which were earlier internalized by manufacturing enterprises, are now being outsourced from firms that are specializing in providing services [Gershuney and Miles (1983) Daniels (1985) and Coffey and Bailly (1992)]. This suggests that it is the inter-temporal and spatial variations in the organization of production practised by manufacturing firms that poses problems in conceptualization of services as service industries.

Another strand of thought has emerged amongst scholars regarding appropriateness of using conceptualization of services based on service industries. The scholars who have evolved this new strand of thought believe that services are, in fact, a misclassified form of manufacturing which do not have independent existence as distinct and separable economic activities [Walker (1985) and Castells (1996). They suggest that instead of looking at services as consumer services or producer services, one should look at them from the perspective of their process of production. For this they suggest that "we must deal with complex production system or what Marx called collective labour" [Walker (1985) p. 43]. Therefore, according to these scholars, the distinction between goods and services lies in the form of labour being used in their production. A good is a material product produced by labour for human use, such as a ship or a bottle of beer. A *labour service,* on the other hand, consists of labour that does not take intervening forms of material products, such as a play or a lecture. This creates a unique transaction between producer and consumer. The mismatch between goods and services emerges due to incorrect understanding of this distinction.

A restaurant provides a joint product, consisting of a part good and a part service. However, this is not true in the case of McDonald's where service component has been substantially eliminated through standardization of its product for mass marketing. Similarly, transportation, education and health cannot also be classified as services because in their case there does not exist a close relationship between consumer and producer. These industries are supplying their products to impersonal customers who are not known to the producer personally. Moreover, classification of these activities into services also undermines the theory of public good: public goods are products which cannot be easily divided for individual consumption and ownership. Therefore, such collective products cannot be individualized and measured. Hence, it is difficult to treat them as service industries [Walker (1985) p. 49].

The logical explanation given by these scholars makes it obvious that the computer software produced for an impersonal customer is a material good in the same way as a chair, but customized computer software prepared for a particular customer is labour service. Therefore, popular standardized computer programmes like Windows or Lotus are unquestionably goods. These scholars also claim that some consultancy firms are erroneously classified as services because they are, in fact, producing goods. For example a legal brief on a paper is like a woodcraft applied to lumber to make furniture. As long as the brief or advise of a consultant remains in his mind, it amounts to labour services, but once it is recorded on a piece of paper, it takes a material form and it, therefore, ceases to be a service [Sayer and Walker (1992) pp. 62-63].

These various examples, given by scholars belonging to this stramd of thought, describe them as different mismatches and these mismatches form a certain part of the new service economy. They suggest that these mismatches can be better understood in the context of division of labour evolved by the new capitalist industrialism. This division of labour has been created by the revolutionary forces of capital which has given rise to new extended division of labour. This has happened because the division of labour has been extended from direct labour to the realm of indirect labour; this has not only improved the efficiency of the system, but also the speed of accumulation. In the process of *extended division of labour*, the indirect economy (i.e. the service industries) has emerged as a consequence of indirect division of labour. Now this indirect economy has become the focus of production, feeding on itself, as an engine of growth [Walker (1985) p. 82].

There are other scholars who view services from the perspective of the process of production of services. They have identified that production of services requires cooperation between producers and consumers, i.e. *coproduction*, to bring about desired results. This specific character of service production has been incorporated in the writings of Fuchs (1968) and Singleman (1978). This peculiarity in the process of production of services has also been highlighted by Bell (1973), when he writes that "individuals now talk to individuals rather than interact with machines" [Bell (1973) p.163]. However, it has been pointed out that coproduction cannot be used as a criterion for defining services because it is not a unique feature of services alone but a distinguishing characteristic of the flexible manufacturing system. The success of this system depends on cooperation between, producer, suppliers of components, suppliers of specific services and customers to achieve economies of scale and scope [Piore and Sabel (1984) and Womack et al (1991)]. It is also worth mentioning here that similar peculiarity also existed in the craft based manufacturing system where customization of product was the main distinguishing feature. It was the need for customization that necessitated the cooperation between producer and customer [Seth (2003)].

III. Conceptualization of Services as Service Occupations

To overcome the shortcomings associated with the conceptualization of services as service industries, some scholars tried to look at services as service occupations. Some service occupations are distinct and can easily be located amongst occupations, for example, doctors, lawyers, teachers, painters, performing artists etc. Some other service occupations are present across different sectors of the economy, for example, farm managers, agricultural scientists, veterinary doctors etc. in the primary sectors; managers, lawyers, accountants, sales and marketing personnel, clerks etc in the secondary sector.

Service occupations have a very strong presence in the secondary sector. The evolutionary process of development in industrial societies has created certain objective conditions which facilitate the emergence of new categories of workers and occupations in the manufacturing sector. Since the beginning of the industrial revolution, there has been a tendency to increase the representative size of the firm. Due to various technological and managerial reasons; this has necessitated changes in the organizational structure (from simple to complex), managerial hierarchy, division of labour and job classifications to run and coordinate activities. The process of transformation of the inner structure of an enterprise results in employment of a large array of technocrats and administrators.

These technocrats and administrators consist of occupations which generally belong to services. The bulk of factory managers who manage different functional areas, specialized engineers and scientists working in R&D section of the enterprise, along with secretaries, clerks, typists and salesmen belong to these categories of occupations. Some of these occupations have emerged in manufacturing enterprises due to separation between ownership and control, which provided objective conditions for the emergence of new specialized managerial functions and hierarchy [Berle and Means (1932), Williamson (1970)]. Some other service occupations have emerged in the modern manufacturing sector due to the process of vertical integration. These occupations have been variously described by different scholars as *managerial revolution* [Burnham (1941)], *pecuniary class* [Veblen (1961)], *New industrial middle class* [Drucker (1956) and Deherendorf (1957)], *techno-structure* [Galbraith (1967)], *industrial bureaucracy* [Bandix (1956), and *non-production workers* [Delehanty (1968), Seth and Bhasin (1978), Seth and Aggarwal (2004)].

However, after the 1980s, when massive restructuring occured in industrial enterprises in response to the stagflation that was experienced by most developed market economies, some of these occupations have shifted to new independent standing organizations. The shift to flexible manufacturing system has resulted in this process of emergence of several specialized service enterprises formed by persons belonging to those occupation which were earlier embedded within manufacturing enterprises. This phenomenon has already been discussed above in greater details.

IV. Conceptualization of Services as Service Situations

Observing that most of the conceptualizations of services evolved by different scholars are not comprehensive, Hill (1977) made an attempt to conceptualize services in a unique way which is distinct from all existing conceptualizations for defining services: he started looking at services in the context of *service situations* or *service relationships*. After analyzing different service situations, he identified one common characteristic which is unique to all service situations, a common thread that binds all the services together—that each service brings about some changes in the condition of *persons* or *goods* with the prior consent or agreement of persons concerned or owners of the goods. Moreover, he observed another important condition which is unique to services—changes in the goods or persons is made by another economic agent. These two important commonalities that exist in all service situations, or in all service relationships, have been used by him to conceptualize services.

According to Hill (1977) "service is a change in the condition of a person or a good, belonging to some economic unit, which is brought about as a result of economic activity of some other economic unit" [Hill (1977) p.318]. This definition of service provides an appropriate description underlying the notion, *service*, namely, "that one unit performs activity for the benefit of another unit" [Hill (1977) p.318]. He states that in most cases the change in the consumer unit (consumer or good) can be observed by comparing its condition before and after the provisioning of the service. Therefore, he suggests that "the amount of service produced by the service provider be measured by recording the magnitude of changes in a good or person brought about by the service, and not by observing the activity of producer of the service" [Hill (1977) p. 319].

In the case of goods, distinction between *product* and the *process of its production* is quite obvious. However, in the case of services, the process of producing the service is sometimes mistaken for its output. In the context of services, the production process consists of activity which is being used to bring about change in product or a person, whereas, output is given by the extent or magnitude of change resulting from the service activity. Similarly, in the exchange of services, nothing is actually exchanged which amounts to change in ownership. He also suggests that it is not appropriate to think of services as immaterial goods which can be traded in the market. For instance, while transporting products or persons, we alter their location. The change in location is not an immaterial good. A surgical operation is not an immaterial drug, similarly, cleaning of cloth is not some kind of immaterial detergent. Repair of a car makes permanent changes in it and the durability of a repaired car can be estimated on the same time scale as durable goods. This may also include redecoration of a house. Even transportation can bring about permanent changes in location like shipping of the Statute of Liberty from New York to Paris. Similarly, changes in location can also be reversible, like transportation of passengers.

Hill (1977) also questions the premise which accepts that services are perishable products which cannot be stored or stocked. The fact that services cannot be stocked has nothing to do with ther durability. Many services bring not only permanent changes in persons and goods, but also irreversible changes, like education, health, repair etc. Services cannot be stored because output of services consists of changes in the conditions and a stock of changes is a contradiction in terms. Thus services cannot be held as stock is, in fact, a logical impossibility [Hill (1977) p. 319].

Most services which bring changes in goods are those which are already owned by some other economic unit. Services that affect goods make physical transformation in goods which is intrinsically not different from those characteristics that were embodied in it at the time of its initial production. Hence, difference between goods and services does not arise from technology being used in their production. For example, repairing of car may require exactly the same kind of technology, materials, components and processes as are being used in its original production. Therefore, the essential difference between goods and services does not emanate from differences in the technology employed in their production, but due to the important distinguishing feature that, in the case of services producer, the unit operates on goods already owned by the consumer unit. In the case of manufacturing of goods, manufacturing unit acquires all materials, components etc and then sells the finished product to the owner after making it. In the case of services, consumer unit retains the ownership of the good, should be able to recognize its goods and claim it at any point in time. This suggests that goods which are being serviced receive fairly small changes (i.e. not beyond recognition). Hence, services affecting goods are often in the form of maintenance for goods originally produced in earlier time periods.

It is also believed by some scholars that production and consumption of services is instantaneous. This is because a producer of services works on goods owned by the consumer unit. This belief has created maximum confusion in defining services. It has also created an impression that services cannot be stocked. This erroneous belief pertains to only *transitory services*. Instantaniety of consumption and production does not mean that services are "physically consumed or are being extinguished or annihilated" [Hill (1977) p. 320]. This inappropriate emphasis on instantaniety of production and consumption of services created an illusion that benefits of services remain confined to the period in which they are is being produced. Several examples have been given above about circumstances in which benefits from a service continue to occur for several subsequent periods. Therefore, there is a need for drawing a distinction between *permanent* and *transitory* services analogous to the distinction between durable and non-durable goods.

The services that effect changes in a person consist of changes in the *physical* as well as *mental* conditions of the consumer unit made on its request by the producer unit. For instance, passenger transportation, haircut and medical treatment bring physical changes in persons, while services like education, communication, entertainment and sports bring about changes in the mental condition. According to Hill (1977), there is very little correspondence between *services affecting people* and *personal services* as defined conventionally in economic literature. Services affecting people can also be transitory as well as permanent. For example, surgery and education make permanent irreversible change in persons, whereas passenger transportation is transitory as well as reversible.

The merit of Hill (1977), conceptualization of services, rests on its logical strength which it derives from economics rather than from formal characteristic of services. Despite its robust nature it does leave certain gaps while defining services. For instance, a purchased videotape (a good) may bring about the same kind of change in a person as a transmitted television programme (service); Hill (1977) also includes, in his approach, some of the services which are preventive e.g. police, fire services and guards. These services, in fact, try to prevent the occurence of change in the condition of goods and persons [Drechsler (1990)].

Hill further refined his conceptualization of services in a paper which he wrote roughly two decades after his earlier paper [Hill (1999)]. Here he evolved a new taxonomy to distinguish between goods, tangible and intangible, and services. He suggests that most of the confusion which has emerged while conceptualizing services can be attributed to the fact that scholars erroneously included intangible goods in services. He believes that the new taxonomy evolved by him can help in minimising the confusion regarding defining of services. He defines goods as those economic entities over which ownership rights can be established because of which they can also be traded. Goods can also be separated from their producers and owners and, therefore, they have an independent existence from their producers and owners. Goods also have capacity to maintain their existence over time and space. Therefore, their production and consumption can also be separated in time and space. These characteristics of goods make it possible to organize their trading separately— to be carried out at different locations and at different times.

Goods also differ in terms of their process of production. When goods are produced, their production process possesses two distinct important characteristics (a) the entire output from the process of production, including all the intermediate inputs which are needed in production, are owned by the producer, and (b) the sale of the good by its producer is a distinct activity from its production and occurs subsequent to production. If it is not sold it can be kept as inventory. Even if a contract to sell the good has been made prior to production, exchange occurs only after the completion of the process of production. The ownership of the good may change several times during its existence.

Most goods are tangible and have material existence, but it is not necessary that all the goods are material or tangible. There exist so many goods which have non-material existence, yet they possess all the characteristics of goods that have been described above. These intangible goods are produced by persons, or enterprises, which are "engaged in creative or innovative activities which are literary, scientific, engineering, artistic or entertainment in nature" [Hill (1999) p. 438]. These intangibles are produced in the form of *originals* which are either a contribution to knowledge and information or are a creation of artistic or literary nature. These originals appear in different forms, viz, the text of a book, whether scientific, literary or educational, a new musical composition, a new film produced by a film studio, or the recording of a performing artist. It can also be in the form of a new formula for a new chemical or generic production process, a new architectural design, design of a new machine, vehicle, aircraft or a product, a blueprint for a new production process, new blend of a fibre or cloth or a new computer software.

The originals might be the creation of a single or a group of individuals working on it for a considerable period of time, incurring substantially higher costs while creating them. These creations are intangible and would have 'perished in the very instant of their creation' but modern technology has made it possible for them to continue to exist for a considerably longer period. Even the creation of these original intangibles has been recognized explicitly in the broad category of 'production' in the 1993 systems of National Accounts evolved by U.N.O. Modern technology has made it possible to separate them from their original creators after being recorded or stored on some medium, such as paper, films, tapes, disks etc. Therefore, these intangibles which had no physical dimensions become tangibles once they are recorded or stored in a physical media. In their intangible reincarnation, they can be separated from their original creators or owners and can be traded and exchanged over time and space. Hence, originals must be differentiated from the objects on which they are recorded or stored—they exist independent of the medium on which they are stored. Moreover, each original can be stored or recorded in several mediums.

When the original is recorded on a medium like a blank page, tape or disc, nothing material is altered in the process; only blank space of the medium is filled but nothing tangible is added. This establishes that the original is an immaterial or intangible good. The original also does not perish or get consumed in order to provide copies. However, making many copies from the original needs usually negligible costs. Copies of the originals, whether in the form of books, films, tapes, disks are ordinary goods. Therefore, they pass through the same channels like wholesale and retail distribution. As the copies can be used several times, they have the same characteristics like that of a consumer durable or a producer durable.

On the contrary, an original is an intangible good, yet, over the original, ownership rights can be exercised. The ownership right of the original is recognized legally in the form of copyright and patents which gives the owner the right to include or exclude others from using it. The ownership rights on originals are described as *Intellectual property Rights* and are well accepted by law. Hill (1999) suggests that these originals should be treated as fixed assets if they are being used over a longer period of time: fixed assets are defined as those assets which are produced and repeatedly used in the process of production. Originals can also be used separatedly for several years until they become obsolete.

In comparison to tangible goods and intangible goods, services cannot be produced without the involvement of consumers. This is because a service is provided by one economic unit (i.e. producer unit) to another economic unit (i.e. the consumer unit). Hill (1999) suggests that the confusion has been added by economists like Mills (1920) and Marshall (1929), in fact, described services as 'immaterial products'. This concept of services pertains to intangible goods which have been described above, which are in fact goods, not services. Services, in fact, cannot exist independent of their producer; they consist of changes brought about in the condition of one economic unit by the activities of another economic unit. Many services are capable of bringing material changes in persons or products. Since services are not entities, they cannot be stored, for example, "a hospital can stock medical goods and equipment ready for use, but it cannot hold stock of appendectomies to meet an epidemic of appendectomies. The notion of a stock of appendectomies that exists independent of both (surgeons and patients is pure non-sense" [Hill (1999) pp. 441-442]. The fact that hospitals cannot store appendectomies follows from the logic emanating from the concept of services.

Since services are not entities, it is impossible to exercise ownership rights over them. Therefore, unlike goods, services cannot be traded independently of their producers. Hill (1999) makes the difference between goods and services quite obvious by comparing two different economic activities—car making, and car repairing. He states that despite the fact that car making and car repairing need similar materials as well as processes, they are different. The difference between them arises because the output of the car manufacturer consists of separate entities, cars; whereas output of a garage does not have a separate entity. The output of the car manufacturer can be stored as inventories and can be sold to the entire world from a single location. The servicing of cars, on the other hand, must be widely diffused following the spatial spread of ownership of cars. The value addition made by the car servicing station is the value of the repairs. The production of repairs are subject to two important constraints (a) the time of the production of repair is largely determined by the preferences of the consumers, and garages cannot stock repairs in order to meet peak-load demand (b) garages must be located near the customers. These constraints apply to all the services, even if they are owned by the same establishments. Some service establishments, which have even become multinational service providers, cannot concentrate their entire activity at a single location. These service multinationals also follow, while locating their services, spatial distribution of their customers globally. These constraints are not applicable to intangible goods, like the location of production of goods, which can be highly localized. Film production, for instance, is localized in Hollywood, software production at Silicon Valley, similarly R&D activities to generate patents are localized at few locations.

The example given above by Hill (1999) aptly brings about the basic difference between goods and services. It is clear that this difference does not emanate from the fact that one is tangible and the other is intangible or material and immaterial, because output of many services is tangible; similarly there are also intangible goods. The difference between them exists because services are performed by one economic unit for the benefit of another economic unit. The difference also depends on who owns the goods involved, who controls the timing and location of production and, finally, who bears the costs of capital and bears risk.

After providing a conceptual basis to explain the difference between goods and services, Hill (1999) points out that "the traditional assimilation of intangible goods with services has unfortunate consequences for statistical systems, standards and classifications underlying the data used for economic analysis" [Hill (1999) p.444]. For instance, he points out that the 1993 System of National Accounts recognizes artistic originals and computer software as intangible assets and implicitly accepts them as intangible goods; it does not accept scientific originals produced by R&D as intangible goods. In 1993 systems of National Accounts, intangibles have also been erroneously classified as services as also in the International Standard Classification of Industries. The inclusion of intangible goods in services makes it difficult to obtain appropriate data on goods and services. Hill (1999), therefore, concludes that intangible goods should not be considered as a grey area or 'twilight zone between goods and services', but should be considered as goods because they have all the characteristics of a good. However, since they are also sufficiently different from goods on the basis of certain characteristics "there may be a case for identifying them separately by having a *trichotomy* of tangible goods, intangible goods and services" [Hill (1999) p. 445].

Gadrey (2000) describes this conceptualization of services as a synthesis between technical and social factors. This definition includes all those technical operations which are carried out on the reality (i.e. goods or persons) to bring about change, and also includes two types of social relationships (a) 'request for intervention' and (b) property or, ownership relationship [Gadrey (2000) p.375]. This synthetic definition of services received critical assessment also in his earlier work [Delauney and Gadrey (1992)]. In this writing also authors describe the basic anomaly in the definition of Hill (1977). According to these authors, if one accepts the validity of the definition proposed by Hill (1999), then it follows that employees working in a manufacturing firm, who are employed to transform the goods belonging to the owner of the enterprise, can be regarded as service providers to their employers. To remove this anomaly from the conceptualization of services evolved by Hill (1977), they suggest that Hills' conceptualization needs revision and expansion. For this, they drew inspiration from the work of a sociologist [Goffman (1961) and (1983)]. Goffman's work is related to the understanding of social interaction which occurs in different situations. These social situations could be factory premises, airports, hospitals and public thorough- fares where they provide different behavioural settings to create variety of interaction orders. He has spent considerable amount of time in understanding "class of events in which the *server*, in a setting prepared for this purpose, perfunctorily and regularly provides goods of some kind to a series of customers or clients" [Goffman (1983) p. 14].

Gadrey (2000) makes modifications in the definition of Hill [(1977) and (1999)] by using Goffman's (1961) concept of the *service triangle*. Using this concept, he defines services "as activities or operations intended to bring about a change of state in a reality *G* that is owned or used by consumer *B*, the change being affected by the service provider *A* at the request of *B*, and in many cases in collaboration with him or her without leading to the production of a good that can circulate independent of the medium *C*". This definition uses the service triangle consisting of a *practitioner*, an *object* and an *owner* [Goffman (1961) p. 285]. In this definition the statement that "the output of which cannot circulate independently of *C*" is quite crucial. The use of this condition removes the anomaly that exists in the definition of Hill and helps in excluding, from his definition, the productive activities of employees of a manufacturing enterprise.

The comprehensive conceptualization of services evolved by Hill [(1977) and (1999)], alongwith the modification in this conceptualization made by Gadrey (2000), does provide applicability to a wide range of service situations, yet, it is not all encompassing; it is not capable of including the services in which service provider, instead of making available *technical capacities*, provides *human capacities* which he puts on stage in the form of performing arts. In such situations the service provider is neither providing his or her technical capacities, nor is making intervention of any kind but is, in fact, responding to the demand of service seekers. These kinds of services include not only live performances but also services provided by educational institutions. Mostly, these services are delivered in the *platform format* in which the activity is set before the audience like lecture or a talk, a contest, performance of dance, play or musical composition. Modern technology has exploded this interaction within an institutional setting to include a vast *distal* audience [Goffman (1983) p. 7].

To include in the definition of services these kinds of service situations, Gadrey (2000) modified his definition given above by adding that "any purchase of services by an economic agent *B* (whether individual or organization) would, therefore, be the purchase from individual or organization *A*, of the right to use, generally for a specified period, a technical and human capacity owned or controlled by *A* in order to produce useful effect on agent *B* or good *C* owned by agent *B* or for which he or she is responsible" [Gadrey (2000) p. 383].

Callon et al (2004) have further extended the conceptualization of services evolved by Gadrey (2000) to make it all inclusive and capable to accomodate all kinds of products that are being exchanged and traded at the market-place. Objective of Callon et al's (2004), in extending the concept of service, is to emphasize the increasing importance of services' inputs even in the manufacturing of goods. While analyzing the increasing importance of services in the production of goods, they are making, in the process, the role of services explicit in the emerging service economy. They explain this phenomenon by describing how services have got embedded in the production and marketing of goods, which converts these goods into products. This conversion of goods into products has emerged due to pressing need of sellers of goods for positioning these goods in the market-place. The positioning of goods necessitates the identification of qualities or characteristics of a good to project its similarities or dissimilarities (i.e. the extent of product differentiation) with respect to other similar goods available in the market. Callon et al. (2004) suggest that the process of classification or position of a good is similar to the concept of service as evolved by Gadrey (2000).

To explain the similarity between the process of positioning of goods and services, they begin their analysis by creating a distinction between a *good* and a *product*. Goods, according to them, are produced to satisfy needs, and their production and circulation involves mobilization of resources. Goods are attached with property rights which are transferable from one economic agent to another. The concept of economic good implies a degree of stabilization of characteristics that are associated with it. These stabilizing characteristics of a good help in explaining why it is being demanded and why it is being traded [Callon et al (2004) pp.60-61]. It is the combination of qualities and characteristics of a good that help in establishing its extent of differentiation from other goods. Therefore, defining a good essentially amounts to positioning it, in a specific location in the space of goods. This connectivity of goods with each other is measured with the help of *cross-elasticity*. It is a measure which shows how demand of a good is affected by changes in the prices of other goods. Each good is positioned in the market-place in terms of its *intrinsic* and *extrinsic* qualities. Intrinsic qualities of a good are invariant to economic agents, whereas extrinsic qualities are evaluated differently by different users of the good.

A *product,* on the other hand, is an economic good seen from the perspective of its production, consumption and distribution. This consists of sequences of actions, a series of operations that transform it, move it, cause it to change hands across a series of metamorphoses that end up putting it into a form to be judged useful by its users, who pay for it. It must be noted that during these transformations the characteristics of goods undergo changes. Hence, product is a description of different networks, coordinating agents, the actors involved in the design, distribution and consumption. In this sense, product singles out different agents which add qualities to goods and binds them together, in the process of iteration and transformation to define its place under the sun. Hence "product is a process, whereas a good corresponds to its state" [Callon et al (2004) p. 63].

These authors have used the expression *economies of qualities* for the *dynamic* economics of product as opposed to a more *static economy of goods* [Callon *et al* (2004) p. 65]. The economics of qualities help in creating singularity of goods offered to consumers. In the process of singularization of goods, consumer participation is very crucial. However, these authors have used the term *distributed cognition* instead of the term consumer's preferences: the former stands for consumer's ability to precieve differences that exist among goods and also their ability to evaluate these differences [Hutchins (1995)]. They have extended this dichotomy between goods and products to services because they believe that services, or service activities, closely correspond to form of organizations of market in which qualifications of products are central and a constant concern. They describe that "service economy is just another name given to the economy of qualities" [Callon et al (2004) p. 70]. They also believe that economy of quality also corresponds to the conceptualization of services evolved by Hill [(1977) (1999)] and Gadrey (2000).

Gadrey's conceptualization of services, as it has been explained above, is based on the concept of service triangle, and takes into account three service logics (a) *request* for intervention (b) *making available* and (c) *show*. According to the logic of request for intervention, *B* (i.e. owner of car) requests for intervention to *A* (a garage owner), who owns a set of human and technological capacities, mobilization of which will allow *B*'s demand to be realized. In the case of logic of making available, *B* uses techno-human capacities established by *A* which *A* makes available to *B* on certain agreed terms. Finally, according to the logic of show (or spectacle), *B* makes a decision to attend a play, an act or performance by artist, or a sports event organized by organization *A* on agreed terms, generally supported by technical and human capacities at the disposal of *A*.

This way of conceptualization of services, and its description in terms of three service logics, has advantage in establishing a correspondence between service activities and the economics of qualities. For instance, in making available logic, public utilities like electricity connection, telephone or water supply can be made available after establishing a complex arrangement of human and non-human capacities that can be adjusted to one another. Similarly, in the logic of show organisers of performing art event or pleasure trip they bring together a group of participants, prepare a programme in advance and the event will not be possible without making material objects necessary for the show like stage, auditorium, proper seats, sound system etc. These material objects also play an important role in the experience of a show. Therefore, when services are defined in this fashion, they are not significantly different from other forms of goods placed in the market. It also established that Gadrey's (2000) concept of socio-technical capacities is quite similar to terms like distributed cognition used by Callon *et al* (2004).

This explanation makes the distinction between products and services quite apparent and establishes the growing importance of input of services in the emerging economics of qualities. This conclusion of Callon et al (2004) is quite close to the understanding of Marshall about goods and services. He described that "man cannot create material things: in both goods and services he produces utilities. Thus, all productive activities by man can be seen as producing services" [Marshall (1929) p.63]. This concept is very close to the term *bien* used in French language, which denotes both goods and services, and stands for things which are useful, profitable and attractive [Lengelle (1966) p.20].

Callon *et al* (2004), though, bring about clearly the increasing role of input of services in the process of transformation of goods into products and establishing certain amount of similarity between products and services, but have not been able to provide a comprehensive concept of services. Therefore, it seems that the concept of service as evolved by Hill [(1977) and (1999)], alongwith its modification by Gadrey (2000), can provide a useful guidance for conceptualizing services.

Chapter 3

Categorization of Services

In the earlier chapter, we focused our attention on the different ways of conceptualizing services that have been evolved by economists to understand their characteristics. In the present chapter, we are focusing our attention on an inter-related problem—to identify different conceptual bases which have been evolved by scholars for categorization of services. This knowledge is essential for evolving a consistent framework for grouping services into different sets, where each set has certain distinct characteristics. These distinctions are necessary for developing analytical frameworks and theories pertaining to different services. It has been mentioned in Chapter I that each stage of social and economic transformation creates new services and, in the process, causes decline in some other services. Due to this ongoing process of 'creative destruction' the composition of services, at different stages of development, keeps changing. Therefore, at a point of time, an economy may have some services that are remnants of earlier stages of economic transformation; some might have emerged as a consequence of the existing stage of economic development; some others might be an early manifestation of future course of economic evolution.

This suggests that to study the composition of services at a point of time, we need consistent sets or categories where each set may include services that manifest their origin during different stages of economic growth. Moreover, services might differ from each other in terms of complexity of technology being used and skills required to operate equipment necessary to deliver them. Services may also differ from each other in terms of technology embodied in the equipments being used to deliver them. Services may also differ on the basis of their suppliers i.e. whether they are being supplied by the government, corporate sector, non-profit organization or individuals, and also in terms of who are their buyers (i.e. producers or consumers). Therefore, in the present chapter, an attempt has been made to understand different conceptual bases which have been developed by different economists, as well as by different official data collecting organizations, to categorize services. This categorization is quite essential to study various aspects of the service economy, and also to know which set of services is experiencing a decline and which set registers growth with changes in the level of economic development.

Several attempts have been made to evolve a conceptual basis for categorization of services into distinct sets. These categorizations vary depending upon the objectives of the scholars. The simplest and most popular categorization is given by the industry based classifications of services. This is given by the Standard Industrial Classification, which is generally being used to collect data on measuring contribution of different service industries to national income and employment. Most national and international statistical organizations generally use this classification for collecting data: the same has also been used in most of the empirical works conducted by economists. This classification of services is also consistent with the classification used in the United Nation's Systems of National Accounts. Since its inception in the 1960s, this classification has been revised upto three times. These classifications are reported in the Appendix to this chapter (See Appendix 3.1 and 3.2). Similarly, there exists an international classification of occupations, which also include service occupations.

The systematic analysis of categorization of services began with the work of Foot and Hatt (1953). Their objective was to study the phenomenon of social mobility. In the absence of a formal model of social mobility, they adopted the approach of Clark (1940) as it indirectly provides a useful framework to analyse changes occuring in social stratification through the increasing levels of income which facilitates the flow of labour into tertiary industries. Hence, with economic development, the shifts in occupational pattern towards services provides a beginning for the study of social mobility. However, observing that services consist of different heterogeneous categories, to study in depth the issues concerning social mobility, they further sub-divided tertiary industries into three distinct categories. Their each category of services represents a distinct social strata and income level [Foote and Nelson (1983)]. This suggests that mobility towards service industries *per se* does not show the upward social mobility of persons.

Their *first* category is defined as tertiary industries, consisting of domestic and quasi-domestic services like restaurants, hotels, barbers and beauty-shops, laundry and drycleaners, repair and maintenance. All these activities were once performed within the household and represent low-end services.

The *second* category of services have been defined by them as *quaternary* services, consisting of transport and communication, commerce, finance and administration. The distinguishing feature of this group of services is that "these facilitate or effectuate the division of labour" [Foot and Hatt (1953) p. 365]. They mention that, in popular opinion, these services are non-productive "Henry Ford used to fire clerical workers in droves on this account, only to hire them again in a few weeks" [Foot and Hatt (1953) p.365].

In their list, the *third* category of services has been defined as *quinary services*. These services comprise of medical care, education, research, recreation (including arts). The common characteristic of this category of services is that all of them have to do with the refinement and extension of human capacities; they are not devoted simply to the maintenance of individuals into conditions in which they are accustomed to live. These services, in fact, help in inculcating behaviour to which they are not used to. They also act as feedback into the working of all other kinds of services through increments in human ability, skills and knowledge. In turn, these increments bring about improvements in quality of all kind of services. They suggest that these services grow at a rapid rate with economic development and truly reflect the upward social mobility of the working classes. Similar classification of services has been used in writings of several scholars [Gottman (1961), Bell (1973) p. 580 and p. 774]. Some scholars have broadened the scope of quarternary services by including in it information activities. Some others have singled out the information sector as a separate sector consisting of information goods (books and computers), information channels (communication) and information *per se* [Abler, Adam and Gould (1977)].

There also exists a group of scholars which derives inspiration from the pioneering work on services sector done by Fisher and Clark, which is popular now as a Fisher-Clark hypothesis. According to this hypothesis, as industrialization gets internalized in an economy, the share of the primary sector in total national output and employment, generally, registers a decline, while the share of the secondary sector goes on increasing. However, as the economy registers economic growth accompanied by increases in per capita income, the relative share of services increases in total income and employment. The weakest hypothesis of the theory of stages of development is when its premises are extended to the service sector [Leibenstein (1962)]. This relative rise in income and employment in the secondary sector, and relative decline in the primary sector, are supported by historical experience of developed economies and several empirical studies. But the same cannot be established regarding a shift towards relative growth of the service sector. Scholars argue that the service sector consists of a heterogeneous group of services emanating from different stages of development as has been explained in the Introduction to this book. Therefore, some of the services decline with development whereas some others register growth with development. This suggests that a clear understanding regarding the relationship between economic development and share of services in total income and employment depends on the composition of services. This necessitates the study of changes in income and employment at a disaggregated level accounting for individual services.

To capture the impact of heterogeneity in services, both in terms of production and consumption, their sub-division into different categories becomes necessary. Therefore, scholars have developed categorization of services where each set is expected to have a unique relationship with the process of economic development [Katouzian (1970) p. 365]. These scholars have also divided services into three different categories (a) new services (b) complementary services, and (c) old services.

New services include all those services which grow at the Rostowian stage of *high mass consumption* [Rostow (1960)]. It is mainly the nature of their consumption, i.e. mass consumption, which makes it appropriate to label them as new services. These services are those which were included in Fisher's definition of tertiary products [Fisher (1935)] and include "education, consumption of modern clinical and medical services, entertainment in general (including holiday resorts, hotels and restaurants, cinemas, concerts, night clubs and the like) and such other services as may be appropriately included in this category" [Katauzian (1970) p. 366]. Historically, demand for such services was associated with elites or aristocratic minority section of the society. However, during the stage of high mass consumption, considerable increases are noticed in the demand for these services. The emergence of mass consumption of these services happens because their demand is highly sensitive to income elasticity. As per capita income grows substantially, accompanied by scientific and technological developments, these services become available at relatively less prices with enhanced supply. The increasing levels of income also increases the amount of per capita availability of leisure time. These factors, together, explain how these services become part of high-mass consumption.

In the second category of services, which is being described here as complementary services, scholars include all those services which are complementary to the manufacturing sector; some scholars use the term *producer services* for this category of services. Since they are complementary to the manufacturing sector, their growth is linked with growth in manufacturing activities. These services either did not exist or had a minor role in pre-industrial economies and started growing faster alongwith the process of industrialization. This category includes banking, finance, transportation and communication, wholesale and retail trade. These services evolved a strong linkage with the manufacturing sector and grew faster due to the emergence of two intertwined processes. The emergence of round-about method of production increased the demand for intermediate services and necessitated the integration of markets into unified national and global markets. The integration of market-expanded-demand for services, including complementary services on the one hand and increasing size of representative firms in manufacturing and their concentration in certain geographical areas, on the other, led to economies of agglomeration which, in turn, faciliated the birth of industrial cities, which intensified the process of urbanization. Demand for some of these services is also intimately linked with the process of urbanization [Seth (1987) pp. 95-102].

This suggests that the process of industrialization, which led to the integration of markets, expanded demand for these services directly; and the process of urbanization, which grew as a consequence of industrialization, on the other hand, also helped in the growth of demand in these services indirectly [Kuznets (1954), Leibenstein (1962) and Katauzian (1970)]. Scholars also include, in this category of services, services provided by the state, like bureaucratic activities and law enforcement services. This is because provisioning of these services expands due to complexities arising in industrialized and urbanized societies. Historical experience suggests that some of the complementary services experienced dramatic growth rates in quantity, quality as well as efficiency (like transportation and communication), much faster than manufacturing during the early phases of industrialization. In fact, railways have been described as the *leading sector* in the growth of American economy [Fogel (1964)]. Scholars have also not observed any significant differences in the growth of productivity in the goods producing sector and complementary services [Dhryms (1963) and Fuchs (1968)].

Finally, in the category of old services are included those services which originated and flourished in pre-industrial societies. These services were essentially remnants of the old feudal social order. Since these services are rooted in the old feudal economy, they experienced a decline after the beginning of the process of industrialization.

However, to understand the time sequence of structural changes in service activities, experienced by different economies, economic historian, Hartwell (1973), evolved a new taxonomy of services in response to his need to understand the historical process of relative dominance of different services at different points in time. This objective required to identify a meaningful historical path for analysing chronological changes in employment in different category of services. He felt that the existing categorization of services was not appropriate in answering his needs. Therefore, he evolved a new taxonomy to categorize services which could help in providing a "reasonably appropriate framework for historical account of growth in services in modern economic history" [Hartwell (1970) p. 363].

To achieve this objective, he segmented the entire gamut of service activities into five different categories (i) social overhead services (ii) business services (iii) personal services (iv) community and cooperative services, and (v) recreational and cultural services. In the category of *social overhead services*, he includes (a) transportation, communication, post and telegraph, and (b) public utilities like education, public health, police, defence, justice and welfare services. In his category of services described as *business services*, he includes (a) wholesale and retail trade (b) finance and banking, insurance and brokerage, and (c) professional services like accountancy, surveying, architecture, engineering and other technical services. In the category of *personal services* he includes (a) domestic services (b) artisan personal services of barbers, cleaners, plumbers, gardeners, cafes, hotel etc, and (c) medicine and law. In the category of *community and cooperative services* are included (a) religious services (b) professional associations (c) cooperative societies of various kind (d) trade unions and (e) voluntary associations. Finally, in the category of *recreational and cultural services*, he has placed services like (a) entertainment and sports and (b) cultural services like theatre and museums.

Hartwell (1973) believes that categorization of services in this particular format will not only provide an understanding regarding the size and relative importance of different services at different points in time, but also provide changes in the relative importance of services in chronological order. He believes that the use of this taxonomy of services will help in seeking answers to important questions like—"How much and why did the service sector expand with industrialization? What was the effect of this expansion on economic growth? How did the growth in services influence the quality of life in industrial societies? What are the national differences in the pattern of growth in services? What are the probable explanations to explain these diverse experiences in the pattern of growth of services in different economies? Finally, what important lessons can be learnt from these historical patterns of growth in services?" [Hartwell (1973) p. 364].

To differentiate services from each other, some scholars use the market based categorization of services. This framework is based on the premise that services can be differentiated on the basis of who are the *clients* of different services. Depending on their clients, services can be classified into (a) *producer services*, if their clients are business enterprises (i.e. business to business services) (b) *consumer services* or personal services, if the services are purchased directly by the consumer or households (i.e business to consumer services) [Marshall et al (1988)]. Some economists believe that just as we divide goods into consumer goods and producer goods, services should also be divided into consumer and producer services. They believe that this particular categorization of services provides a better understanding regarding identification of factors that determine growth in their demand i.e. whether they are linked with supply side or demand side of economic growth [Greenfield (1966)].

Categorizing services on the basis of their clients (i.e buyers) is quite difficult in real life situations because some services are being purchased by consumers as well as producers. Moreover, when scholars use this categorization for empirical work, the magnitude of errors becomes larger when services are aggregated at the industry level. It has been noticed that services which were classified as producer services also sold a very substantial proportion of their services to households. For example, more than fifty per cent of the revenue of legal services, insurance and real estate is earned from households [Greenfield (1966)]. Sometimes service firms sell their services to each other also than to producers or consumers. Therefore, it becomes quite difficult to identify the clients of services. The only way to use this method for empirical work is through a painstaking micro-level study involving individual firm interviews [Beyer and Alvine (1985) and Kirn, Canway and Beyer (1990)].

In the recent past, some scholars have made attempts to classify services on the basis of their *mode of delivery*. Using this criteria, they broadly divide services into two categories (a) equipment centric, and (b) people centric. Depending upon the combination of quality of equipment and quality of manpower being used in the delivery of service, these two broad categories are further divided on the basis of (a) quality of people involved in handling the equipment being used in the delivery of service i.e. whether the equipment being used is handled by unskilled, semi-skilled or skilled person, and (b) whether people centric service is being delivered by unskilled, semi-skilled, skilled or knowledge worker [Thomas (1978) p. 161]. This taxonomy of services has been described in Figure 3.1.

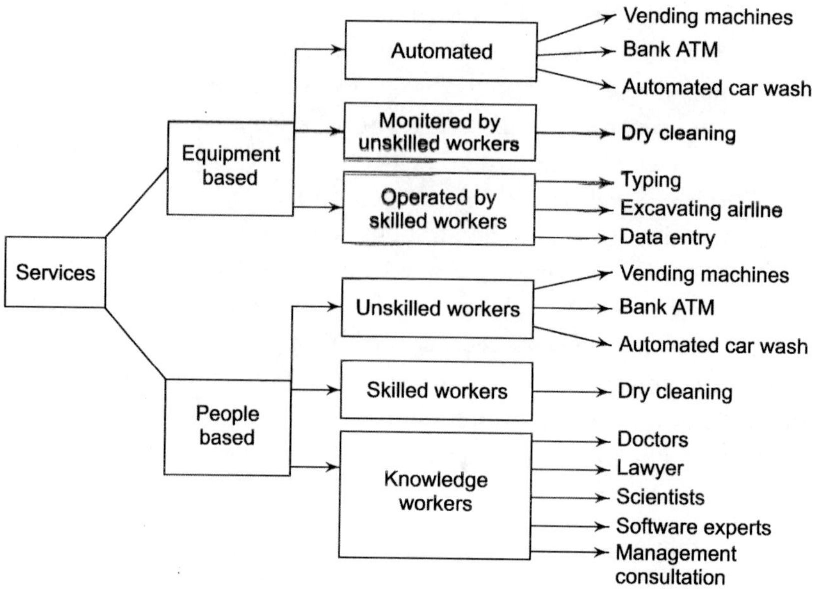

Fig. 3.1 Taxonomy of Services.

Source: Thomas (1978), p. 161

Tradability of services across geographical and political boundaries has also been used as a criterion for classification of services by some scholars. Tradable services are those services which can be separated from their supplier in time as well as in space i.e. service which can be consumed at locations different from the location where they are being produced. These are the services which can be separated from the service providers in the same way as it is possible in the case of goods. This means that the service can have an existence independent from its producer [Boddewyn Holbrich and Perry (1986) and Enderwick (1987)]. These services are, in fact, those which can be either converted in the form of computer software or can be stored in a VCD, DVD and cassette. In these forms lots of services can be separated from their suppliers, like information, knowledge, entertainment etc. The possibility of their separation creates opportunities for global trade in these services. Services which are location bound can be traded through the presence of foreign consumers (like hotels, tourism etc). This categorization of services is quite useful for studying the location decisions of service firms and to know the pattern and magnitude of trade in services [Sauvant (1986)]. However, this categorization does not take into account all modes in which services are being traded globally; these different modes have been discussed in greater detail in Chapter VII of this book.

Economists have tried to categorize services on the basis of *dimensionality constraint*. These are defined constraints imposed by the dimension of *time* and *space* in the production and consumption of services [Melvin (1990)]. The continuum which surrounds us has very obvious facets—time and space—which are the basic context of human existence and his activities. Space and time are modes of existence of matter, where space reflects its *extension* and time reflects its *duration*. If one accepts space as distance, then space becomes important for social analysis because (a) overcoming distance involves costs (b) overcoming distance involves time (c) distance constraints available information and (d) distance constraints opportunities [Seth (1989) pp. 2-3]. This constraint becomes more complex in the case of services because in their production and consumption there is a need for double coincidence of time and space.

For instance, in the case of personal services, double coincidence is essential. These services are beauty salons, hairdressing, surgery etc., where direct contact between service provider and consumer is necessary at the same time and at the same place. These services are categorized as *contact services* which cannot be delivered at long distances—"you cannot get a haircut unless a barber is where you are. Doctor can diagnose on T.V. screens from elsewhere but nurses have to be in hospital where you are with tubes in your arms and in your nostrils and your wind pipes" [Bhagwati (2004) p. 212]. However, integration of technology in the delivery of services has made it possible to overcome the dimensionality constraint in case of some of them. These services are where it has become possible to separate production and consumption in either time or in space; therefore, they do not need double coincidence. Revolutionary changes in the means of communication and information have helped in overcoming the limitations imposed by dimensions of time and space. Services which help in overcoming these two constraint have been categorized as *intermediate services,* for example, transportation, wholesale and retail trade, communication, information, banking and financial services [Melvin (1995)].

This suggests that the dimensionality constraint creates differentiation between two sets of services: the one set consists of those services for which double dimensional coincidence is necessary for their production and consumption; the other set consists of services where technology has made it possible to separate their production and consumption in time and space. Therefore, the activities themselves, which have made it possible to achieve separation between dimension of space and time, become services. These two set of services are not all inclusive; there are also those services which help in overcoming the constraints imposed by knowledge. In this category are included the services of lawyers, accountants, educationists and consultants. These services help in overcoming the constraints imposed by ignorance [Melvin (1989) (1990) and (1995)].

Attempts have also been made to categorize services on the basis of information content required in performing the service occupations. Here, each service occupation is being classified on the basis of the extent of information processing necessary while performing them. This kind of exercise has been done to analyse the relative importance of information economy in contemporary societies. In the information economy, role of manpower in manipulation of symbols and information assumes greater significance [Hepworth (1990)]. He classifies occupations in the service economy into (a) *information producers* (e.g. scientists, scholars and lawyer etc.) (b) *information processors* (viz. teachers, librarians, managers, office supervisors, and (c) *information workers* (like computer operators, data entry persons, printers etc). However, this classification categorizes some services while ignoring several service occupations like that of beautician, bus driver, barbers, shop assistants etc.

Singleman (1978) has evolved a system of categorization of services using a multiple criterion to avoid weaknesses that exist in the classification of services that use a single criteria. He differentiates services on the basis of (a) market criteria (i.e. identifying services according to their clients) and (b) on the basis of the nature of service provider i.e. whether service provider is public organization owned by the state, private organization or non-profit organization. Singleman's categorization provides a structuralist view of services, by dividing them according to the place of activity in the chain of linkages that began with their production process [Castells (1996) p. 207]. He has divided services into four broad categories, viz., business, distributive, personal and social services. In the category of *business services* he includes, financial services, insurance, real estate, business related professional services like accountancy, consulting, marketing, legal, engineering and design. These services employ higher proportion of technical, professional and managerial personal.

Distributive services include wholesale and retail trade, transportation and communication. These services become significant as a consequence of mass production and mass consumption requiring mass distribution and transportation services. There growth has been strongly related to the process of industrialization.

Personal services consist of services that are, in a way, remnants of the feudal social order. These services are modern equivalents of erstwhile servitude of butlers, maids, cooks, gardeners and other domestic help. Initially, these services registered a decline with the disintegration of feudalism into new social formations. This happened due to changes in the methods of production, social relations and family rights and obligations. This also happened due to the end of slavery and different kinds of servitudes, which were replaced by the emergence of the labour market. Domestic services are probably the best example of this group. According to calculations made by scholars "the ratio of servants to families fell by 36 per cent in the United States between 1900-1940 and that this ratio also decreased in U.K., Germany and France [Stigler (1946) p. 24]. In the initial stages of the industrial revolution, these services registered significant growth in their demand because they were a substitute for work that households generally performed through their own inputs (self service). Households started buying these services from the market because of a growing desire for spare time and leisure or to have additional hours at their disposal to supply them in the labour market for additional income. Therefore, demand for these services increased substantially with increases in women's participation in the labour market.

However, when the labour market provided better employment opportunities to the persons engaged in these low-end services, they became quite costly. On the other hand, increasing supply of household capital goods helped in the substitution of these services with inputs of self services. Researchers have shown that households, by combining the purchase of household capital goods with the inputs of self services, substituted the purchase of personal services from the market. There are several examples to illustrate this process. For instance, demand for the services of barbers reduced with the use of razor and inputs of self service, servants by kitchen machines, laundry by washing machine and other personal services by the purchase of electrical and electronic household capital goods [Gershuny (1978), Gershuny and Miles (1983), Driver (1984)]. Analysis regarding personal services has been conducted in greater detail in the chapter on changing composition of employment in services, in this book.

Finally, in the category of *social services,* singleman (1978) includes healthcare, education, social care services like baby sitting or domestic help services. These services generally grow with economic growth and prosperity. Some scholars consider the stage of economic growth, in which the relative importance of these services emerge, as an indicator of the emergence of service economy.

The categorization of services, evolved by Singlemann (1978), is much broader and facilitates the scholars in analysing the process of expansion and decline of relative importance of different services with economic development. Moreover, Singlemann's classification of services is based on the standard industrial classification of official statistical organizations of different countries. Therefore, this classification makes it possible to obtain comparable time series of data on different services which can be used for the study of changes in the composition of services in time and space [Castells (1996) p. 208]. Due to these advantages, his classification of services has been used in several important empirical studies conducted by different scholars [Marshall (1988), Castells (1996), Gershuny and Miles (1983) and, Aoyoma and Castells (2002)]. Despite its innovative approach, singlemann's (1978) classification has all those weaknesses that are inherent in any standard industrial classification based categorization of services. However, in this particular shortcoming is also one of its important strength, because his categorization of services is well adopted to the usual statistical categorization used by official data collecting agencies in most countries. His detailed classification has been given in one of the appendices of this chapter.

Baumol (1967) believed in a certain kind of homogeneity in all kinds of services, therefore, he did not evolve any criterion for differentiating them. According to him, all services have similar characteristics, i.e., they are devoid of any kind of technological change, innovations and economies of scale. Hence, according to him, all services belong to the stagnant sector of the economy and suffer from *cost desease* [Baumol (1967)]. However, his ideas on services changed with the passage of time. He, later on, evolved a categorization of services based on the possibility of growth in productivity [Baumol (1985)]: only those industries can experience changes in the level of productivity in which there are possibilities of technological change, innovation or economies of scale. Based on this criteria, he evolved a classification of services into three distinct categories (a) stagnant services (b) progressive services and (c) asymptotically stagnant services. The same classification has also been used in the work of Inman (1985).

a. *Stagnant services* are services where the delivery of the service and its quality is related to human content and not necessarily with complementary technology being used by the service provider, for example, haircutting, teaching, healthcare and live performances by performing artists. For these services, the hour of service provided by the service provider, or human content, are a measure of quality. For instance, the quality of health services is measured in terms of doctors per thousand of population, nurses per thousand of population; and quality of education is judged on the basis of student-teacher ratio. Hence, even if technological change makes it possible to provide better services to more consumers with less hours of work with reduced human content, the service provider cannot reduce the human content to maintain the precieved quality of service amongst its consumers.

b. *Progressive services* are those which have developed a symbiotic relationship with information technology. They are also being described as Information Technology Enabled Services (ITES). These services do not suffer from double dimensionality constraint, and in them there is no personal contact between user of service and service supplier. There is also absence of human content in the supply of these services. They are capital intensive, technology intensive and experience innovations and economies of scale. Due to these reasons these services experience high rates of productivity growth. Baumol (1985) has defined them as progressive services; and includes in this category services like telecommunication, e-commerce, transportation and multi-media,

c. *Asymptotically stagnant services* have been described by him as those services which experience sporadic growth in productivity but eventually stagnate. This happens because these services contain the seeds of their own stagnancy in their structure. This category consists of services like broadcasting, data processing and R&D. Technology being used in these services consists of a fixed set of inputs which occasionally experience technological changes that enhance their productivity. They contain the seeds of their own stagnancy because they need complementary and matching inputs of stagnant services. For example, to produce a programme to be telecast on T.V. for one hour, one needs one hour of inputs from progressive segment of services i.e. electronic equipment to record the one hour event and telecasting and transmitting equipment for the same duration. These progressive services need matching inputs from stagnant services i.e. contents developed from live performance of performing artists, news readers, VJ's and DJ's etc. Therefore, these services experience growth in productivity as and when equipment and technology used by the service providers experience technological change or innovation. However, unless and until new innovation and technological changes occur continuously in the capital-equipment being used, these services stagnate. This classification is quite appropriate for analysing growth in productivity, efficiency, technological change and innovations among different services. The changing composition of these three categories of services can also be used to explain whether overall productive efficiency of the economy will increase or decrease.

The analysis given above shows that different scholars, who made attempts to study various aspects of the service economy, evolved different bases to categorize services to suit their requirement. The analysis also shows that the classification of services also varied, depending on whether scholars were studying services as products, services as occupations or services as industries. These three conceptual bases have already been discussed in the earlier chapter. However, it is also being observed that categorization of services evolved by Singlemann (1978) has been used in most empirical studies. Its popularity depends on its compatibility with International Standard Industrial Classification which facilitates the availability of comparable time series data for different economies which is necessary for the study of inter-temporal and spatial variations in the composition of services.

APPENDIX 3.1

International Standard Industrial Classification of all Economic Activities (ISIC-Rev. 2, 1968)1

Major Division 1. Agriculture, Hunting, Forestry and Fishing

11 Agriculture and Hunting
- 111 Agricultural and livestock production
- 112 Agricultural services
- 113 Hunting, trapping and game propagation

12 Forestry and Logging
- 121 Forestry
- 122 Logging

13 130 Fishing

Major Division 2. Mining and Quarrying

21 210 Coal Mining
22 220 Crude Petroleum and Natural Gas Production
23 230 Metal Ore Mining
29 290 Other Mining

Major Division 3. Manufacturing

31 Manufacture of Food, Beverages and Tobacco
- 311-312 Food manufacturing
- 313 Beverage industries
- 314 Tobacco manufactures

32 Textile, Wearing Apparel and Leather Industries
- 321 Manufacture of textiles
- 322 Manufacture of wearing apparel, except footwear
- 323 Manufacture of leather and products of leather, leather substitutes and fur except footwear and wearing apparel
- 324 Manufacture of footwear, except vulcanized or moulded rubber or plastic footwear

33 Manufacture of Wood and Wood Products, including Furniture
- 331 Manufacture of wood and wood and cork products, except furniture
- 332 Manufacture of furniture and fixtures, except primarily of metal

34 Manufacture of Paper and Paper Products, Printing and Publishing
- 341 Manufacture of paper and paper products
- 342 Printing, publishing and allied industries

35 Manufacture of Chemicals and Chemical, Petroleum, Coal, Rubber and Plastic Products

351 Manufacture of industrial chemicals
352 Manufacture of other chemical products
353 Petroleum refineries
354 Manufacture of miscellaneous products of petroleum and coal
355 Manufacture of rubber products
356 Manufacture of plastic products not elsewhere classified

36 Manufacture of Non-metallic Mineral Products, except products of Petroleum and Coal
361 Manufacture of pottery, china and earthenware
362 Manufacture of glass and glass products
369 Manufacture of other non-metallic mineral products

37 Basic Metal Industries
371 Iron and steel basic industries
372 Non-ferrous metal basic industries

38 Manufacture of Fabricated Metal Products, Machinery and Equipment
381 Manufacture of fabricated metal products, except machinery and equipment
382 Manufacture of machinery except electrical
383 Manufacture of electrical machinery apparatus, appliances and supplies
384 Manufacture of transport equipment
385 Manufacture of professional and scientific and measuring and controlling equipment not elsewhere classified, and of photographic and optical goods

39 390 Other Manufacturing Industries.

Major Division 4. Electricity, Gas and Water

41 410 Electricity, Gas and Steam
42 420 Water Works and Supply

Major Division 5. Construction

50 500 Construction

Major Division 6. Wholesale and Retail Trade and Restaurants and Hotels

61 610 Wholesale Trade
62 620 Retail Trade
63 Restaurants and Hotels
631 Restaurants, cafes and other eating and drinking places
632 Hotels, rooming houses, camps and other lodging places

Major Division 7. Transport, Storage and Communication

71 Transport and Storage
711 Land transport
712 Water transport
713 Air transport

719 Services allied to transport

72 720 Communication

Major Division 8. Finance, Insurance, Real Estate and Business Services

81 810 Financial Institutions

82 820 Insurance

83 Real Estate and Business Services

831 Real estate

832 Business services except machinery and equipment rental and leasing

833 Machinery and equipment rental and leasing

Major Division 9. Community, Social and Personal Services

91 910 Public Administration and Defence

92 920 Sanitary and Similar Services

93 Social and Related Community Services

931 Education services

932 Research and scientific institutes

933 Medical, dental, other health and veterinary services

934 Welfare institutions

935 Business, professional and labour associations

939 Other social and related community services

94 Recreational and Cultural Services

941 Motion picture and other entertainment services

942 Libraries, museums, botanical and zoological gardens, and other cultural services not elsewhere classified

949 Amusement and recreation services not elsewhere classified

95 Personal and Household Services

951 Repair services not elsewhere classified

952 Laundries, laundry services and cleaning and dyeing plants

953 Domestic services

959 Miscellaneous personal services

96 960 International and Other Extra-territorial Bodies

Major Divsion 0. Activities not Adequately Defined

00 000 Activities not adequately defined.

APPENDIX 3.2

International Standard Industrial Classification of all Economic Activities (ISIC-Rev. 3)1

Tabulation category A: Agriculture, Hunting and Forestry

01 Agriculture, Hunting and related service activities
02 Forestry, Logging and related service activities

Tabulation category B: Fishing

05 Fishing, Operation of Fish Hatcheries and Fish Farms; Service activities incidental to Fishing

Tabulation category C: Mining and Quarrying

10 Mining of Coal and Lignite; Extraction of Peat
11 Extraction of Crude Petroleum and natural Gas; Service activities incidental to Oil and Gas extraction, excluding surveying
12 Mining of Uranium and Thorium Ores
13 Mining of Metal Ores
14 Other Mining and Quarrying

Tabulation category D: Manufacturing

15 Manufacture of Food Products and Beverages
16 Manufacture of Tobacco Products
17 Manufacture of Textiles
18 Manufacture of Wearing Apparel; Dressing and Dyeing of Fur
19 Training and Dressing of Leather; Manufacture of Luggage, Handbags, Saddlery, Harness and Footwear
20 Manufacture of Wood and of Products of Wood and Cork, except Furniture; Manufacture of articles of Straw and Plaiting Materials
21 Manufacture of Paper and Paper Products
22 Publishing, Printing and Reproduction of Recorded Media
23 Manufacture of Coke, Refined Petroleum Products and Nuclear Fuel
24 Manufacture of Chemicals and Chemical Products
25 Manufacture of Rubber and Plastics products
26 manufacture of other Non-metallic Mineral Products
27 Manufacture of Basic Metals
28 Manufacture of Fabricated Metal Products, except Machinery and Equipment
29 Manufacture of Machinery and Equipment NEC2
30 Manufacture of Office, Accounting and Computing Machinery

31 Manufacture of Electrical Machinery and Apparatus NEC2
32 Manufacture of Radio, Television and Communication Equipment and Apparatus
33 Manufacture of medical, Precision and Optical Instruments, Watches and Clocks
34 Manufacture of Motor Vehicles, Trailers and Semi-trailers
35 Manufacture of other Transport Equipment
36 Manufacture of Furniture; Manufacturing NEC2
37 Recycling

Tabulation category E: Electricity, Gas and Water Supply

40 Electricity, Gas, Steam and Hot Water Supply
41 Collection, Purification and Distribution of Water

Tabulation category F: Construction

45 Construction

Tabulation category G: Wholesale and Retail Trade; Repair of Motor Vehicles, Motorcycles and Personal and Household Goods

50 Sale, Maintenance and Repair of Motor Vehicles and Motorcycles; Retail Sale of Automotive Fuel
51 Wholesale Trade and Commission Trade, except of Motor Vehicles and Motorcycles
52 Retail Trade, except of Motor Vehicles and Motorcycles; Repair of Personal and Household Goods

Tabulation category H: Hotels and Restaurants

55 Hotels and Restaurants

Tabulation category I: Transport, Storage and Communications

60 Land Transport; Transport via Pipelines
61 Water Transport
62 Air Transport
63 Supporting and Auxiliary Transport Activities; Activities of Travel Agencies
64 Posts and Telecommunications

Tabulation category J: Financial Intermediation

65 Financial Intermediation, except Insurance and Pension Funding
66 Insurance and Pension Funding, except Compulsory Social Security
67 Activities auxiliary to Financial Intermediation

Tabulation category K: Real Estate, Renting and Business Activities

70 Real Estate Activities
71 Renting of Machinery and Equipment without Operator and of Personal and Household Goods

72 Computer and related activities
73 Research and Development
74 Other Business Activities

Tabulation category L: Public Administration and Defence; Compulsory Social Security

75 Public Administration and Defence; Compulsory Social Security

Tabulation category M: Education

80 Education

Tabulation category N; Health and Social Work

85 Health and Social Work

Tabulation category O: Other Community, Social and Personal Service Activities

90 Sewage and Refuse Disposal, Sanitation and similar activities
91 Activities of Membership Organizations NEC**
92 Recreational, Cultural and Sporting activities
93 Other Services activities

Tabulation category P: Private Households with Employed Persons

95 Private Households with Employed Persons

Tabulation category Q: Extra-territorial Organizations and Bodies

99 Extra-territorial Organizations and Bodies

Additional category X: Not Classifiable by Economic Activity

Notes

[1] For full details see United Nations: Statistical papers, Series M, No. 4/Rev. 3 (New York, 1990).

[2] Not elsewhere classified.

APPENDIX 3.3

An extended sectoral classification (Browning-Singlemann)

I. Extractive

1. Agriculture, fishing and forestry
2. Mining

II. Transformative

3. Construction
4. Food
5. Textile
6. Metal
7. Machinery
8. Chemical
9. Miscellaneous manufacturing
10. Utilities

III. Distributive Services

11. Transportation and storage
12. Communication
13. Wholesale trade
14. Retail trade (except eating and drinking places)

IV. Producer Services

15. Banking, credit, and other financial services
16. Insurance
17. Real estate
18. Engineering and architectural services
19. Accounting and bookkeeping
20. Miscellaneous business services
21. Legal services

V. Social Services

22. Medical and health services
23. Hospitals
24. Education
25. Welfare and religious services
26. Non-profit organisations
27. Postal services
28. Government
29. Miscellaneous professional and social services

VI. Personal Services

30. Domestic services
31. Hotels and lodging places
32. Eating and drinking places
33. Repair services
34. Laundry and dry-cleaning
35. Barber and beauty shops
36. Entertainment and recreational services
37. Miscellaneous personal services

Chapter 4

Inter-sectoral Shifts in Employment

As has been described in Chapter 2, the attraction of economists towards employment in services was drawn during the Great Depression of the 1930s. It was felt at that time that services can provide employment to a sizeable part of the working population that had been rendered unemployed due to recession. It was indeed a great realization on the part of policy-makers, as well as economists, that the classification of economic activities into primary and secondary sectors does not completely exhaust all the possibilities of employment. Therefore, all other economic activities, other than those included in the primary and secondary sectors where employment existed at that time, were provided with a *single signpost* called the *tertiary sector* [Fisher (1933) and Clark (1940)]. Since then several attempts have been made to define these residual economic activities, which are now broadly categorized as services. These attempts have been discussed in detail in Chapter 3. Whether services can be conceptualized appropriately or not is more of an academic issue; however, expansion of employment in services in the short-run, and in the long-run, and emergence of a service economy as a consequence of economic growth have become a part of folk-lore in economics.

The emergence of the service economy can be understood only in the context of structural changes that occur in the inter-sectoral composition of employment accompanied by economic growth. Economists have studied, in greater detail the inter-sectoral shifts in employment; unlike economists, sociologists have shown greater interest in the study of shifts in occupational patterns. This is because changes in the inter-sectoral distribution of occupational pattern reflect the changes occuring in social mobility and social stratification. However, there exists a close relationship between inter-sectoral changes in the composition of employment and shifts in occupational patterns.

In the present chapter, an attempt has been made to study inter-sectoral shifts in employment to understand the relationship between employment in services and economic development. The chapter has been divided into two sections and each section deals with certain specific issues related to inter-sectoral changes in the employment structure. Section I deals with the inter-sectoral shifts in employment experienced by different economies and offers an identification of the determinants of these shifts. Section II deals with different empirical studies that have made an attempt to conceptualise the relationship between inter-sectoral shifts in employment and economic development.

I. Inter-sectoral Shifts in Employment

Some development economists have evolved certain generalizations or stylized facts regarding inter-sectoral shifts in employment based on empirical investigations of experiences of developed economies. Their empirical observations gave birth to certain broad patterns regarding the relative proportion of employment in different sectors of the economy, at different stages of economic development. The sectoral theory of employment shifts– pays attention on structural changes occuring within an economy in terms of shifts in employment pattern—initially from primary to secondary, and later on to the services sector [Fisher (1935), Clark (1940), Kuznets (1966) and Chennary (1960)].

Empirical studies regarding evolution of employment structure amongst developed economies suggests that there have been three distinct phases experienced by these economies during three distinct historical periods. All the developed economies were primarily agrarian economies where a substantial proportion of working population was engaged in the primary economic activities. The second phase, i.e. the period between 1880 to the 1960s, is described as the post-agricultural period, in which these developed economies experienced (at varying dates) that the proportion of working population engaged in primary activities declined and shifted to the secondary sector. The third phase began after the 1960s, when these economies entered the post-industrial phase. In this phase they experienced a decline in employment in the secondary sector and rise in the proportion of working population engaged in services. Some economists described the post-industrial phase as the rise of the *service economy* [Fuchs (1968), Bell (1973), Castells (1996) and Aoyama and Castells (2002)].

The existing data regarding the shift in employment among different sectors of developed economies shows that during 1920-1970, in England and Wales, manufacturing employment increased marginally from 42.1 to 43.8 per cent, whereas in U.S.A. manufacturing employment increased from 32.9 to

33.9 per cent, in Canada from 26.1 to 30.0 per cent. Japan and Germany showed a remarkable shift in employment towards manufacturing from 19.8 per cent in 1920 to 34.3 per cent in 1970 and from 38.9 per cent to 49.0 per cent respectively (see Table 4.1). This suggests that during 1920-1970, secondary sector was expanding in all the developed economies. Therefore, whatever expansion these economies experienced in employment in services was occuring at the cost of primary sector during this period [Singlemann (1978)].

However, it should be noted that England and Wales had entered the post-agricultural stage much before 1920 (in fact in 1821). Therefore, it had only 4 per cent of working population engaged in primary activities in 1970 and it also registered a decline in the proportion of working population in the manufacturing sector (from 46 per cent in 1960 to 43.8 in 1970). This has emerged as a consequence of early industrialization. Despite this divergent experience, trends in their employment structure show remarkable similarity during the period. This commonality in the structural change in sectoral composition of employment is the simultaneous expansion in employment in secondary as well as services sector at the cost of declining employment in the primary sector. This convergence occured because of rapid industrialization that caused a shift in surplus manpower from primary to secondary as well as services sector [Castells (1996) p. 209]. However, the economy of U.S.A. had already crossed more than 50 per cent share of working population employed in services in 1960s. Therefore, U.S.A. can be described as the first economy which got transformed into a service economy [Fuchs (1968)].

In the post 1970 period, the process of economic growth, accompanied by rapid technological change, helped in reducing employment in the secondary sector in all the developed economies. However, the decline in employment in the secondary sector was not uniform, indicating the role of diversities in economic policies and strategies of development pursued by different economies. The process of relative decline in employment in the secondary sector is also being described as the process of *de-industrialization* which occured very rapidly in the United States of America, United Kingdom and Italy. These economies registered a decline in secondary sector employment from 25.9 to 17.5 per cent (U.S.A.), 38.7 to 21.8 per cent (U.K) and from 27.3 to 21.8 per cent (Italy) during the period 1970-1990. This process was quite slow in other developed economies where relative decline in employment in the secondary sector was recorded in the post 1990 period. This suggests that the economies of U.S.A., U.K. and Italy have entered a stage in structural shifts, in sectoral employment, when the service sector starts growing at the cost of primary as well as secondary sector.

The post 1990 period has been characterized by globalization and liberalization of markets for factors of production as well as for goods and services. This period also witnessed the end of the longest period of continuous expansion experienced by developed economies punctuated by stagflation. These changes resulted in a dramatic decline in manufacturing sector employment in economies like U.K. and U.S.A. between 1990-2000, from 22.5 to 15.2 per cent in U.K. and from 17.5 to 14.7 per cent in U.S.A. Similar deceleration in employment in the secondary sector was registered by even the rapidly growing manufacturing economies of Germany and Japan during this period. Despite the fact that Germany still has a very significant proportion of working population employed in the secondary sector, in comparison to other developed economies, it recorded a decline in the secondary sector employment from 32.2 to 25.2 per cent. A moderate decline was also noticed in the employment in the secondary sector in Japan from 23.6 in 1990 to 19.6 per cent in 2000 [Aoyama and Castells (2002)]. This suggests that both Japan and Germany have also experienced structural changes in the organization of production in their manufacturing sector.

Attempts have been made by different scholars to identify the reasons for the occurence of these structural changes in the sectoral composition of employment. The beginnings in this direction were made by Fisher [(1933) and (1935)] and Clark (1940) to study how economic growth affects employment pattern across different sectors of an economy. Fisher-Clark identified that employment in services was growing as a result of structural changes occuring in the employment pattern experienced by economies. From their studies, a broad generalization emerged that "a high level of income per head is always associated with higher proportion of working population engaged in the tertiary sector" [Clark (1940) p. 341]. Even though this generalization has become almost like a received wisdom or stylized fact regarding the consequences of economic development, it needs explanation.

The generalization evolved by Fisher-Clark also has a historical legacy. William Petty anticipated this trend in 1690 when he observed the existence of a very large share of employment in trade and shipping in Holland [Hull (1899)]. Almost after a century, another economist belonging to the German Historical School, Freidrich List, also formulated a stage theory of development which anticipated a similar pattern regarding inter-sectoral shifts in income and employment as identified by the Fisher-Clark hypothesis [Bremer (1966) and Hoselitz (1960)]. However, a rigorous empirical and logical explanation to the pattern was given by Engel, known as *Engel's Law of Consumption*, which established that with rising level of income (i.e. economic growth), consumption of primary products increases less than proportionately and, therefore, composition of demand shifts in favour of products of services [Hauthakker (1957)]. Therefore, with economic development, consumption pattern shifts in favour of services which explains the growth proportion of working population engaged in their production. This hypothesis is further extended to explain the changes in the composition of services because rising levels of income also affect the consumption pattern of different services differently.

Although Fisher and Clark both accepted the generalization that with economic growth largest proportion of working population will be employed in services, but they provided different explanations for this pattern. Fisher [(1933) and (1935)] identified the reason regarding shifts in inter-sectoral composition of employment from the *demand side*, whereas clark (1940) sought the answer for the same from the *supply side*. According to Fisher, the expected pattern of inter-sector shifts in employment pattern emerge because services have very high *income elasticity of demand* i.e. their demand grows more than proportionately to rise in income. This rising demand leads to shift in employment in favour of service industries. On the contrary, clark explained that structural changes in the inter-sectoral distribution of working population emerge because of *inter-sectoral differences in productivity*. According to him, services suffer from low productivity in comparison to other sectors of the economy. This necessitates a shift of large proportions of working population towards services.

Similar understanding regarding inter-sectoral differences in productivity and elasticity of demand of services was expressed by a French economist, Fourastie, in 1950 in his book, *The Great White Hope of the Twentieth Century* [Delauney and Gadrey (1992) p. 79]. While explaining inter-sector differences in productivity, he has selected certain products as proxies for the characteristics of the output of that sector. For example, in his analysis, potatoes represent the primary sector, bicycle is used as a proxy for the secondary sector and a hotel room is used as a proxy for the tertiary sector. He describes that labour productivity in case of potatoes increased from 100 in 1880 to 130 in 1950. Its consumption increased continuously throughout the period of 1920, experienced negative income elasticity in 1950. In the case of bicycle, productivity increased from 100 in 1900 to 700 in 1950, and is still increasing. The consumption also increased nine times during the same period and, in 1950 it began to level-off. In the case of hotel rooms, productivity of labour practically remained unchanged from 1800 to 1950, but demand increased from 100 in 1800 to 10,000 in 1930. Fourastie used these inter-sectoral differences, in productivity and elasticity of demand, to explain how inter-sectoral terms of trade and changes in demand will favour growth of employment in services, in comparison to other sectors of the economy [Kindleberger (1958)].

Studies conducted by Fisher and Clark led to several such studies to evaluate the validity of the expected shifts in the inter-sectoral distribution of working population observed by them [Kuznets {(1955)} and (1966)}, Dowie {(1960) and (1970)}, Chennary and Taylor (1968), Fuchs (1968) and Haig (1973)]. These studies also observed similar patterns in inter-sectoral shifts in working population. However, these scholars differed from each other in their approach—whether they used the supply side factors or the demand side factors. The scholars who used a logical explanation based on supply side factors emphasize inter-sectoral differences in productivity as the main reason for the existence of the observed pattern. Believing that services have lower labour productivity in comparison to other sectors of the economy makes it inevitable for the shift of a large proportion of working population in favour of services. These scholars implicitly assume that services have unlimited capacity to absorb working population. On the other hand, scholars who lay stress on demand side factors attach importance to higher income elasticity of demand for the products of services, in comparison to products produced by other sectors of the economy.

It is not only demand for final services which grows with development but also demand for intermediate services because of emerging strong inter-sectoral linkages between sectors. These linkages also increase the demand for services because other sectors also require larger inputs of services for their proper growth [Turnham (1971) and Sapir (1982)]. Several empirical studies have established that the *demand-led* growth is a better explanation than supply led growth in explaining inter-sectoral shifts in employment in favour of services as a consequences of economic development. These studies explain the growth in employment in services as being led by such demand side factors as industrialization, urbanization, rising real income and increasing employment in the rural non-farm sector. These factors increase the demand for final services as well as intermediate services [Gershuny and Miles (1983), Marshall (1988) and Britton (1990)].

Fuchs (1967) identified three hypothesis, which he used while explaining the relative growth of employment in services sector. The *first* hypothesis is that service sector products have elasticity of demand greater than unity. Therefore, as real income grows, the employment in services sector grows more than proportionately in comparison to other sectors of the economy. The *second* hypothesis is that increasing specialization, mechanization and automation, as a result of economic growth, facilitates the emergence of independent and efficient service providers like management consultancy, accounting, data processing, transportation and distribution. These specialized services substitute some of the services which were earlier available in-house within manufacturing enterprises. The high degree of specialization not only increases the quality of these services but also reduces their costs because of economies of scale which arise because specialized service providers supply these services to several enterprises. The *third* hypothesis is inter-sectoral differences in productivity. Through his empirical work, Fuchs (1967) tried to understand the relative importance of each of these hypotheses in the context of growth in service employment in the U.S. economy. He observed that each hypothesis did provide explanation for the growth of employment in a particular segment of services, but the hypothesis which was valid in the case of most of the services was low-productivity of services.

Based on his understanding regarding the determinants of employment in services given above, Fuchs (1967) evolved a formal model to explain inter-sectoral shifts in employment [Fuchs (1967), Appendix A pp. 201-202)]. He developed a model based on these factors, with the understanding that the difference between the rate of growth of employment in services in comparison to the goods producing sector depends on the differential rate of growth of output in different sectors (i.e. services producing and goods producing sectors), and the inter-sectoral differences in the productivity measured in terms of output per-worker in each sector. This is expressed in the following equation

$$\dot{E}s - \dot{E}g \ (\dot{Q}s - \dot{Q}g) - (\dot{P}s - \dot{P}g) \qquad \text{(i)}$$

Where Es and Eg stand for employment in service producing (s) and goods producing sectors (g); $\dot{Q}s$ and $\dot{Q}g$ stand for output in services and goods producing sectors respectively, Ps and Pg represent productivity per man in the respective sectors and the dot stands for percentage change. This formulation assumes that these differences in output and productivity in each sector are independent of determinants which cause differences in the rate of growth of output and productivity. If we incorporate these determinants in the model, the model becomes a nontautogical description of differential sectoral growth in employment.

The changes in output of different sectors are determined by the rate of growth of per capita income ($\dot{Y}$), the income elasticity of demand for the product of each sector (Is and Ig), changes in the relative prices of services ($\dot{R}s$) and goods ($\dot{R}g$) and the elasticity of substitution (esg) between good and services

$$(\dot{Q}s - \dot{Q}g) = f\left[\dot{Y}, Is, Ig, (\dot{R}s - \dot{R}g), esg\right] \qquad \text{(ii)}$$

On the other hand, the price differentials among the products of different sectors depends on different rates of changes in their nominal prices ($\dot{N}$), the rate of growth of real wages ($\dot{w}$), and the time intensity of goods relative to services (t)

$$(\dot{R}s - \dot{R}g) = f[Ns - Ng), \dot{w}, ts, tg] \tag{iii}$$

Under the conditions of perfect competition, the differential rate of change of the nominal prices will be approximately equal to the differential rate of change of output per unit of total factor output ($\dot{T}$). The changes in the output per unit of factor input will depend on rates of technological change ($\dot{A}$) and economies of scale (c) that can be realized from changes in the level of output (Q)

$$(\dot{N}s - \dot{N}g) = -(\dot{T}s - \dot{T}g) = f[(\dot{A}s - \dot{A}g), Qs, Qg, cs, cg] \tag{iv}$$

The inter-sectoral productivity differential, ($\dot{P}s - \dot{P}g$), on the other hand, depends on the all the determinants which influence sectoral changes in output and inter-sectoral difference in the use of capital (both physical and human) per man ($\dot{K}$) in two sectors, and the initial hours per man (H) and changes in per hour (ΔH).

$$(\dot{P}s - \dot{P}g) = f[(\dot{T}s - \dot{T}g), (\dot{K}s - \dot{K}g), Hs, Hg, \Delta Hs, \Delta Hg] \tag{v}$$

Combining all the five equation into one, we get the following equation

$$(\dot{E}s - \dot{E}g) = f[\dot{Y}, (\dot{A}s - \dot{A}g), (\dot{K}s - \dot{K}g), ms, mg, Cs, Cg,$$
$$Csg, ts, tg, Hs, Hg, \Delta Hs, \Delta Hg] \tag{vi}$$

In this formulation, it is assumed that the price of labour (w) and price of capital (Kp) change at the same rate i.e. prices of the factor do not influence factor use. Therefore, changes in the factor intensities in technology can be attributed to only factor biases embodied in the technology (B). If factor prices vary at different rates, the changes in capital per man will depend on inter-sectoral differences in the elasticity of substitution between capital and labour (m) and factor proportions in the initial year (k).

$$(\dot{K}s - \dot{K}g) = f[(\dot{B}s - \dot{B}g), Ks, Kg, \dot{W}, Kp, ms, mg \tag{vii}$$

From these equations, Fuchs suggests that the inter-sectoral differences in the growth of employment will depend on (a) the rate of growth of per capita income in the economy (b) inter-sectoral differences in the rate of growth of technological changes (c) inter-sectoral factor intensity bias in the technology (d) inter-sectoral differences in factor proportions (e) relative changes in factor prices (f) income elasticity of demand for goods and services (g) inter-sectoral differences in the elasticity of substitution between capital and labour (h) elasticity of substitution between goods and services (i) inter-sectoral differences in the economies of scale (j) the time intensity between goods and services (k) initial hours of work and changes in hour of work in each sector.

William J. Baumol (1967) developed a two sector model based on inter-sectoral differences in productivity. The model consists of manufacturing (m) and services (s) sector, where services have lower average productivity in comparison to manufacturing sector. He defines production technology for each sector, where output level Qm and Qs (of manufacturing and services) entirely depends on the amount of labour used, (Lm) and (Ls), and rate of increase in productivity of labour in each sector (rm and rs). In his model, total employment is given by the amount of labour employed in each sector i.e. $L = Lm + Ls$. The demand for the output of each sector i.e. Qm and Qs is determined by the budget constraint, which is represented by the wages per work (w). Therefore, demand for service workers will be

$$(Qs/L) = t(Ps/Pm)^{\beta}\, w^{\alpha}\, e^{\Delta t} \qquad \text{(i)}$$

This equation suggests that the demand for service workers depends on relative prices (Ps/Pm) of services and manufacturing, wage income per worker (w), and also by the exogenous shifts in the demand ($e^{\Delta t}$) over time. Here β provides price elasticity of demand for services and α provides the measure of income elasticity of demand.

In Baumol's (1967) model, wage rates are determined by equating demand for labour with the supply of labour (i.e. market clearing level of wage rate). Since a profit maximizing firm will demand labour inputs until the value of marginal product of last unit of labour is equal to wages, the marginal product in manufacturing (mpm) and in services (mps) is defined by

$$dQm/\partial Lm = mpm$$

and

$$\partial Qs/\partial Ls = mps$$

The market prices of manufacturing (pm) and services (Ps) are determined by competitive market forces, where their respective prices are determined by marginal costs. The marginal cost in the case of manufacturing industries is given by (w/mpm), and in the case of services by (w/mps). According to the conditions of competitive market equilibrium, the marginal cost differences between services and manufacturing sector should correspond to the relative prices of manufacturing (pm) and services (ps) i.e. (ps/pm).

The most important premise on which the model is based is that the rate of change in labour productivity in manufacturing sector (*rm*) is greater than the rate of productivity change in services (*rs*)) i.e. $rm > rs$. Therefore, the relative price of services increases over time $[\partial(ps/pm)/\partial t > 0]$. These relationships are used in the model to determine the time path of the growth of employment in services in the economy. If we define the share of services in the total employment of the economy by

$$Is = Ls/Ls + Lm = Ls/L$$

then the main conclusions of Baumol's (1967) model can be represented by the following relationship to understand as to how the relative share of service employment will grow over time

$$Is = (\alpha - 1)rm + \Delta + (rm - rs)(1 + \beta) \qquad (ii)$$

With the help of this equation, Fuchs first hypothesis (mentioned above) can be tested by using first term in the equation (*ii*) i.e. $(\alpha - 1)rm$. In Baumol's model, wages per worker increase at the rate of *rm*. This percentage change increase in wage rate generates additional demand for services output at the rate of $rm\alpha$. This suggests that the share of employment in the economy increases if increase in the demand for services is more than proportionate to the change in aggregate demand i.e. $rm\alpha > rm$ or $rm(\alpha - 1) > 0$. Fuch's second hypothesis can be explained with the help of the second term in the model, i.e. Δ, which accounts for all exogenous changes that can occur in the demand for services which occur due to factors like changes in the size of family, changes in the labour force participation rates of women or the extent of business process outsourcing by enterprises. Finally, the last two terms of equation (*ii*) measure the role of inter-sectoral differences in productivity in determining the share of employment in services. These terms are $(rm - rs)$ $(1 + \beta)$.

However, it must be mentioned that Fuchs (1969) revised his understanding regarding hypothesis on lagging productivity in services. He writes "This assumption is probably wrong for most of the service industries. Where we have decent independent measures, output per man in services usually goes up. Moreover, many factors that have increased output per man in agriculture and industry, such as capital per worker and improvement in the quality of workers, were operative in at least a few service industries. Also, the benefits of economies of scale and growth of transaction size probably helped some service industries. Finally, it is hard to believe that there has been no advance in knowledge concerning production of services" [Fuchs (1969) pp. 10-11]. These findings regarding productivity estimates in services by Fuchs (1969) also compelled Baumol (1985) to revise his two sector model given above.

Baumol (1985) included another sub-sector in his new three sector model consisting of some of the progressive services which experience productivity growth in the short-run, but eventually stagnate in the long-run. These services have been appropriately described by Baumol (1985) as *asymptotically stagnant services* (see, for detail, chapter on Categorization of Services in this book).

Several attempts have been made by different scholars to evaluate the empirical validity of Fuchs-Baumol's explanation regarding inter-sector shifts in employment [Levson (1985), Saxonhouse (1985), Summers (1985), and Hesten et al (1992)]. These studies provide evidence for the inter-sector shifts in employment experienced by different economies to lend support to the Fuchs-Baumol hypothesis regarding lagging productivity as the main determinant of worldwide drift towards service employment. Regarding the demand side explanation for the growth of employment in services, Summers (1985) observed that the value of income elasticity (α) for the aggregate of all services was equal to $\alpha = 0.98$, which was not significantly different from unity. However, his study does show that the income elasticity of demand for services like housing, medical care and other consumer services was significantly different from unity [Summer (1985) Table 1.6 p. 41].

Contrary to the accepted pattern of inter-sectoral shifts in employment envisaged by Fuchs-Baumol hypothesis, based on the premise that services suffer from low productivity but have an income elasticity of demand for their output greater than unity, have been disputed by Appelbaum and Schettkat (2001). They challenge the premise on which Fuchs-Baumol hypothesis is based—that demand for services expands solely on the basis of increases in income and psychologically explained hierarchy of needs. This approach neglects the role of prices in the decision making process of consumers. The role of prices have appeared indirectly in several studies which have observed that the share of services in real output has remained constant despite the fact that per capita income has increased [Baumol, Blackman and Wolff (1989), Rowthorn (1992) and Ramaswamy and Rowthorn (1997)]. They observed that income elasticity of demand for many services was greater than unity and also that demand for services was also price sensitive. Therefore, they reached an unusual conclusion: an increase in productivity of services, that brings productivity growth in line with or above the level of overall productivity growth in the economy, will accelerate the growth of demand for services and increase their real output and employment share. "Thus, improvements in productivity in services emerge as the key not only to raising per capita income but also to expand employment" [Appelbaum and Schettkat (2001) p. 129].

The analysis of Japanese service economy provides an important example regarding the role of lagging productivity of Japanese services and peculiar structure of Japanese wholesale and retail trade which have been responsible for the expansion of employment in the services sector. The persistence of lagging productivity in the Japanese economy can be attributed to the protection given to small retailers by the government due to which the share of distribution activities in Japanese economy is 25 per cent of the active population and almost 70 per cent of this segment consists of establishments employing less than ten workers [Saxanhouse (1985)].

The demand and supply side explanations given by Fuchs-Baumol hypothesis, in terms of Engel's law of consumption (demand side) and inter-sectoral productivity differentials (supply side), have also been used by Bell (1974) as basic determinants for the emergence of service economy or *post-industrial society*. The explanation based on these factors ignores the role of intermediate services or producer services in generating employment in services. The most important historical fact is that intermediate services have expanded very rapidly in most developed economies. The intermediate demand for services grew as a consequence of the evolving division of labour within manufacturing as well as due to the increasing component of intangibles in the production of goods. To understand the extent of intermediate services in an economy, final output of the economy can be viewed with the help of input/output framework.

Fuchs (1968), ther analysed the service industry output that enters as inputs in other sectors of the economy, he observed that they accounted for around ten per cent of the expansion in service sector employment in 1950, in the case of the U.S. economy. Studies based on input-output analysis for different economies found that service sector output, that takes the form of inputs in other sectors of the economy, is around 22 per cent in U.K. and 38 per cent in U.S.A. [Gershuny and Miles (1983) p.31]. However, it should be noted that input-output analysis gives information only regarding the magnitude of inter-sectoral production linkages rather than the linkage between the final output and services sector employment. To know the relative importance of intermediate demand for services and growth in service sector employment, one can also use the approach evolved by Singlemann (1978). He assesses the role of intermediate demand for services in expanding employment in services by estimating the percentage share of employment growth which can be attributed to producer services. His estimates show that the percentage growth in the share of employment in producer services during 1960-1970 was 24 per cent for England and Wales, 15 per cent for Germany and 52 per cent for France [Singlemann (1978), Tables 2.1 and 2.3].

Some of the scholars attribute the phenomenon of increasing share of employment in service sector to the breakdown of the methods of mass production, also described as demise of Fordist methods of production. This view has been evolved by (a) *French Regulation School* [Aglitte (1979), Coriat (1979) and Bayer and Saillard (2002)] (b) *Neo-Schumpetarian Approach* [Dosi *et al* (1958)], and (c) flexible specialization approach [Sabel (1982) Piore and Sabel (1984) and Sabel and Zeitlin (1997)]. These different theoretical formulations believe that a serious crisis has been experienced by methods of mass production, which provided competitive advantage to the manufacturing sector of the developed market economies for almost a century. These methods emerged initially in the U.S.A, following the use *of continuous process-flow assembly line* method of production used in the Ford motorcar company. The methods of mass production are based on economies of scale and *vertical integration* to maximize *internal economies*. The increasing size of firms, to achieve economies of scale, integrated several service functions within manufacturing enterprises. These service function related employment was recorded as employment in manufacturing in the official statistical data. However, after the oil crisis of 1973, and subsequent emergence of *stagflation* in developed market economies, the methods of mass production became inefficient and needed restructuring to achieve flexibility in the process of production.

The basic characteristics of flexible production system are (a) flexibility of the production system (b) flexible factor markets and (c) increased dependence on *external economies* in the organization of production. The essential characteristic of flexible production system is *vertical disintegration*. These characteristics help firms to respond quickly to market forces.The process of vertical disintegration creates an inter-firm and inter-plant transaction structure which gives rise to a network of firms in a supply chain. Hence, the production system becomes more and more externalized and the notion of "firm as an organization" gets transformed into "the organization of firms" [Scott (1988)]. This process of externalization has significant consequences on the growth of employment in services.

Some of the services are intermediate inputs in the production of goods or other services. The efficiency of the system, both upstream and downstream, depends on the quality of services. This has been established by several empirical studies [Daniels (1985); Baily and Maillart (1985); Illeris (1988) and Beyer (1989)]. These service inputs can be either provided internally in the manufacturing enterprise through vertical integration, or externally from free-standing service firms through outsourcing [Coffey and McRae (1989)]. However, since the 1980s, most firms are following the second alternative. Therefore, as a consequence of this strategy, a shift has occured to move service functions out of the manufacturing enterprises. This phenomenon has created employment in services at the cost of employment expansion in manufacturing [Seth (2001), (2002), (2003) and Seth and Aggarwal (2004)].

However, in recent years, a debate has emerged amongst scholars—is growth in employment in services illusory or real ? Some scholars believe that it is essentially a statistical phenomenon because most of it is due to *displacement-effect* [Gershuny and Miles (1983) and McRay (1985)]. Some empirical studies show that the growth in employment and output in services has occured by internal as well as external growth in services simultaneously. They also observed that there is no empirical evidence to suggest that employment in services has grown because of displacement effect. This is because there has not been any significant decline in internalized services in the manufacturing sector [McCrackin (1985), Tschetter (1987), Kutscher (1988) and Illeris (1989)]. In fact, some of the studies suggest that growth in service employment is real and not as a consequence of displacement effect because it has been found that most of theis growth has emerged as a result of certain fundamental changes that have occured in the variety of services being consumed rather than simply due to displacement effect [Beyer (1989)].

Moreover, it has been observed that with increasing diversities in tastes of consumers, modern economies are characterized by growing complementarity between production of goods and services. This has happened because the competitive advantage of the products produced by the manufacturing units no longer depends on their manufacturing quality alone, but also on the extent of customization of their products which has become necessary to reorient the products according to diversities in the consumer's preferences. This has necessitated that the enterprises should pay attention to the design of products, marketing, branding and on complementary services. This requires integration of service inputs, both upstream (R&D) and downstream (marketing, retailing distribution and after scale services). This suggests that manufacturing now also needs specialized inputs of financial and information services. These developments have increased the demand for intermediate services. This possibility was noticed earlier by Osberg, Woolf and Baumol (1989). The argument advanced to explain the growing employment possibilities in services is that now manufacturing sector needs larger proportion of inputs of services. Therefore, expansion in the manufacturing of goods creates more than proportionate growth in employment in services. This argument has been propagated by those economists who still believe that 'manufacturing' matters.

The Economic Council of Canada (1991) examined the validity of the premises on which this argument is based. They used input-output analysis to know the increases in the linkages between inputs of services in the production of goods. However, the study did not observe any substantial increase in the inputs of services needed to produce the final output so it did not lend support to the argument that expansion in manufacturing goods leads to more than proportionate growth in employment in services. Even if one accepts the validity of this argument than it would be expected that whenever an economy experiences recession, the service sector should register greater fall in employment than the manufacturing sector. However, reality does not lend support to this premise. In the 1980s, when most developed economies were experiencing stagflation, which significantly affected employment in manufacturing enterprises, it did not significantly affect employment in services.

We have explained above the experience of developed economies regarding inter-sectoral shifts in employment. Some scholars believe that the experience of developed economies provides a future mirror-image of the pattern of inter-sectoral shifts in employment. However, information available regarding the experience of developing economies shows quite a different pattern. It has been observed that even at a premature level of economic development, these economies employ a significant proportion of their active population in services and have experienced transition from primary to service sector, without experiencing a transition of employment from primary to secondary sector. Some of them have a higher proportion of active population engaged in the service sector in comparison to secondary sector. It is shown in Tables 4.2B and 4.2A that a significant proportion of their work force is engaged in services and its magnitude is increasing over time. This growth is attributed to the decline in the rate of labour absorption in the primary as well as in the secondary sector because they are using relatively higher capital intensive technologies in both sectors in comparison to developed economies in the comparable stage of development [Seth and Seth (1994)].

According to some scholars most of the employment generated in the services sector of developing economies can be attributed to the supply side factors, that is, the existence of low productivity in services accompanied by higher rates of growth in population. In developing economies, services generally have low productivity which helps in accommodating larger proportion of their working population in services. As these economies have relatively lower per capita income in comparison to developed economies, a very small proportion of employment in services originates due to high income elasticity (i.e. demand-led growth in service employment). This formulation suggests that every addition to the workforce in developing economies creates employment for himself in service sector by sharing certain amount of work [Bhalla (1970)].

Some other scholars have questioned the appropriateness of this formulation. They believe that developing economies are also experiencing shifts in the inter-sectoral composition of employment as predicted by Fuchs-Baumol and Fisher-Clark hypotheses and empirical work of Kuznets (1966). They believe that both supply-led factors (like low productivity levels in services) and demand-led factors (like high income elasticity of demand for services) are playing important roles in influencing inter-sectoral distribution of the active population. Alongwith low productivity of services, in the case of developing economies, a high income elasticity of demand for some services, created by expanding population growth in cities, is also responsible for their growing importance. Such services are transportation and communication, wholesale and retail trade [Udall (1976)]. Some scholars also explain the rate of growth of employment in services with the help of excessive growth of employment in administration in developing economies alongwith increasing role of government in achieving the objectives of employment generation and reduction of poverty. They also explain this process with the help of factors like rising middle-class households in developing economies which creates demand for services like retail and wholesale trade, education, health and entertainment. Even increasing rate of growth of manufacturing sector creates supply-led growth in employment in intermediate services and through income elasticity of demand emanating from the incomes of workers employed in the manufacturing sector [Panchmukhi et al (1986), Bhatacharya and Mitra (1997) and Seth and Aggarwal (2004)]. Therefore, as has been experienced in the case of developed economies, growth of employment in services in developing economies has also been determined by demand induced as well as supply induced factors.

It should also be noted that the emergence of higher proportion of working population employed in the services sector, in developing economies, can be attributed to one important fact that some of the services which grew in developed economies alongwith the process of development have now become preconditions for achieving modern economic growth (like education, banking, insurance etc.). The emerging necessity of these services at the initial stages of development has resulted in the excessive growth of employment in services in these economies.

Due to the commonality of experience of developed as well as developing economies, as revealed by the empirical evidence generated by the three sector division the economy, it has now become a mainstream understanding that as a consequence of economic growth, economies follow a well defined sequence of inter-temporal shifts in their inter-sectoral distribution of working population. However, the three sector model ignores the differences in the process of creation of final products of each sector at different stages of economic growth. This is based on a very simplistic structure of organization of production. It assumes that primary sector delivers final products produced with the help of primary sector occupations like forming and fishing directly to the consumers. Similarly, manufacturing sector supplies products produced with the help of blue-collar workers directly to the consumers, while services provide direct service to the household with the help of primarily white-collar workers. If reality had been so simple, then the three sector model provides an excellent explanation regarding inter-sectoral shifts in employment. This explanation is, however, not appropriate for those economies where production is organized, in all the sectors of the economy, with complex organizational structures. In technologically developed economies, we cannot visualize the production of primary sector products without the help of services of agricultural scientists, farm managers, wine and tea-tasters, modern farm equipment and chemical fertilisers. Similarly, manufacturing activities are also linked with several services like advertising, marketing, sales and distribution etc. Some of the services also cannot be visualized in modern economies without the complementary technology and equipment made available by the manufacturing sector. Can we visualize modern health care services without CAT scans and x-ray machines, modern banking without ATM's ? It is due to the emerging strong inter-sectoral linkages that it has become difficult to predict intersectoral shifts in working population with the help of the three sector model.

Moreover, it is also envisaged that human beings have a hierarchy of needs which change with different levels of income. Three sector model implicitly assumes that there exists a correspondence between each sector and human needs. Therefore, changes in the hierarchy of needs explains the shift in employment in different stages of development among different sectors of the economy. This premise ignores the possibility of technological change and *social innovation* [Gershuny and Miles (1983) pp. 83-91]; the latter can redefine the production function and influence the final uses of different products. The characteristics of end-use of products change because other commodities are produced by means of other commodities which, in turn, influences inter-sector distribution of working population. In the production of commodities we need inputs of goods as well as services; however, technological change and social innovation may alter the requirement of either. It has been observed that economies have experienced innovations in the production of services which has changed the mode in which final services are obtained. The social innovation of services has not influenced their formal production but has significantly influenced their informal procurement in *self-service* mode. This innovation has been achieved by reorganizing the final service function. This process has been described as *social innovation* in services.

In this mode of provisioning of services, individual households purchase equipment or consumer capital goods related to services and combine them with collective investment made in infrastructure and their unpaid self-service to obtain final services [Gershuny and Miles (1983) pp. 84, 85].

The process of social innovation breaks the linkage between employment in services and hierarchy of needs. Thus, as services have low productivity, their growing demand increases their prices which, in turn, reduces demand for final services. This reduction occurs because instead of increasing the demand for services, it increases demand for consumer capital goods (i.e. consumer durables) which can be combined with free-inputs of self-service within the household to satisfy the need of services. This mechanism of substitution of goods, which enjoys greatest economies of scale and productivity growth, for services has been ignored in the three sector model. It is unable to anticipate that the growing demand for services can be met not by increasing employment in services, but by increasing demand for goods which can be combined with self-service.

Apart from issues related to growing employment in services, scholars have also identified several important characteristics of employment in services. For instance, it has been observed that employment in services is more stable over business cycles, but its productivity is more unstable in comparison to the manufacturing sector. This is explained by the fact that services cannot be stored. This eliminates the possibilities of fluctuations in the output of services caused by changes in the holding of inventories of goods by firms as well as consumers. This is also related to the fact that for a very significant proportion of persons employed in services, their earnings are sensitive to business cycles but their hours of work do not vary with business cycles. For self-employed persons engaged in services, like legal experts, consultants, brokers in real estate, insurance and stock market, waiters, barbers, beauticians and salesmen, their earnings output and commissions and tips are sensitive to business cycles, but their hours of work are not sensitive to such fluctuations [Fuchs (1968) pp. 160-182 and Elfring (1989) p. 435].

Another important distinction between employment in services and manufacturing sector, that has been identified by scholars, is that most of the work in service sector does not require physical attributes. This characteristic of employment in services results in a situation when men and women can compete with each other on equal terms. Moreover, some of the service jobs require flexible timings. These characteristics have helped in the increasing participation of women in services; some of the work has already been feminized in services, like school education, nursing, front office work, clerical positions, public relations etc. [Warren and Gilroy (1976) and Wheat (1977)].

It has also been emphasized that with increasing rates of women's participation in the labour market, demand for personal services has significantly increased: this further increases the employment of women in services because they are well equipped to work in services that they earlier provided in the household [Grubel (1987) and Silver (1987)].

II. Empirical Studies for Analysing Inter-sectoral Shifts in Employment

Several attempts have been made to study the inter-temporal shifts in the inter-sectoral distribution of working population, to verify the expected changes in them as predicted by the three sector division of economic activities. Most such empirical studies have obtained mixed results regarding the relationship between sectoral shares in employment and economic growth as predicted by this approach. These studies have related shifts in sectoral distribution of working population with per capita income to test the validity of this approach. Fuchs (1968) tested this relationship with the help of the following equation

$$Ei = \alpha + \beta / x$$

where Ei stands for share of employment in the ith sector of the economy, and x stands for per capita income [Fuchs (1968) p. 25]. If Ea stands for the share of employment in the primary sector, Em for employment in the secondary sector, and Es for employment in services sector, and x stands for per capita income, than the hypothesis implicit in the three sector division of the economic activities can be tested and expressed as

i. $\partial Ea/\partial x < 0$ $\quad$ $d^2 Ea/\partial x^2 > 0$

ii. $\partial Em/\partial x > 0$ $\quad$ $\partial^2 Em/\partial x^2 > 0$

iii. $\partial Es/\partial x > 0$ $\quad$ $\partial^2 Es/\partial x^2 < 0$

It is interesting to note that Fuchs (1968) obtained support regarding the validity of the hypothesis in his empirical exercise (see Figure 4.1). The figure shows the pattern of shifts in employment experienced by each sector. According to the figure, agricultural employment declines faster in the early stages of development and employment shifts to secondary and services sectors. However, the decline in the share of employment in agriculture sector slows down with development, approaching asymptotically, a share around three per cent of employment of working population. In the case of secondary and services sectors, their share becomes asymptotically about 40 per cent and 57 per cent respectively [Fuchs (1968) pp. 24-31].

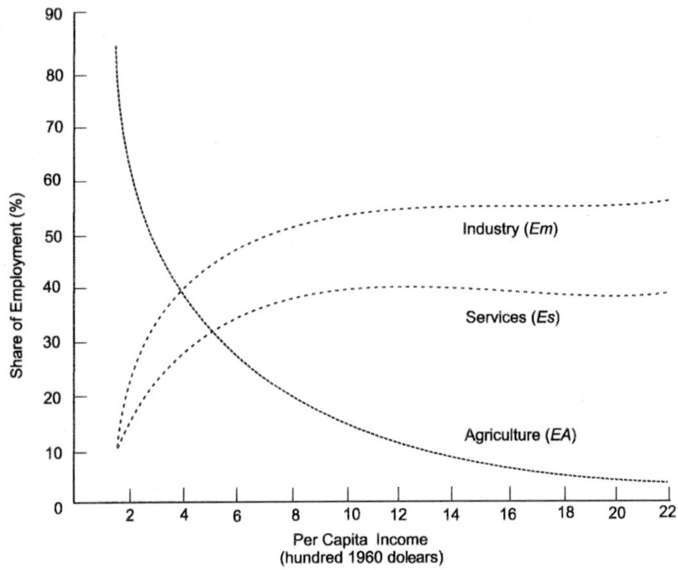

Fig. 4.1 Relationships Between Sector Shares and Per Capita Income (Fuchs, 1968)

Source: Fuchs (1968), pp. 32-33

To study the shifts in the inter-sectoral composition of employment, Chenery and Taylor (1968) used a cross-section data of 54 countries and covered the period between 1950-1963. They used the following equation to test the relationship between inter-sector shifts in employment and economic development

$$\log Ei = \alpha + \beta \log x + \phi \log x^2 + \delta \log P$$

Here Ei is the share of the ith sector in terms of employment, x stands for per capita income and P stands for population [Chenery and Taylor (1968) p. 393]. This single equation assumes that the effect of each variable is additive in logarithms and independent of the value taken by the other variables. They have used two separate methods to obtain better results. In one method they have used continuous variable and grouping of countries into different levels of development with one or more indices [Chenery and Taylor (1968) p. 373]. To evolve different setcs of countries, they have divided them into large and small countries and have used population as the basis of determining the size. According to their criteria, countries having population below 15 million are small and above 15 million are large countries [Chenery and Taylor (1968) p. 393]. Later on, a modified model was used by Chenery and Syrquin (1975). The empirical exercises done in both the studies also lent support to the expected shifts in the inter-sectoral distribution of working population in industry and agriculture. However, they did not obtain any plausible results in the case of services. It has been suggested that they have obtained an insignificant relationship for the services sector because they have included the variable log *P* representing population of the economy [Gemmell (1981) p. 62].

The choice of form of relationship presented in the equations of Fuchs (1968), Chenery and Taylor (1968) and Chenery and Syrquin (1975) have been dictated by a *priori* economic logic underlying the sectoral shifts in employment. The literature on economic development suggests that a relative shift of employment occurs from primary sector to other sectors of the economy, as per capita income grows in an economy, and also predicts that the pace of the shift eventually slows down as income per capita rises. This suggests that a predominantly agrarian economy, with very low productivity in agricultural sector, experiences a faster shift towards non-agricultural sector then when the sector becomes smaller with relatively higher productivity. This phenomenon can be well represented by logarithmic specification of variables as in the case of Chenery and Taylor (1968) and Chenery and Syrquin (1975) and also by reciprocal specifications of the variable [Fuchs (1968)].

Similarly, a relative shift of employment from secondary sector to services is explained with the help of the argument that services enjoy a high income elasticity of demand as compared to the manufactured goods, therefore, as per capita income increases with economic growth, it will initially increase demand for manufactured goods and subsequently, with higher changes in per capita income, it will increase demand for services. It has also been accepted in economic theory that productivity in services generally lags behind the secondary sector [Baumol (1967) and (1983)]. Therefore, at higher income levels when surplus labour from the primary sector is exhausted, a shift from industrial sector to services becomes inevitable. This logic suggests that structural changes in the sectoral composition of employed workers occur in the beginning when employment in secondary and services sectors grows at the cost of employment in the primary sector. However, when agricultural sector reaches the stage of asymptotically stagnant share, service sector employment increases at the cost of secondary sector employment (i.e. de-industrialization) [Gemmell (1981) p. 41]. Figure 4.2 provides the pattern of structure changes that are expected to be followed by an economy based on this logic.

To accomodate this new insight into a computable framework, Gemmell (1981) evolved an alternative methodology: while specifying the equation for different sectors of the economy (i.e. *Ea*, *Em* and *Es*), he has used separate all functional forms. He has used the specification of Fuchs (1968) for primary sector employment (*Ea*) i.e.

$$Ea = a_1 + b_1/x$$

However, he believes that Fuch's equation, which he has used for all the sectors, does not represent structural changes in the services sector, that have been explained above. Therefore, he evolves an equation which represents the pattern of shifts in employment in services, expected as a result of structural changes. Thus, he uses the following equation for services

$$Es = a_2 + b_2x + C_2x^2 + \partial_2x^3$$

This function is cubic in x and provides sigmoid shape, which appropriately captures the expected structural changes in the employment in services. He did not specify any independent functional form for the secondary sector because, according to him, specifying three independent functional forms for three different sectors would not yield values for three sectors which meet the essential condition that $Ea + Em + Es = 1$. Therefore, he treats employment shifts in secondary sector (Em) as residual shifts and has specified its share as

$$Em = 1 - (Ea + Es)$$

He is also aware of the fact that specifying an equation for service sector, which is cubic in x, may not be able to show that point where the share of service sector employment will approach some maximum value asymptotically. Therefore, he approximates the Es function with a single infletion point which may occur when $a_2 + a_2 + c_2 = 0$. This can be obtained by shifting the origin in Figure 4.2 to the point of inflection (see Figure 4.3).

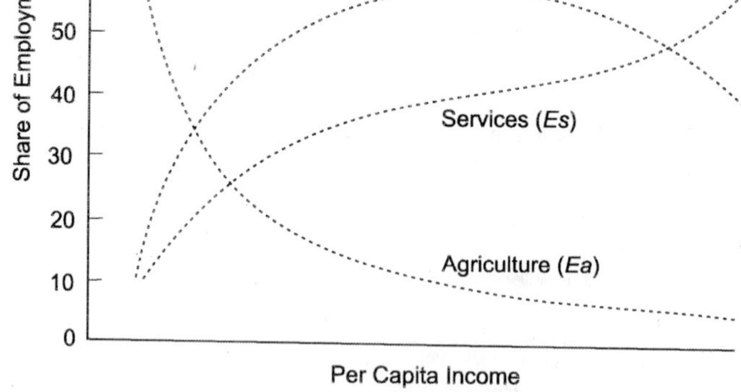

Fig. 4.2 Alternative Relationships Between Sector Employment Shares and Per Capita Income.

Source: Gemmell (1981) p. 40

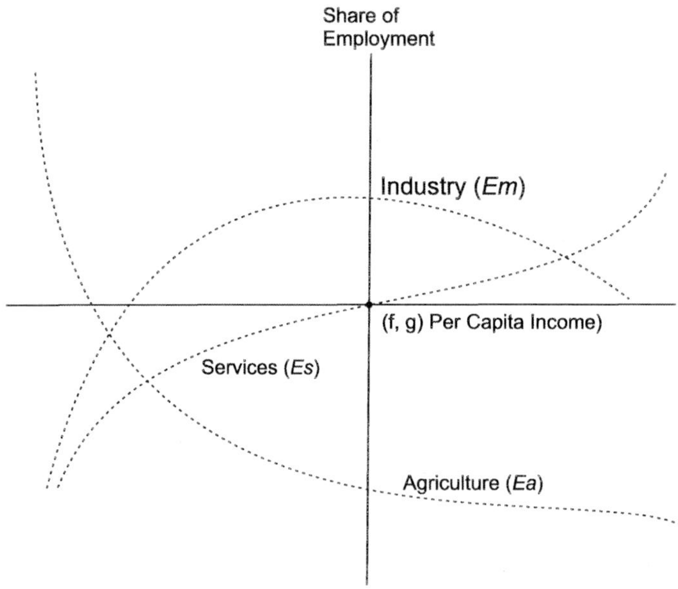

Fig. 4.3. Origin as the Point of Inflection.

Source: Gemmell (1981) p.42

After fixing the point of inflection, i.e. new origin of *Es* described as (*f*, *g*), new variables for employment and per capita income can be generated in the following manner

$$e = E - g$$

$$x = X - g$$

This will give new functions for *ea*, *em* and *es*, such that

$$ea + g = a_1 + b_1 \{1/(x + f)\}$$

$$es = d_2\, x_3$$

$$em = 1 - 3g - es - ea$$

The main weakness of this specification is that even though employment shares of secondary sector (*em*) and services (*es*) are endogenous variables, in this specification either of the sector can be used as residual sector.

Gemmell (1981) has obtained quite plausible results with the help of this specification. His results show that service sector share in employment begins to grow at the cost of industrial sector share at about 37 per cent and 34 per cent of the two sector share respectively. This suggests that services sector share is already larger relative to the share of the secondary sector, when it begins to grow at the cost of manufacturing employment. Moreover, he observes that as the share of secondary sector begins to decline, the share of social services increases faster than the rate of growth of aggregate employment in services. This conclusion is quite consistent with the expected inter-sectoral composition of employment in a *post-industrial society* where proportion of persons employed in social services, i.e. engaged in the provisioning of public welfare services, substantially increases with higher levels of income. The most important conclusion of his study is that *de-industrialization* phase is not a *transient* phenomenon in developed economies, arising from slower growth or recession, but a *permanent* one. Therefore, his exercise lends support to the proposition that the employment in service sector expands faster than secondary sector during early and later stages of the process of economic development.

The analysis presented above gives a detailed account regarding advances made in the understanding of inter-sectoral shifts in employment which economies experience as a consequence of economic growth. A beginning in this direction was made by the studies of Fisher (1933, 1935) and Clark (1940). In earlier studies, emphasis of the scholars was on identifying the pattern of shifts in inter-sector distribution of working population. Once the pattern was identified, emphasis shifted towards identifying determinants which influence the pattern of inter-sector shifts in employment. Some scholars identified these determinants from the supply side, while some others identified them from the demand side. Finally, scholars shifted their attention to empirically predict these patterns to provide knowledge to policy makers regarding expected future scenarios. These findings establish that at an aggregate level inter-sectoral shifts in employment follow a predictable path, and deviations from this path may arise due to differences in the policy regime prevalent in different economies.

We have already mentioned about different categories of services in this book, in the chapter on *Categorization of Services* (Chapter 3). These categories originate at different stages of economic development. Therefore, composition of services keeps changing with the process of economic development. This happens because each category of services has a unique relationship with development; some of them grow in importance with economic development, while some others register a decline. Therefore, aggregate growth of employment in services depends upon the composition of employment in different services. This knowledge can be obtained by analysing shifts in the composition of employment in different services. This is the subject matter of the chapter that follows.

Table 4.1 Percentage Distribution of Working Population in Different Sector's Among Developed Economics (1920-1970)

Sectors and Countries	*About 1920*	*About 1930*	*About 1940*	*About 1950*	*About 1960*	*About 1970*	*About 1980*	*About 1990*	*About 2000*
Primary Sector									
U.S.A.	28.9	25.4	21.3	14.4	8.1	4.5	4.0	3.5	2.9
Canada	36.9	34.4	31.7	21.6	14.7	9.1	7.1	5.7	5.6
England	14.2	11.8	*	8.9	6.6	4.2	4.3	3.2	1.9
Germany	33.5	31.5	*	16.1	9.0	5.1	4.1	4.1	2.9
France	43.6	38.3	40.2	31.9	23.0	17.0	8.7	6.4	4.1
Italy	57.1	48.1	*	42.9	29.8	17.2	11.7	9.5	5.1
Japan	56.3	50.9	46.3	50.3	34.1	20.0	11.2	7.2	5.4
Secondary Sector									
U.S.A.	32.9	31.5	29.8	33.9	35.9	33.9	29.6	25.6	22.6
Canada	26.1	24.7	28.2	33.7	31.2	30.0	26.8	22.3	21.6
England	42.1	39.3	*	45.4	46.0	43.8	35.7	27.3	20.6
Germany	38.9	38.3	*	47.3	51.3	49.0	40.3	40.3	33.1
France	29.7	32.8	29.6	35.2	37.3	39.3	34.8	29.5	24.7
Italy	24.2	29.2	*	32.0	40.9	44.3	40.5	29.7	29.9
Japan	19.8	19.8	24.9	21.0	28.5	34.3	33.7	33.7	30.1
Services									
U.S.A.	38.2	43.1	48.9	51.7	56.0	61.2	67.4	70.9	74.5
Canada	37.0	40.9	40.1	44.6	54.1	60.9	66.1	72.0	72.8
England	43.7	48.9	*	45.7	47.4	52.0	60.0	69.5	76.5
Germany	27.6	30.1	*	36.6	39.7	45.9	55.6	55.6	64.0
France	26.7	28.9	30.2	32.9	39.7	43.7	56.4	63.1	71.2
Italy	18.7	22.6	*	25.1	29.3	39.5	47.8	60.8	65.0
Japan	23.9	29.3	28.8	28.6	37.4	45.7	55.1	59.1	64.5

Source: Derived for the period (1920-1970) from Singlemann (1978) Table No. II P. 1227 and for the period (1980-2000) from Aoyama and Castells (2002)

Table No. 5p.136.

* Not available

Table 4.2 Inter-sectoral Composition of Employment in Developing Economies (1970-2000)

Country	*Sectors* / *Years*	*P*	*S*	*T*
Egypt	1970	54	15	31
	1975	49	17	24
	1980	42	21	37
	1985	–	–	–
	1990	44	21	35
	1995	34	21	45
	2000	28	23	49
Mauritius	1970	42	08	50
	1975	37	16	47
	1980	30	22	48
	1985	25	25	50
	1990	17	42	41
	1995	–	–	–
	2000	09	29	62
Zimbabwe	1970	41	19	40
	1975	40	20	40
	1980	39	20	41
	1985	31	20	49
	1990	29	23	48
	1995	29	22	51
	2000	–	–	–
Mexico	1970	43	22	35
	1975	42	22	36
	1980	41	23	36
	1985	29	25	46
	1990	28	22	50
	1995	25	21	54
	2000	18	26	46
Brazil	1970	32	23	45
	1975	31	21	48
	1980	30	20	50
	1985	30	20	50
	1990	24	22	56
	1995	27	26	47
	2000	25	26	49
Korea Republic	1970	49	17	34
	1975	46	23	31
	1980	35	28	37

	1985	26	29	45
	1990	19	34	47
	1995	13	33	54
	2000	11	28	61
Pakistan	1970	58	16	26
	1975	55	18	27
	1980	53	17	30
	1985	52	19	29
	1990	51	19	30
	1995	47	21	32
	2000	48	17	45
Malaysia	1970	58	20	22
	1975	59	20	21
	1980	55	14	31
	1985	38	22	40
	1990	32	22	46
	1995	24	31	45
	2000	18	32	50

Source: Year Book of Labour Statistics of different years.

P → Primary Sector

S → Secondary Sector

T → Tertiary Sector

CHAPTER 5

SHIFTS IN THE COMPOSITION OF EMPLOYMENT IN SERVICES

We have discussed and analysed, in detail, the inter-sectoral shifts in employment in relation to economic development in Chapter 4. It was observed that the inter-sectoral shifts in employment, at the aggregate level, follow a predictable path as an economy develops. These predictable changes in the employment structure have become a part of received wisdom regarding inter-sectoral composition of employment at different stages of development. However, it was also noted that services consist of quite heterogeneous economic activities that have roots in different stages of economic evolution. Therefore, each category of services has a unique relationship with the process of economic development. This suggests that certain services experience growth along with economic development, while some others register a decline. It is expected that whether service employment will grow or decline at the aggregate level depends on the composition of employment among different categories of services. Hence, knowledge regarding the same is quite relevant in understanding the relationship between employment in services and economic development as also to know at which stage of development the economy is.

Since each stage of development, or economic transformation, creates some new services and destroys some older ones through an ongoing process of creative destruction, in the present chapter, an attempt has been made to analyse the shifts in the composition of employment in different services. This exercise pertains to analysing intra-sector shifts in employment in services. For a better analysis, this chapter has been divided into two broad sections—Section I deals with explanations regarding shifts in the composition of employment among different services. For this, the study is trying to seek answers to the nature of relationship between different categories of services and economic growth. Section II deals with the results obtained by different empirical studies regarding intra-sectoral shifts in employment in services.

I. Relationship Between Economic Development and Different Categories of Services

As has been mentioned above, services, like other economic activities, are also subject to the process of creative destruction, which causes changes in the composition of employment at different stages of development. This suggests that at any point of time, the composition of services includes some that are remnants of a past distinct socio-economic structure alongwith those that emerge as a consequence of contemporary changes in the economy. This process of continuity and change explains the existence of quite a heterogeneous set of services in an economy at a point in time. Therefore, shifts in the composition of services can be used to represent the level of development of an economy. Hence, the relationship between service employment and economic development, which is being observed at the aggregate level, may not be manifest at the level of the individual or for a group of services.

It is not only the heterogeneity of services which explains why employment in services at the aggregate level might move on the expected path while movement of employment in individual services might be different; this might also emerge due to differences in the institutional framework in which the process of development is embedded. In different economies the process of development is embedded in different set of policy regimes and institutional setting which also significantly influence the divergence between the behaviour of employment at the aggregate level and its movements at the individual level. For example, if the process of development is embedded in a free-market economy with very little state intervention, it might lead to income inequalities. These income inequalities might favour rich households, which may choose to spend a large part of their income on entertainment. On the other hand, if the development process is embedded in a totalitarian regime, it might increase government expenditure on law and order and administration, which might need expansion in police, judiciary and bureaucracy. These examples suggest that in both the cases, employment in services will increase at the aggregate level, but in one case the growth will manifest in the employment of entertainers and performing artists, whereas in the other it will be reflected in a growth in employment in administration and bureaucracy [Baur and Yamay (1951)]. Due to these reasons, some economists believe that relationship between employment in services and economic development does not have a strong theoretical base [Baur and Yamay (1951), Fisher (1952) and (1954)].

Apart from economic development and institutional factors, there are several other factors which might influence the growth of employment in different categories of services. Therefore, it is suggested that due to heterogeneity in services, which causes divergence between pattern of employment at the aggregate level and the fact that sub-groups of services within this aggregate are not *assimilable* by any useful criteria which is relevant for economic analysis, there is a need for studying shifts in the composition of employment in services [Minkes (1955) p. 366]. To understand this process of changes, we need a consistent set of categories of services, which have certain similar characteristics and can be identified with different stages of economic development. In Chapter 3, we have discussed different conceptual frameworks that have been used by different scholars to classify services into various categories. We also observed that these categorizations were largely influenced by the purpose of the scholars while categorizing of services.

Hartwell (1973) evolved a categorization of services which is suitable to study the changes in the composition of services in a historical perspective [see his categorization of services in Chapter 3). This categorization helped him while analysing changes in the composition of employment in different services, and gave an insight regarding the relative importance of different services at different stages of economic development. Pre-industrial societies had evolved a specific category of services which served the needs of the society and economy at that time. In pre-industrial economies, employment in most services was generally part-time or casual employment. Full-time employment in services existed amongst a very narrow base of specialized service providers associated with urban businesses, a tiny bureaucracy and a large army of domestic servants [see Chapter 1]. The professions involved in services, in pre-industrial societies, consisted of divinity, law and medicine. Other professional services were provided by amateurs who were trained under experienced service providers.

In the classification of Hartwell (1973), the social overhead services are very close to what are now defined as producers services. Those services, in his analysis, provide the basic services which are preconditions for the successful emergence of industrialization. Therefore, employment in services like transport and communication, education and other intermediate services like trade and commerce increases with economic development which, according to him, also increases employment in recreational and cultural services. These services grow as a consequence of economic prosperity which increases the demand for such services due to its influence on life-style and quality of life. The rising income, when sustained over a longer period, also influences the demand for most services faster than the demand for goods.

In the existing literature on services, transportation and financial services have been studied in greater detail [Girard (1965), Gille (1965) and Cameron (1967)]; among other services, there also exist detailed accounts on welfare services, trade unions, and religious services, but no attempt has been made to establish a relationship between their individual history with the history of the economy. There is a paucity of studies on different industries. Despite its relative importance, literature on retail and wholesale trade, in historical perspective, is very scanty [Jeffreyns and Knee (1962) and Alexander and Aken Hurst (1998)]. Similar is the situation with regard to professional services [Carrsounders and Wilson (1933)] and domestic services, which occupied great importance in terms of employment but, received very little attention [Stigler (1946)]. On cultural and entertainment services, there is hardly any serious study. No attempt has been made to establish the relationship between cultural achievements of a historical period and the nature of economic life to establish a unique relationship between different kinds of economic structure and artistic achievements of an era [Tawney (1958) p. 28].

Studies by economic historians and development economists have shown that revolution in the means of transportation and communication is a precondition for the emergence of the process of economic development. Railways have been described as a *leading-sector* in the growth of the U.S. economy [Fogel (1964)]. However, thereafter, means of transportation and communication grow in tandem with the process of economic development. The role of transportation in the process of economic development has been in reducing costs—of production and distribution—by evolving linkages between locations of inputs, places of production and markets. It also helped in increasing the mobility of workers by linking village economies with centres of industry and played an important role in increasing the size of the market by linking segmented markets through transportation. The role of revolution in means of communications like post and telegraph, telephone etc has been in reducing the costs of collecting and dissipating information. Therefore, as an economy grows, employment in transportation and communication are bound to increase. However, these services are capital intensive and are able to take advantages of economies of scale and technological change. Therefore, though their contribution to national income increases considerably with development, employment potential might decline. For example, it has been observed that transportation obtained peak level of employment in the 18th century [Vance (1986)] and, subsequently, employment in the sector got stabilized.

One of the observed features of modern economic growth has been that, with economic development, the role of the state in providing variety of services also increased which subsequently led to the belief that only a strong and responsible government can initiate the process of economic growth. The statist ideology is implicit in most theories of economic development which were written after World War II. Following this prescription, most developing economies began their development process through activist state. Therefore, it has been observed that employment in public services and utilities will increase with economic development. However, since the 1980s, with the emergence of the process of liberalization and globalization, this view is being challenged. All those economies which have adopted structural adjustment programmes are minimising the role of state in provisioning of these services. This has led to a broader debate amongst economists—whether the state should provide these services or their provision should be left to the market forces—based on the idea of *government failure* and *market failure* [Bardhan (1990) and Dattachaudri (1990)]. However, all those economies, where provisioning of these services is the responsibility of the state may generate significant employment in these services even at a very low-level of economic development. Moreover, some of these services are now considered as high yielding variety of seeds for economic development; therefore, most governments are spending a high percentage share of their budget on these services. Hence, there are possibilities that even economies at lower level of employment might have proportionally higher-level of employment in services like health, education and administration, in comparison to developed economies at their comparable level of development [Harbinson and Myers (1964)].

Economists have observed a positive relationship between employment in retail and wholesale trading services and economic development. Retail and wholesale trade employ a very large proportion of workers engaged in services. The important function of this service is to provide to the producers of goods and services expanding markets and reliable channels of distribution. Therefore, retail and wholesale trade create *space* and *time* utility and flow of information. With economic growth, economies registered a decline in fairs and weekly local markets and in auctions. The declines in these modes of trading were compensated by a rise in retail outlets, wholesale dealers and forward trading. Economists generally believe that employment in these services grows faster with economic development because productivity in these services is quite low in comparison to other services. Therefore, as the economy grows, which necessitates growth in trade and commerce, it increases demand for labour in these services. Therefore, these services can grow only by expanding employment [Fuchs (1968), Baumol (1967) (1985)].

Modern retail systems have their origin in the late eighteenth and early nineteenth century when there emerged multiple branch operations and cooperative stores in Europe and America [Bamfield (1998) and Fowler

(1998)]. To this end, detailed studies have been conducted by scholars regarding the historical conditions which led to the growth of multiple retailing [Jeffreys (1954)]. Employment potential in retail and wholesale trade depends on the organizational structure of trade. It has been described by business historians that wholesale and retail trade in Britain, until the middle of the nineteenth century, were organized along the old system, that is, according to the needs of pre-industrial economy. However, during the period 1875-1914, these services experienced a transformation—flamboyant window display, advertising, marked and fixed prices clearly displayed, branding of manufactured products and advertisement by producers [Jeffreys (1954) and Alexander (1997)]. Similarly, business historians have identified five distinct kinds of organizational changes experienced by U.S. retailing: the prehistoric India trade; the trading post period; the general merchandise era; the period of rise and development of line speciality stores; and finally large scale retailing [Savitt (1984) and Nytrom (1930)].

With the emergence of big malls and stores, these services have also experienced technological changes. With standardization of services, human element has declined significantly. Stores like Mark Spencer and Wall Mart have become more like an industry than service. Due to these changes, employment potential in these services has significantly declined.

Financial services, consisting of all kinds of financial intermediaries and dealers in different financial instruments, did not exist in large numbers before the emergence of the industrial revolution. There were perhaps few banks of issue in European economies and a few insurance companies dealing with shipping insurance. The beginning of modern industry increased the importance of financial services: it created a demand for money and capital, short-term and long-term credit needs, and the need for financial institutions which could underwrite risks involved in different kinds of business operations and transactions. These needs resulted in the expansion and growth in banking services, money markets, stock exchanges, financial brokers and insurance companies [Guarly and Shaw (1995) and Cippola (1973)]. Growth in demand in financial services led to employment growth in financial services which keeps growing in tandem with economic growth. However, in the recent past, the integration of information and communication technologies with financial services has influenced the employment growth in this sector. Till recently, though, economists believed that due to difficulties in improving the productivity in these services, their employment potential will continue to growth.

For several centuries, societies were able to sustain themselves with the help of a narrow base of professional services. Professional services, in the sense that we precieve them today, also emerged alongwith the process of industrialization. Not only the demand for old professional services, the process of industrialization also created demand for new professions like engineers, managers, accountants, consultants, architects, dentists, doctors, veterinary doctors, journalists, advertisers etc. [Carrsaunders and Wilson (1933)]. The emergence of these professions increased the stock of human capital in the economies. These professions emerged as a new strata in society, which did not fit into the *two class model* of Marxian analysis. Concepts like *technostructure* [Galbraith (1967)]; *managerial revolution* [Burnham (1941)]; *new middle class* [(Drucker (1956)] and *pecuniary class* [Veblen (1961)]; and *industrial bureaucracy* [Bendix (1956)] have been used to describe these professions by different scholars. Due to increasing employment in these professions, they have become objects of new sociological and economic analysis. Famous sociologist, Talcott Parsons, describes the increasing significance of these professions "as the most important change that has occured in the occupational system of modern societies" [Parsons (1968) p. 536].

Despite the fact that the demand for these professional services continuously grows with economic development, there do emerge certain institutional impediments which try to arrest the growth of employment in these professions. It has been observed that to maintain their social importance, the professional bodies in which these professions get organized create several kinds of entry barriers to maintain relative scarcity of personnel in professions. It has been noticed though that employment keeps growing in these professions, but at a relatively lesser pace. Moreover, it is growth of employment in these professions which increases the demand for higher education and also creates additional demand for educational services and persons engaged in teaching and research.

It has been mentioned earlier, in Chapter 2, that in agrarian economies a dominant part of services existed in the form of personal services of domestic servants employed by middle and upper classes. In pre-industrial societies, agricultural activity did not have high productivity; this created a very high percentage of underemployed masses who were available at very low wages and were hired as domestic servants [Landes (1969) and Bell (1974) p. 126]. Adam Smith, who was more influenced by the physiocratic framework of economic analysis and Scottish philosophy of thrift and austerity and had political hostility towards aristocracy's wasteful expenditure on several domestic servants for their upkeep, declared all services as unproductive. Rich people have always benefited from personal services, either by hiring domestic servants or being attended by workers working in hotels and restaurants etc. Such relationships are more prevalent in poor economies of Asia and Africa. In the United States and Britain the golden age of domestic servitude was nineteenth century, when domestic servants were almost as numerous as industrial workers [Sayer and Walker (1992) p. 86]. The number of persons employed in household services dropped from 1.8 million in 1910 to 1.41 million in 1920 while the number of households enumerated in the census rose from 20.3 millions to 24.4 million in U.S.A. In the process, the number of paid domestic servants per 1000 population dropped from 98.9 in 1900 to 58 in 1920 [Cowan (1997) p. 330]. The increasing proportion of personal services continued during the early phases of industrialization. The increased income levels, broadening of middle class and rapid urbanization also increased the demand for personal services of barbers, plumbers, cleaners, laundry and gardeners. The growth in personal services, in the initial phases of industrialization, helped in realising the time and talent of professional middle classes for substituting personal services for more productive work outside the household. It also helped in increasing the rate of women's participation in the labour market.

The implicit logic advanced to propagate that demand for personal services will continue to increase with economic development was based on the concept of *hierarchy of needs* evolved by Maslow [Maslow (1954)] which consists of (a) physiological needs (b) safety and security needs (c) belonging and living needs (d) esteem needs and (e) self-actualization needs. This suggests that with increasing prosperity, people develop more sophisticated tastes that can be better obtained through personal attention. This notion is quite historical because human needs, and objects to fulfil these needs, evolve in a society in a complicated feedback relationship. Therefore, what has been observed is that, even though with economic growth, income as well as availability of leisure time with households has increased, there is no evidence of a significant shift towards an economy of hair saloons and mud-baths. On the contrary, personal services have grown little over the course of this century [Walker and Greenberg (1982), Stanback et al (1983) Sayer and Walker (1992)].

The decline in the growth of some of the personal services has occured, on the one hand, due to the process of industrialization of services as has already been described in Chapter 2. This happened because of the emerging standardization in the delivery of services which has reduced the service content in personal services. The working of fast food outlets of McDonalds, Wimpy and Pizza Hut, the working of Malls and Departmental stores are examples of such services. On the other hand, the evolution of the *self-service economy* has also reduced the demand for personal services.

The development and growth of the self-service economy, where individuals combine the purchase of consumer durables with self-service to satisfy their need for personal services, is a consequence of social innovation in the provisioning of services. In the present dispensation, final services to consumers are not directly supplied by the single service industry; instead, households obtain these services through combining products of several industries alongwith their self-service to satisfy their service need. This happens by combining some of the consumer durables produced by manufacturing industries, with intermediate services of infrastructure developed by the public/private company, and self-service of the household to produce their own services. For instance, car manufacturers, dealers of cars, garage services, together with a network of roads developed by infrastructure providers, and driving skills of unpaid householders produce a significant proportion of transport services. Similarly, television set manufactured by a manufacturing firm, with electricity supplied by public utility companies alongwith intermediate service inputs of T.V. channels and software provided by service companies who developed programmes for telecasting, provide the bulk of entertainment services. Moreover, large number of household appliances alongwith electricity supplied by public utility providers and unpaid self-service provided by householders have replaced large number of personal services, viz., razor has reduced the frequency of visits to the barber's shops, kitchen machines have reduced the demand for domestic help, washing machines have reduced the demand for laundry services [Gerghuny (1978), Gershuny and Inman (1983)].

The emergence of the *self-service* economy can also be explained with the help of a demographic transition towards lower rates of population growth accompanied by near-full-employment conditions in most developed market economies during the post-war boom. These trends shifted the persons engaged in low-paid domestic services to higher income jobs in other growing sectors of the economy. This reduced the availability of workforce for low-paid personal services and provided conditions for substitution of consumer durables and self-service for personal services. Baumol (1985) has classified personal services into the category of stagnant services (see Chapter 3). These services include all those economic activities in which quality of service is assessed on the basis of labour time expanded by the service provider and also need direct contact between the consumers and those who provide services. They also consist of those economic activities where standardization of service is quite difficult. Due to these reasons, they have experienced very little changes in productivity and technological change. It is due to the existence of relative stagnation in these services that they have been substituted in whole or in part by other products which have higher performance in terms of productivity [Baumol (1985) pp. 302-303].

Composition of employment in recreational and culture related services also changes with economic development. Since most of these services are final services, their demand is income induced: as income per capita increases, demand for these services also increases. The pursuit of wealth and accumulation has always been culturally embedded and culturally driven. With the process of development there occurs mass commodification of culture which converts different aspects of culture into commodities which provide new opportunities for their commercial exploitation. This process gives rise to services like tourism, leisure activities, media, arts, music and literature. All these cultural products create new enterprises which provide employment to large numbers of people. Some of these enterprises are now supplying global popular music, cinema and software for different T.V. channels. Not only this, the consumption demand of the emerging global middle class has provided basis for the emergence of fashion and design industry including print-media and advertising [Du Gay and Pryke (1999), Scott (2000) and Amin and Thrif (2004)].

The emergence of these services, on the one hand, has caused decline of rural folk music, folk performing arts, which earlier used to provide part-time employment to several individuals in rural areas. On the other hand, they have created full-time specialized service providers of cultural products in urban settings.

The popular sources of entertainment, which in the eighteenth century were localized in theatre companies, taverns and streets, got transformed, in the nineteenth century into institutional settings of concert halls and cinema houses. Thereafter, music and entertainment entered the sitting rooms of households in the form of radio, followed by T.V. and now other electronic devices. In the film industry itself, the impact of technological changes has been enormous. From the days of the silent movies, it moved to talkies in 1920s. With advances in camera projection, emergence of computer aided designs, multi-media, electronic editing and composition devices, it became possible to make films like *Spiderman, Terminator, Independence Day, Titanic* and *Star Wars*. These developments have helped in continuously sustaining the film industry and in providing employment to large numbers of workers. Music industry also underwent several technological changes which began with Thomas Edisons, *phonograph* in 1877; subsequent improvements were made in it by Graham Bell and with the introduction of *gramophone* or *vitrola* by Victor Talking Machine company in 1890. The latest technological changes have been the development of VCD and DVDs etc [Pessman (1994), Millard (1995), Clark (1995) and Vogel (2001)]. These changes have affected employment in the music industry.

One of the important characteristics of the cultural and entertainment business is that most of the employment in this industry is flexible employment of artists and performers; however, it does provide regular employment to a very insignificant proportion of workers. Therefore, whether it is making of films, cassettes or T.V. serials and other software, most artists engaged in directing, acting, providing music and other technical fields like cameramen etc are hired on contract. Once that assignment is over they have to look for another assignment to continue to make a living. Same is true of employment in the fashion industry, where fashion designers and fashion models are also hired on flexible terms [Storper (1994), McRobbie (2004)].

II. Empirical Studies on Changing Composition of Employment in Services

The analysis given above, regarding changes in intra-sectoral composition of employment in services, was intended to provide a broad understanding of the shifts in employment in different services as a consequence of economic development. The analysis suggested that different services have different kinds of relationship with the process of development. Therefore, to have a better knowledge about employment in services and its future potential, it is essential to know that the aggregate growth in employment is qualitatively different at different stages of economic development. Quality of service employment changes because the development process alters the composition of employment in services. Several attempts have been made to empirically analyze the changes in employment in services occuring due to the process of economic development. However, here we are analysing empirical studies conducted by Singlemann [(1974) and (1978)], Elfring (1989), Castells [(1996) and (2002)] and Aoyama and Castells (2002). These studies have been identified because (a) they are using the same method of categorization of services, therefore, they are comparable, and (b) they together encompass the time period from 1920 to 2002.

Singlemann (1978) has made an attempt to analyze inter-industry as well as intra-industry shifts in employment in the case of seven most developed economies of the world—Canada, U.S.A., England and Wales, Germany, France, Italy and Japan. To analyze the shifts in composition of employment in different services, he has used a new classification scheme for services [Singlemann (1974)] which has been discussed in detail in chapter 3 of the present study. According to him, services can be categorized in four categories (a) distributive services (b) producer services (c) social services, and (d) personal services. His study covers the period between 1920 to 1970.

From the analysis of data, he found that the overall share of employment in distributive services has been increasing in all developed economies.

However, they recorded a decline in their relative share of employment during World War II and Great Depression of the 1930s [see Table 5.1]. He observed that employment in this service, when studied at a more dissaggregated level, shows two divergent trends—a continuous decline in employment in transportation and a continuous increase in employment in trade in the case of all developed economies. A very large part of expansion in trade is accounted by rapid increase in employment in retail trade, whereas wholesale trade registered a marginal increase. He also observes differences in employment in retail trade in the U.S.A. in comparison to Germany, France and England. He explains that these differences emerge because in England, France and Germany retail has been labour intensive whereas in U.S.A, it has been organized on capital intensive lines. Despite these differences in their retail trade, employment is not significantly different because in comparison to small retails stores of these countries, where working hours are less, in U.S.A. capital intensive stores work for longer hours in different shifts.

Producer services employed not a very significant proportion of workforce in 1920 in all the seven developed economies. However, employment in producer services experienced some decline during the Great Depression of 1930s but, ever since, employment in these services has been growing—in fact it doubled during 1920-1970 in all the seven countries. However, employment in producer services increased threefold in U.S.A. and France and six times in Japan. Singlemann comments that these services may employ more and more proportion of workforce in future because employment in these services has not yet achieved its peak.

The data reported by Singlemann (1978) suggests that employment in social services increased continuously in all the seven developed economies, and it is interesting to note that growth in employment in social services did not experience any downturn either during the depression of 1930s or during World War II. Therefore, record of employment in social services is unique. However, singlemann (1978) anticipates that in future employment in social services might slow down in developed economies like U.S.A., England and Canada (a) because these economies have already grown very large, and (b) due to fiscal constraints that are likely to emerge in them. Singlemann (1978) suggests that the proportion of working population engaged in social services should be used as an important indicator to study the transition of an economy into a service economy [Singlemann (1978) p. 1231].

Relative employment in personal services increased in most developed economies only up to the 1960s. During 1960s and 1970, employment in these services only expanded in Germany and Italy. To understand these trends regarding employment in personal services, Singlemann (1978) studied these services by decomposing employment in them into two sub-categories i.e. (a) domestic services and (b) other personal services. He observed that the employment in domestic services continuously declined in all the developed economies since 1920 and became almost negligible by 1970. As has been mentioned in Chapter 2 that domestic services employed a significant proportion of working population engaged in services during pre-industrial stage, therefore, the employment in domestic services was expected to decline with the process of development. Amongst the personal services, employment is increasing in automobile repair shops and lodgings, eating and drinking places. The latter group are experiencing higher growth in employment. This, perhaps, has emerged as a consequence of increasing participation of women in the labour market, which has shifted household production to purchases of substitutes of household services from the market.

A similar kind of attempt has been made by Elfring (1989) to study the changing composition of employment in different services. For his study he selected U.S.A. and some European economies (France, Germany, Netherlands, Sweden and England) and Japan. The main objectives of his study was to identify which of the services were experiencing acceleration and which ones were experiencing slow down in terms of employment. Unlike the study of Singlemann (1978), he also made an attempt to study the importance of self-employment among different services and also the impact of recession on employment in services. He followed the system of categorization of services evolved by Singlemann [(1974) and (1978)] and divided the service industries into four major groups i.e. producer services, distributive services, personal services and social services. However, he also made a slight modification—he has classified postal services in the category of communication services under the major group distributive services, as against Singlemann (1974) who classified them in the social services group [Elfring (1989) p. 411].

Elfring's (1989) study covers the period 1960 to 1985. His study begins in 1960 because he thought that the period prior to 1960 was an abnormal period to study the shifts in employment among different services due to phenomenons like Great Depression of 1930s followed by World War II which created shifts in employment patterns. He divided his time series study into two sub-periods (a) 1960-1973 and (b) 1973 to 1985. He called the former sub-period as the Golden Age; the latter sub-period represented the period followed by the first OPEC shock.

According to broad findings of his studies, producer services more than doubled their employment share between 1960 to 1985. In 1960, they accounted for only 4.1 per cent of employment which continued to grow, between both sub-periods. During Golden age, employment in producer services grew at the rate of 2.3 per cent, while, following the oil shock, it grew at the rate of 2.8 per cent point. After the first oil shock, the annual growth of employment in producer services slowed down in Europe and Japan, but it did not slow down in the case of U.S.A. because of impressive growth rates recorded in some of the producer services, like insurance, professional services and real estate [see Table 5.2].

According to Elfring (1989), the experience of employment in the insurance sector of U.S.A. is quite contrary to expectations. It was expected that it will decline due to the integration of information technology with insurance and increasing automation in the sector. Contrary to this expectation, information technology led to expansion in the market due to greater diversities made possible by information technology in insurance products. Despite certain amount of job losses that occured due to automation, they were more than compensated by job creation due to expansion in the market [Elfring (1989) p. 418)]. His contention is supported by earlier studies also [Browning (1986) and Rajan and Cook (1986)]. Similarly, business and professional services grew at the rate of 6.7 per cent in U.S.A. This rate of growth in both services was three times above the rate of growth of employment registered by the services at the aggregate level. The rate of employment in professional and business services in European economies and Japan was more or less the same but much lower than the rates of growth recorded in U.S.A.

Elfring contradicts the opinion held by several economists that by the middle of 1970s the growth rate of employment in professional and business services slowed down due to the emerging reorganization of these services after their integration with information technology. He suggests that the shift in the developed economies towards service economy has helped in the faster expansion of employment in professional and business services. Moreover, integration of IT services, alongwith professional and business services, has further increased employment in these services due to creation of additional demand for persons related to computer softwares. These services are (a) softwares which make the computer work (b) engineering services which show how to use the computer and integrate it within the framework of existing management in production system (c) system consultants to customize software according to the needs of customers (d) training services to train the workforce in how to operate systems (e) to provide information to organizations regarding new developments in the IT areas, and (f) maintenance services to facilitate the automated operations of hardware. Moreover, it has also been experienced that the introduction of IT also necessitates reorgnization of organizations. The need for these organizational changes also increases demand for consultancy services. The demand for producer services also grew in most developed economies due to externalization of producer services, which were previously provided in house, in the manufacturing sector.

The analysis of data collected by Elfring (1989) shows that employment in distributive services has remained more or less stable over time. Retail trade was a more important employer in the category of distributive services—it accounted for around 10 per cent of the total employment in them. He observed that Germany and Japan represented two extreme cases of employment in distributive services; in Germany the employment in distributive services was smaller than all the other economies studied by Elfring (1989), while in Japan he observed that ethe same was very large. To understand these extreme cases, he analysed the behaviour of employment in different services that are grouped under the category of distributive services.

Elfring (1989) found the explanation regarding lower employment level in distributive services in the geography of Germany. Since Germany is land locked, many goods for the main industrial areas of Germany are shipped to Rotterdam and transported through Netherlands. Thus the geographical location of Germany increases employment in wholesale trade and transportation in Netherlands (i.e. 10.4 per cent), while it reduces share of employment in these services in Germany (i.e. 7.2 per cent). In the case of Japan, relatively large number of persons are employed in retail trade because there is a lot of stress on the quality of services. Also, in Japan, there exist large number of retail stores. In the middle of 1970s, a Japanese retail store served only 70 households; in U.S.A. this ratio was twice as high while in Germany it was 179 households [Woronoff (1983)]. The prevalence of small family enterprises which used flexible and cheap family labour and their protection by the Japanese government policies, which discouraged the opening of large retail stores, led to over manning of retail business in Japan [Saxonhouse (1985) and Woronoff (1983)]. Moreover, Japanese retail business is labour intensive due to the absence of self-service and the operation of retail outlets for longer hours, whereas in U.S.A. capital intensive big retail outlets depended largely on self-service [Elfring (1989) p. 423].

In the case of United Kingdom, Elfring (1989) also observed the role of government policy in influencing employment in retail trade by way of *Selective Employment Tax on Services* (SET), which was introduced in UK in 1966. This was a tax on employment in labour intensive services like retailing. The objective of this regulation was to stop the growth of employment in retail services and forcing the retail outlets to use labour saving measures to increase productivity and efficiency. This was evolved to discourage labour intensive small stores and encourage capital intensive big retail stores with better productivity. This piece of legislation had an adverse effect on registered employment in retailing because store owners started under-reporting employment in their stores to minimize the incidence of taxation under SET. This phenomenon has also been observed by other scholars [Raddaway (1973)].

Employment in personal services grew at an average annual growth rate of 0.4 per cent during the Golden Age (i.e. 1960-1973) and 1.3 per cent subsequent to the oil shock of 1973. Elfring (1989) observed that most of the employment in personal services is accounted by employment in hotels and restaurants. In U.S.A. employment growth in hotels and restaurants occured at the rate of 4.5 per cent per annum. The trends observed regarding the ratio of growth of employment in personal services do not lend support to the hypothesis advanced by several scholars [Skolka (1976), Singlemann (1974) and (1978), Gershuney (1978) and OECD (1984)] who believe that employment in personal services will decline with economic growth because these services will be substituted by *self-service* in the long-run [see for details Chapter 4 and 5]. Elfring (1989) accepts that there has been a certain amount of substitution of self-service activities for purchased personal services, facilitated by the availability of household consumer durables like washing machines, kitchen equipment and television. He, however, suggests that growth in self-service economy has not been able to significantly reduce employment in personal services due to increased female workforce participation rates. This has affected employment in personal services through two interrelated processes. Initially, growing participation rates of women take them away from the household and, subsequently, reduces wage rates in those occupations where women look for employment. Since women generally look for employment in services, the costs of services do not increase subtantially. Moreover, personal services like restaurants have increased efficiency through standardization of services and use of machines. This has also reduced the cost of such services thereby encouraging the substitution of household production of services by purchased personal services. For example, the services of domestic servants, restaurants, laundry and day care are substitutes for cleaning, cooking, washing and baby-sitting.

Some other scholars have also observed the relationship between women labour force participation rates and demand for personal services [Fuchs (1980) and Grubel (1987)]. This is because households with working women spend more money on the purchase of personal services. The reason is that with women actively participating in the work force, the amount of time available in a household for self-service has declined significantly. Demographic factors—ageing of population on the one hand and reduced size of the household on the other—have further reduced the availability of time which a household can spare for self-service. Moreover, each household now spends a very large proportion of available time on paid as well as unpaid work out of the household. Due to all these influences, the time available with the household for providing in-house self-service has declined substantially [Silver (1987)].

The importance of personal services can be judged from the fact that in 1985, the persons employed in these services were minimum (6.1 per cent) in Sweden and maximum (12.4 per cent) in U.S.A. Elfring (1989) explains this with the help of an important fact that, in Sweden, a large number of personal services are provided by the government. Therefore, employment in personal services gets registered as employment in social services in official statistics.

In the case of social services, data collected by Elfring suggests that the proportion of working population employed in these services is quite substantial— varying between 21.3 per cent in Germany in 1985 (lowest in Europe) to 35.3 per cent in Sweden (highest in Europe). U.S.A. has employment in social services comparable to average European level (i.e. 25.8 per cent). However, Japan has the lowest share of employment in social services in comparison to all the developed economies (12.7 per cent). Amongst the sub-groups of social services, in most economies, 'general government services' employed highest number of persons in all the economies (i.e. 7.6 per cent on average), whereas persons employed in health care and education were slightly lower.

As has been mentioned above, Sweden had the highest proportion of working population employed in social services, whereas Japan had the lowest amongst all developed economies. To explain this paradox, Elfring tried to study this phenomenon at a disaggregated level, by dividing social services into four sub-groups (a) government proper (b) health services (c) educational services and (d) miscellaneous services. While studying the composition of employment in these sub-groups in Japan, he observed that Japan has a relatively lesser number of persons employed in the category of government services. This is because military employment in Japan is very insignificant. Moreover, a substantial part of social services are provided by Japanese firms to their employees. This is because Japanese enterprises also integrate the social life of their employees within the domain of corporate governance. Since a large part of social services are purchased by the enterprises on behalf of employees, they do not get reflected in the data separately on social services.

Japan also has less proportion of working force employed in educational services in comparison to other developed economies. This is despite the fact that the enrollment ratios in schools are not very different in comparison to other developed economies. Elfring (1989) explains this characteristic of educational services in Japan by suggesting that Japan has a highly efficient educational system—it has the capability to provide better educational standards with small labour inputs. This could be achieved because in Japan most of the effort is directed at education proper, while in the case of other countries additional labour inputs in educational services are required to achieve the objective of equality of opportunity [Elfring (1989) p. 430]. On the other hand, to explain why Sweden employs a very high proportion of its working population in social services, in comparison to other developed economies, Elfring mentions the policies to promote social welfare and educational services which are embedded in the active labour market policies pursued by the government of Sweden. These policies result in higher employment growth in social services [Elfring (1989) p. 433].

Elfring (1989) also made an attempt to explain the incidence of self-employment in services and also the sensitivity of service employment to recessions. This he has done to explore the appropriateness of a common belief amongst scholars that the incidence of self-employment is quite significant in the case of employment in services and that it is also not affected by business cycles. From the analysis of data, he found that the incidence of self-employment declined during the Golden Age (1960-73) and registered growth after the first oil shock (1973-1985).

However, he observed that the incidence of self-employment was more in producer services, in most economies. This happened because here individuals are sometimes pulled into self-employment to form independent businesses in response to favourable opportunities to exploit their specialized knowledge. There are also cases where individuals are pushed into self-employment out of compulsion. In the absence of social security, some individuals take up activities like retailing, peddling, repair services, shoe-shining or working in restaurants.

Unlike other scholars who believe that employment in services is less sensitive to recession, Elfring (1989) states that services sector consists of heterogeneous sub-group of services where each group responds differently to recessions. He found deceleration of employment in producer services which was quite sensitive to recession as these services have close linkage with investments in the manufacturing sector. He also suggests that this happens because the demand for producer services fluctuates with fluctuation in income levels. He found that social services were insensitive to recessions. However, by and large, service employment was less sensitive to recessions in comparison to industrial employment. To explain this he provides the following arguments (a) the existence of disguised unemployment in services due to higher incidence of self-employment, which explains why services experience changes only in working hours during different phases of business cycle, rather than unemployment (b) the flexibility of compensation system in services like commissions, consultancy fees and tips, income of self-employed persons and absence of trade unions, in comparison to industrial employment.

Castells (1996) made an attempt to study the changes in the structure of employment of G7 countries, consisting of economies of U.S.A., Japan, Germany, France, U.K., Italy and Canada, using categorization of services evolved by Singlemann (1974). To analyze changes in the structure of employment he had divided the time series data from 1920-1990 into two sub-periods, 1920-1970 and 1970 to 1990. The first period has been described as the period of *post-agriculture* and the second as *post-industrial*. Later on Aoyama and Castells (2002) expand the analysis to cover the period upto 2000. Therefore, we are presenting here, the findings of both the studies together. The main objective of the two studies was to identify which one of the two concepts is a more appropriate description of the changes in the composition of employment in services experienced by the developed economies—*post-industrialism* [Tomain (1969) and Bell (174)] and *informationalism*. The concept of post-industrialism envisages the coming into being of a new social structure characterized by dominance of services over the production of goods. They question this natural law of economics that suggests that each economy will follow a single path along a trajectory of transitions experienced by U.S.A. [Castells (1996) p. 202].

They argue that there exists a complicated process of interaction between technology, economy and institutions which condition the evolving pattern of employment in the process of economic development between sectors. For them, the real distinction is not between an industrial or post-industrial economy, but between new forms of knowledge–based agriculture, industry and service production. They believe that the most important distinction between economic structure of the first and second half of the twentieth century is the revolution in information technology and its diffusion to all spheres of economic activity. Therefore, they lay more stress on informationalism instead of post-industrialism [Castells (1996) p. 204].

To understand the process of transformation of employment structure, they analysed the differential evolution of employment in each type of services in G-7 countries (see Table 5.3). Their data reveals that due to the strategic location of producer services in the new economy, increasing sophistication and productivity, these services have recorded an impressive growth in employment. In the 1920s, most G-7 countries employed less than 3 per cent of their working population in producer services; its share increased to around 5 per cent in 1970; around 10 per cent in 1990 and 15 per cent in 2000. In both

Japan and Germany, the proportion of working population employed in production services is quite low upto 1990 and has become comparable in 2000 to other developed economies. The authors suggest that the manufacturing sectors of Germany as well as Japan use substantial amount of producer services, but with different pattern of organization of production in their manufacturing firms where producer services are internalized by the manufacturing firms. They argue that the integration of producer services within the manufacturing enterprises is a more efficient combination for achieving higher rates of productivity and global competitiveness. It is due to this reason that the two most dynamic industrial economies have a lower percentage of working population engaged in producer services. Moreover, this proportion is also low in other economies, in comparison to proportion of persons employed in other services. This is perhaps due to the possibilities of integration as well as disintegration of producer services with manufacturing.

The employment in social services, which epitomizes the emergence of post-industrial society, has grown significantly in all the G-7 countries, though in varying rates. They argue that the higher proportion of working persons employed in social services is not because of the coming of post-industrialism, but due to the emergence of several social movements. They notice that Japan is the only economy which employed quite lower proportion of working population in social services in comparison to other developed economies—lately this has become comparable to other G-7 countries. The lower proportion of working population employed in social services in Japan, they say, can be attributed to the fact that the social support system in Japan existed in a highly decentralized form in firms and family. However, after Japan emerged as a major industrial power, it now follows similar social distribution policies which are followed by other developed economies; this has helped in creating more employment in social services. However, from the analysis of employment in social services in the G-7 countries, authors have realized that the *extent of employment in social services neither depends on the rates of growth of the economy, nor on post-industrialism: it depends essentially on the relationship between the state and society.*

It is generally expected by scholars that employment in some distributive services will decline with economic development. This is because on some distributive services like transportation and communication, labour can be substituted by capital and there are also possibilities of experiencing technological change. However, the data collected by Aoyuma and Castells (2002) shows that the proportion of working population employed in distributive services continued to increase in all the developed economies and it varies between one fifth and one quarter. Amongst all the developed economies,

Germany has a lower proportion of workforce employed in distributive services (17.5 per cent in 2000). Although the authors do not explain this important fact, it seems that the explanation provided by Elfring (1989), which has been mentioned above, is appropriate to explain the existence of lower percentage of working force employed in distributive services.

Scholars believe that personal services are remnants of the pre-industrial phase or feudal economic structure (see Chapters 2 and 3). Therefore, it is expected that, with economic growth, the proportion of working population employed in personal services will decline. It is also expected that some personal services will be replaced by self-services [Skolka (1976) and Gershuny (1978)]. This will also reduce employment opportunities in personal services. However, analysis of data provided by Castells (1996) and Aoyama and Castells (2002) suggests that personal services have continued to grow even in post-industrialism or informationalism. The percentage of persons employed in personal services is comparable to the percentage of working population employed in the producer services. A very large part of growth in employment in personal services is accounted by hotels, eating and drinking places. This has happened partly due to the increasing participation of women in the labour market and partly due to rising incomes, which has given rise to a leisure society.

To analyse the transition of developed economies from industrialism to informationalism or from industrialism to post-industrialism, authors have computed the ratio of service sector to industrial employment and ratio of goods production to information handling [see Tables 5.4A and 5.4B]. They state that a shift from industrialism to informationalism cannot be equated with the emergence of the service economy. They have observed that the ratio of service sector to industrial employment continued to increase; 1990s was the period in which most developed economies achieved the ratio 2.0: this was also the period when services started dominating the employment structure. In U.K. this ratio increased from 2.4 in 1990 to 3.7 in 2000. Even the economies of Germany and Japan, which were primarily considered as industrially dynamic, registered significant rise in this ratio from 1.4 to 2.0 per cent in Germany and from 1.8 to 2.2 per cent in Japan in 1990 and 2000 respectively. During this period, developed economies showed, for the first time, a reversal in importance between goods handling and information handling employment. The data regarding the year 2000 reveals that Canada, United States, France and England had greater proportion of working population employed in information handling than in goods handling. The exception is the economy of Japan which continues to employ more persons in goods handling. Therefore, they conclude that post 1990, the structure of employment in most G-7 countries shifted from goods handling to information handling employment.

On the basis of their empirical work, Aoyuma and Castells (2002) describe that there have emerged two distinct paths regarding changes in the composition of employment among different services. Path one is described by them as the *Anglo-Saxon* model in which shifts in employment pattern occured from manufacturing to advanced services alongwith maintaing employment in traditional services. The second path has been followed by Japan and Germany, where the composition of employment has shifted towards advanced services alongwith preserving employment in manufacturing by integrating a large segment of producer services within manufacturing enterprises. Therefore, according to them, the Anglo-Saxon model represents a process of transition in the employment structure in which economies experience rapid *de-industrialization* accompanied by a rapid employment expansion in producer and social services. On the other hand, in Japan-German path to transition, the composition of employment structure occurs with strong internalization of producer services within manufacturing and more cautious expansion in social services while deliberately maintaining higher employment in distributive services. However, in both the paths of transition, the shifts in the employment structure show expansion in all service categories with the exception of domestic services.

Their analysis also suggests that the economies of Japan and Germany have evolved a more efficient symbiosis between manufacturing, producer services, social services and distributive services which has been absent in the Anglo-Saxon model. The absence of this symbiotic relationship has caused rapid de-industrialization in Anglo-Saxon economies, instead of gradually reducing manufacturing employment. Therefore, they suggest that rapid de-industrialization does not necessarily mean that these economies are more advanced but this only shows that this has happened because these economies followed a specific path of development based on certain specific policies and strategies. This analysis suggests that the change in the composition of employment in different services in different economies is not only determined by their level of development but also emerges as a consequence of policies and strategic options made by different economies.

Table 5.1 Percentage Distribution of Labour Force by Industry Sector: Seven Industrialized Countries, 1920-70

Sectors and Countries	*About 1920*	*About 1930*	*About 1940*	*About 1950*	*About 1960*	*About 1970*
Extractive:						
United States	28.9	25.4	21.3	14.4	8.1	4.5
Canada	36.9	34.4	31.7	21.6	14.7	9.1
England	14.2	11.8	*	8.9	6.6	4.2
Germany	33.5	31.5	8	16.1	9.0	5.1
France	43.6	38.3	40.2	31.9	23.0	17.0
Italy	57.1	48.1	*	42.9	29.8	*
Japan	56.3	50.9	46.3	50.3	34.1	20.0
Transformative:						
United States	32.9	31.5	29.8	33.9	35.9	33.9
Canada	26.1	24.7	28.2	33.7	31.2	30.0
England	42.2	39.3	*	45.4	46.0	43.8
Germany	38.9	38.3	*	47.3	51.3	49.0
France	29.7	32.8	29.6	35.2	37.7	39.3
Italy	24.2	29.2	*	32.0	40.0	*
Japan	19.8	19.8	24.9	21.0	28.5	34.3
Distributive services:						
United States	18.7	19.6	20.4	22.4	21.9	22.1
Canada	19.2	18.4	17.6	21.7	23.9	23.0
England	19.3	21.6	*	19.2	19.7	17.9
Germany	11.9	12.8	*	15.7	16.4	16.9
France	14.4	13.3	15.1	14.4	16.4	15.5
Italy	8.6	10.1	*	10.6	13.1	†
Japan	12.5	15.6	15.2	14.6	18.6	22.7
Producer services:						
United States	2.8	3.2	4.6	4.8	6.6	9.3
Canada	3.7	3.3	2.8	4.0	5.3	7.3
England	2.6	3.1	*	3.2	4.5	5.6
Germany	2.1	2.7	*	2.5	4.2	5.1
France	1.6	2.1	1.9	2.7	3.2	5.5
Italy	1.3	1.8	*	1.9	2.0	†
Japan	.8	.9	1.2	1.5	2.9	5.1
Social services:						
United States	8.7	9.2	10.0	12.4	16.3	21.5
Canada	7.5	8.9	9.4	11.3	15.3	21.1
England	8.9	9.7	*	12.1	14.1	19.4
Germany	6.0	6.8	*	11.5	12.9	17.4
France	5.3	6.1	6.8	9.4	12.3	14.8
Italy	4.1	5.2	*	7.9	9.4	*
Japan	4.9	5.5	6.0	7.2	8.3	10.2
Personal services:						
United States	8.2	11.2	14.0	12.1	11.3	8.6
Canada	6.7	10.3	10.3	7.8	9.6	9.5
England	12.9	14.5	*	11.3	.0	9.0
Germany	7.7	7.8	*	6.8	6.4	6.5
France	5.6	7.2	6.4	7.4	7.4	7.9
Italy	4.6	5.6	*	4.7	5.9	†
Japan	5.7	7.3	6.3	5.3	7.6	7.6

* The European countries did not take a census during World War II (the French census was taken in 1946).

† At the time of this writing, the data for Italy were not yet available.
Singlemann (1978) p. 1229.

Table 5.2 Employment Growth in Producer Services in the 1960-73 and 1973-85 Period (Average annual compound growth rate)

	France	*Germany*	*Japan*	*Netherlands*	*Sweden*	*United Kingdom*	*United States*	*Average*
				1960-73				
1. Producer services	5.8	3.8	7.0	4.7	47	3.3	4.3	4.8
2. Business/ professional services	6.0	3.2	8.3	6.9	5.7	3.9	5.8	5.7
3. Financial services	5.0	4.7	4.3	4.9	4.9	3.7	4.1	4.5
4. Insurance services	5.8	3.6	6.4	-0.4	1.6	1.2	2.1	2.9
5. Real estate services	10.5	2.8	10.5	9.2	3.5	3.6	3.6	6.3
6. Total services	2.1	1.6	3.7	2.4	2.6	1.3	2.6	2.3
				1973-85				
1. Producer services	2.8	2.7	4.1	4.3	2.5	3.0	5.1	3.5
2. Business/ professional services	3.6	4.1	5.3	5.8	3.4	3.3	6.7	4.6
3. Financial services	1.9	2.0	1.7	3.1	2.1	2.9	4.0	2.5
4. Insurance services	1.4	1.5	3.4	0.6	1.2	1.7	2.8	1.7
5. Real estate services	2.6	0.0	3.4	4.2	1.1	3.4	4.0	2.7
6. Total services	1.5	1.2	2.0	1.9	1.9	1.1	2.6	1.7

Source: Elfring (1989) p. 410.

Table 5.3 Sectoral Distribution of Employment, 1920-2000

Canada, 1921-2000[a]	*1921*	*1941*	*1971*	*1971*	*1981*	*1992*	*1996*	*2000*
Extractive	36.9	31.7	9.1	8.3	7.1	5.7	5.6	—
Transformative	16.1	28.2	30.0	27.1	26.8	22.3	21.0	21.6
Distributive services	19.2	17.7	23.0	20.8	22.9	24.0	23.7	23.3
Producer services	3.7	2.7	7.3	6.6	9.7	11.3	12.1	14.6
Social services	7.5	9.4	21.1	22.0	24.0	22.6	24.2	25.1
Personal services	6.7	10.2	9.6	7.5	9.5	13.5	13.5	13.2
Total	100.0	100.0	100.0	100.0	100.0	100.0	100.0	100.0

France, 1921-2000[b]	*1921*	*1946*	*1968*	*1968*	*1980*	*1990*	*1998*	*2000*
Extractive	43.6	40.2	17.0	15.6	8.7	5.5	4.3	4.1
Transformative	29.7	29.6	39.3	37.4	34.8	29.1	24.6	24.7
Distributive services	14.4	15.1	15.5	18.8	19.9	20.1	19.9	19.4
Producer services	1.6	1.9	5.5	5.0	7.8	12.4	14.4	14.8
Social services	5.3	6.8	14.5	15.1	17.1	25.1	27.4	27.1
Personal services	5.6	6.4	7.9	8.2	11.6	6.7	8.1	8.5
Total	100.0	100.0	100.0	100.0	100.0	100.0	100.0	100.0

Germany, 1925-2000[c]	*1925*	*1950*	*1970*	*1970*	*1987*	*2000*
Extractive	33.5	16.1	5.1	8.7	4.1	2.9
Transformative	38.9	47.3	49.0	47.1	40.3	33.1
Distributive services	11.9	15.7	16.4	17.9	17.7	17.5
Producer services	2.1	2.5	5.1	4.5	7.3	12.1
Social services	6.0	11.1	17.4	15.7	24.3	25.8
Personal services	7.7	6.9	7.4	6.1	6.3	8.6
Total	100.0	100.0	100.0	100.0	100.0	100.0

Italy, 1921-1999[d]	*1921*	*1951*	*1960*	*1961*	*1971*	*1981*	*1990*	1999
Extractive	57.1	42.9	29.8	29.8	17.2	11.7	9.5	5.1
transformative	24.3	31.8	40.0	39.9	44.3	40.5	29.7	29.9
Distributive services	8.6	10.6	13.0	15.3	18.7	16.2	23.8	20.4
Producer services	1.2	1.9	2.0	1.1	1.5	4.6	1.8	12.3
Social services	4.1	7.9	9.3	6.9	6.5	19.1	15.5	19.0
Personal services	4.6	4.7	5.9	—	—	7.9	4.1	8.9
Total	100.0	100.0	100.0	100.0	100.0	100.0	100.0	100.0

Japan, 1920-2000	*1920*	*1940*	*1970*	*1970*	*1980*	*1990*	*2000*
Extractive	56.4	46.3	19.6	19.8	11.2	7.2	5.4
Transformative	19.6	24.9	34.2	34.1	33.7	33.7	30.1
Distributive services	12.4	15.2	22.5	22.4	25.1	24.3	24.2
Producer services	0.8	1.2	5.1	4.8	7.5	9.6	11.0
Social services	4.9	6.0	10.1	10.3	12.9	14.3	16.9
Personal services	5.7	6.3	8.5	8.5	9.6	10.2	11.3
Total	100.0	100.0	100.0	100.0	100.0	100.0	100.0

Contd....

United Kingdom, 1921-2001[e]	*1921*	*1951*	*1971*	*1971*	*1980*	*1990*	*1995*	*2001*
Extractive	14.2	8.9	4.3	3.4	4.8	3.2	1.5	1.9
Transformative	42.2	45.4	43.8	45.9	35.7	27.3	23.1	20.6
Distributive services	19.3	19.2	17.9	18.7	20.2	20.4	19.9	21.1
Producer services	2.6	3.2	5.6	5.2	7.5	12.1	17.3	19.0
Social services	8.9	12.1	19.4	18.3	23.9	27.2	27.8	25.8
Personal services	12.9	11.3	9.0	8.1	7.9	9.8	11.0	11.8
Total	100.0	100.0	100.0	100.0	100.0	100.0	100.0	100.0
United States 1920-2000	*1920*	*1940*	*1970*	*1970*	*1980*	*1990*	*2000*	
Extractive	28.9	21.3	4.5	4.6	4.5	4.0	2.9	
Transformative	32.9	29.8	33.1	33.0	29.6	27.2	22.6	
Distributive services	18.7	20.4	22.3	22.4	21.0	20.9	21.0	
Producer services	2.8	4.6	8.5	8.2	10.5	12.7	15.7	
Social services	8.7	10.0	21.9	22.0	23.7	23.6	26.1	
Personal services	8.2	14.0	10.0	10.0	10.5	11.7	11.7	
Total	100.0	100.0	100.0	100.0	100.0	100.0	100.0	

Source: Aoyama and Castells (2002) Table V p. 136.

* The data given in the left side of the dividing line belongs to Singlemann (1978) and on the right hand side to Aoyama and Castells (2002).

Table 5.4A Ratio of Service Sector Employment to Industrial Employment

Years\Centre	*Canada*	*France*	*Germany*	*Italy*	*Japan*	*UK*	*USA*
1920	1.3	0.9	0.7	0.8	1.2	0.9	1.1
1940	1.4	1.0	0.7	0.8	1.1	0.9	1.6
1970	2.4	1.2	1.0	0.8	1.4	1.1	2.0
1980	2.4	1.7	0.9	0.9	1.7	1.5	2.3
1990	3.3	2.3	1.4	1.2	1.8	2.4	2.9
2000	3.6	3.0	2.0	2.2	2.2	3.7	3.5

Table 5.4B Ratio of Employment in Information Handling and Goods

Years\Centre	*Canada*	*France*	*Germany*	*Italy*	*Japan*	*UK*	*USA*
1920	0.4	0.3	0.3	0.3	0.3	0.3	04
1940	0.4	0.3	0.3	0.3	0.3	0.3	05
1970	0.7	0.5	0.4	0.3	0.4	0.5	06
1980	0.7	0.6	—	0.6	0.4	0.6	07
1990	0.8	0.9	0.6	0.6	0.5	1.0	09
2000	1.2	1.1	0.9	0.7	0.6	1.3	1.0

Source: Derived From Aoyama and Castells (2002) Table 6 p. 139.

CHAPTER 6
SERVICES IN THE NATIONAL ACCOUNTING FRAMEWORKS

Accounts provide the basis for recording and classification of transactions, carried out by enterprises and other economic entities, while performing their businesses. The recording and classification of business transactions converts data into information, which can be used to understand the performance and characteristics of organizations. The evolution of national accounting frameworks was also based on the same motivation, i.e. to properly record and classify different transactions to obtain some useful insight regarding the working of the economy. After World War II, there have emerged several improvements in the national accounting framework. These were necessary because most economies started using the information collected through national accounts for formulating macro-economic policies and planning. Therefore, national accounting frameworks have undergone several improvements since their earliest inception in the writings of William Petty of England and Pirre la Peasant Sieur Boisguillbert in France. From its early formulations, these frameworks evolved around certain basic concepts which carried specific meanings for the monetary value of annual output, income and expenditure of an economy.

National accounting frameworks are based on the double entry system of accounts. In the double entry system of book-keeping, all the transactions are recorded twice because every debit entry appears as a credit entry somewhere in the system. Therefore, in this system, there is no possibility for the existence of receipts without the existence of payments or vice versa. Hence, there emerges a perfect balancing i.e. equality between the two sides of the accounts. Due to this equality, the system can be presented in the form of equations and identities.

The changes that have occurred in the national accounting frameworks resulted from either increasing robustness of its conceptual basis or the availability of reliable sources of data and statistical techniques. The conceptual basis of national accounting systems have been significantly influenced by the theoretical understanding evolved by economists on the concept of *production* as it is central to the national accounting framework because these frameworks essentially generate momentary expression of national output. The concept of production has been variously understood by different paradigms of economic analysis. These different premises, for defining output, resulted in not only the evolution of different national accounting frameworks, it also changed the composition of national output because it became essential for each economic activity to satisfy different criterion of production, evolved by different schools of thought, before its contribution is recorded in national output. The debates regarding *economic* and *non-economic* activities and *productive* and *unproductive* activities are associated with these criterions.

There exists a long historical debate amongst the economists of different schools of thoughts on whether services, as a group of economic activities, satisfy different criterion of production or not. These debates are well documented in the encyclopedic works of Studenski (1958) and Delauney and Gadrey (1992) and have also been discussed in Chapter 1 of the book. Therefore, in the present chapter, instead of focusing on these debates, we will concentrate on the impact of these debates on the evolutionary changes in national accounting frameworks and how these changes affected the accomodation of economic contribution of services in the calculation of national output. It is also the objective of this chapter to present to the readers how real contribution of services to national output is estimated for inter-temporal comparisons, and how the differences in the national prices of services are adjusted to make estimates regarding contribution of services useful for international comparisons.

For the purposes of analysis, this chapter has been divided into four different sections, where each section deals with a specific issue. Section I describes different national accounting frameworks evolved by different schools of economic thought. Section II narrates how these different national accounting frameworks accomodate contribution of services. Section III deals with price adjustments made to obtain real contribution of services which is necessary for inter-temporal comparisons. Finally, in Section IV, we suggest methods which are used to adjust national differences in the prices of services for making international comparisons.

I. Different National Accounting Frameworks

The emergence of different national accounting frameworks can be attributed to the basic epistimological problem identified by Aristotle regarding what determines the value of a product [Ethica Nicomachea 1132a-1133b]. This epistimological problem originated from the realization by Aristotle that commodities must possess, in some degree, a measurable common quality to facilitate exchange. This necessitates identification of a unit of measurement which all commodities must possess in equal degree to help the process of exchange. Aristotle identified two such units which can be used for this purpose. The first unit was *consumer's need* and need renders all commodities commensurable. This premise suggests that the value of the product is determined by the subjective evaluation of the user regarding its usefulness. The second unit which he identified was *intrinsic value of the product.* This premise suggests that the exchange value of a product is proportional to the work necessary to produce it.

Economists from the Physiocratic to Classical and Marxian school of thought followed this line of reasoning based on the thinking of Aristotle which stated that the value of the commodity lies in itself. This view gave them the premise that the value of a product is determined by the amount of labour used in its production. This premise gave birth to the *labour theory of value* and is now being described as *commodity fetishism*; it is also the basis of the materialist conception of production. This view remained a dominant view amongst economists for almost two centuries.

There always existed an alternative view, as an undercurrent, which did not accept the validity of the premise on which the materialist concept of production was based. This view believed in the first premise identified by Aristotle, that the value of a product lies in the mind of its user. Therefore, a strong reaction against commodity fetishism emerged amongst some economists, which helped in the formulation of another extreme position. These economists believed that things do not have value because their costs are assumed, but they cost because they have value (in use) [Georgesu Roegan (1968) and Parsons (1968)]. These two premises have resulted in the formation of two different conceptual frameworks of national accounting practices. The scholars adhering to the premise that the value of the thing lies in itself, helped in the evolution of national accounting framework based on *material production-criteria*, whereas the idea that the value of a thing lies in the mind of its user led to the utilitarian approach, which believes that output means creation of utility. The latter approach facilitated the emergence of a national accounting framework based on *the comprehensive production concept.*

It is interesting to note that most estimates of national income made by early economists, like William Petty (1665) and Gregory King (1696) for England and by Pirre le Pesant de Boisguillebert (1697) and Marshall Vaubaun (1707) for France, followed the comprehensive production concept. This concept went into oblivion in the eighteenth century due to the influence of French physiocrats and classical and Marxian economists subsequently. However, eventually the comprehensive production approach became more acceptable amongst the Western market economies [Studenski (1958) and Kendrick (1968)].

Adam Smith was the first economist who systematically propounded the restricted material production approach of national accounting framework. For him only that part of output is justified for inclusion in national output which has been generated by productive labour (which is engaged in the production of marketable material goods). These are the goods which can command a price in the market equal to the amount of labour embodied in them and added value which is sufficient for the maintenance of the labour and entrepreneur's profit. These conditions make it apparent that national output, according to this criterion, consists of only marketed material goods. The labour engaged in the provisioning of services did not fulfil these conditions, therefore, it was not considered part of the national output. This method adds only the 'stock of goods' while calculating national output and ignores 'flows of utilities'.

Marxian concept of material production was essentially based on Smith's concept of national product, but he reformulated it to develop a framework through which he could establish that labour is the source of all the value. Therefore, contrary to the understanding of Smith, which accepted worker as well as entrepreneur (i.e. capitalist) as productive economic agents who collectively contributed to value, Marx attributes productive role to only hired workers. According to the Marxian conceptualization, labour reproduces value for its own maintenance and also creates an additional value which he called as *surplus-value* which erroneously is being appropriated by entrepreneurs through thir ownership of the means of production. In the writings of Marx, the magnitude of surplus value appears as a measure of the extent of exploitation of workers. Hence, in the conceptualization of Marx, material production system emerged as a methodological tool to criticize the capitalist system. This system of national accounts, now known as 'System of Material Balance of National Economy', received support in the U.S.S.R. and other centrally planned economies of Eastern Europe and remained embedded in the Marxist-Leninist concept of production until the 1990s.

The National Accounting Framework based on comprehensive production approach has received wider acceptability amongst all market economies. This system is based on the utilitarian approach which defines production as "the process of creation of utility" (see Chapter 1, Studenski (1958)]. According to this approach, all products, whether material or immaterial, have utility if they are capable of satisfying human needs. Alongwith satisfying human needs, they should also have determinable prices and costs. This conceptualization is based on the premise that goods as well as services are being exchanged at the market place, and production of both needs inputs of capital and labour. It is also accepted that some of the services cannot be delivered without the facility of complementary goods (e.g. medical care without the complementary medical equipment) in the same way as some of the goods may not be useful without complementary services (e.g. computers may not be useful without complementary software). Based on this conceptualization of national accounts, several attempts were made by individual economists to compute the contribution of goods and services to national output. Looking at the economic importance of national accounts, different governments formed specialized agencies to compute national accounts. However, soon it was realized that there is need for standardization of national accounting framework to facilitate international comparisons.

In 1928, the League of Nations held an international conference relating to economic statistics to evolve a system of compilation of national accounts uniformly by all the governments. This resulted in the publication of national income estimates in the annual *World Economic Survey* in 1939. The Great Depression of the 1930s and emergence of Keynesian Revolution increased the importance of national accounting for macro-economic management of the economies. Therefore, immediately after World War II, a sub-committee on National Income Statistics was constituted by the League of Nations. The memorandum prepared by this sub-committee submitted in 1947 led to the origin of Systems of National Account. Because of the pressing need for establishing international standards to facilitate international comparisons, United Nations prepared a report, *A System of National Accounts and Supporting Tables* [U.N.O. (1953)]. This report generated a lively debate amongst the statistical organisations of different countries which led to several improvements and changes in this document. The second edition of the document was published in 1960. The third reincarnation of the document appeared in 1968 which was approved by the Statistical Commission of U.N.O. this and finally accepted as *System of National Accounts* (SNA) [U.N.O. (1968)]. After being used for several years, in 1975, the United Nations undertook a review of SNA 1968 based on the experiences of different countries while applying it in practice. After wide ranging debates by experts and suggestions given by statistical organisations of different countries, a revised draft of SNA was prepared in 1991 for final comments and suggestions. This draft was finally unanimously recommended by the statistical commission for being adopted as System of National Accounts 1993 [U.N.O. (1993)]. This document is being used globally for the purposes of collecting national accounting data till now. However, like earlier systems of accounts, it represents a stage in the evolution of national accounting. Here, we are not interested in providing a detailed understanding regarding these two systems of national accounting frameworks; instead, our purpose is to know how these systems of national accounting differ from each other in accomodating the contribution made by services to national output.

II. Recording of Contribution of Services in Different National Accounting Frameworks

Both the systems of national accounting differ from each other in terms of their approach to accomodating contribution of services to national income. These differences emanate from the philosophical premises on which these systems of national accounting are based. The Material Production System derives its inspiration from the writings of Marx and Lenin and is being used in the U.S.S.R. and other East European planned economies. Soviet economists define national output as that part of total output, expressed in monetary terms, which has been created by the labour of the economy, engaged in the production of material goods, which are made available annually for consumption and accumulation. Therefore, according to this approach, only material production is recorded in national accounts and also that national output consists of net output of primary activities, mining, manufacturing and construction. However, in their calculations, they also include services like freight transportation, trade and some branches of communication (only business to business), on the ground that without these services material production cannot achieve its ultimate purpose which is to make the products available to their end users; therefore, material goods have no value until they reach their users. According to this concept, non-productive services which are not included in the national output are banking, education, art, cultural and medical services [Thalheim (1973) p. 327].

It is also interesting to note that this concept of national accounts very strongly opposes the inclusion of the contribution of services like police, bureaucracy and military because, according to this conceptualization, these services 'protect the system of capitalist hired slavery'. Therefore these services are infact "parasitic servants of the exploitative classes" [S.S.S.R. Institute of Political Economy (1964) p.119]. These ideas were conceptualized in the alternative system of national accounts published by U.N.O in 1971. This framework is now known as the *Basic Principles of Systems of Balances of the National Economy*. As is apparent from its name, this approach is based on a system of balances which includes (a) material balance (b) financial balance (c) balances of fixed capital and indicators of national wealth, and (d) balancing of manpower resources. The balancing of manpower is a unique feature of this system.

According to the framework of accounting used by this system, it decomposes all the economic activities into two broad categories—the sphere of material production (i.e. goods producing) and a sphere of non-material production (i.e. services). The material sphere of production makes available means of production and tangible consumer goods and material services. Material services include all those services which are complementary to material production such as repair, transportation and distribution which, according to this system of account, are in fact the continuation of the process of production. Therefore, according to this approach, material production and material services constitute national output. Non-material services are not part of national output because they are not embodied in any form in any material product. These services have characteristics like (a) intangibility (b) inseparability between service provider and service per se and (c) simultaniety between production and consumption. This suggests that the system of material production balances and accomodates the contribution of only those services which are part of the value chain of material production.

In comparison to the material production balances system of accounting, the comprehensive production system, which has been formulated by U.N.O. as a system of National Accounts in 1968 alongwith its several revisions over time, views production as creation of consumables whether they are material or immaterial. According to this system of national accounting, national output consists of all the goods and services which are being exchanged in the market by either private, government or not-for profit organizations. For the purposes of accounting, it defines services as those inseparable entities for which ownership rights can be established. Services consist of heterogeneous outputs produced to bring about changes in the conditions of consuming units, realized by the activities of producers at the demand of the consumers. Their production and consumption is instantaneous. The production of services is confined to activities that are being carried out by one unit for the benefit of another. The changes that are affected by the producers of the services to the consuming unit may take different forms (a) changes in the condition of consumer's goods by transporting, cleaning repairing and transforming them (b) changes in the physical conditions of the persons by providing medical or surgical treatment by improving their appearance, like beauty treatment or haircut (c) changes in the mental conditions of persons by providing education, information advise, entertainment etc. (d) changes in the general economic state of the individual unit, by providing insurance, financial intermediation, protection, guarantee etc. These changes may be temporary or permanent. However, they cannot be held as inventories by producers or traced as separate entities [U.N.O. (1993) pp. 122-123].

In this system of accounts, all the economic activities which are produced on own account are excluded from the measurement of national income. This is because own account services represent self-consumption of services or non-marketed services. However, it does include some of the services produced within the household through hired domestic servants. While computing the contribution of services, it does not include those services which are intermediate in nature. This is done to avoid double accounting—that only final services are accounted for. To obtain the aggregate of final services, a simple empirical rule is followed.The rule is whether the service has been sold by one business enterprise to another for further production (i.e. intermediate services); or directly to the households (final services) for consumption. However, there are several debates amongst economists regarding what constitutes intermediate services and what constitutes final services [Fisher (1939), Shoup (1947), Gini (1948), Kuznets (1951) and Lowe (1952)].

In the category of intermediate services fall the services of banks, insurance companies and other financial institutions. These services play the role of intermediaries between supplier of funds and actual user of funds. In fact these institutions render services to both business enterprises and to households, therefore, it becomes difficult to identify which kind of services are provided to different groups. For instance, take the case of banking services. All funds and financial transactions pass through the network of banks, whether transacted by business enterprises, households or governmental organizations. Banks charge from their depositors specific fees for some of the services and some other services they provide without charging any fees. Similarly, the interest rates that they charge from the borrowers include true interest rates and costs of administering loans. However, banks do not report information on these charges separately in their accounts. Therefore, it becomes difficult to compute how much of the banking services have been rendered to households (i.e. final services) and how much to business enterprises (i.e. intermediate services). To overcome this problem, banks accounts are redrawn on the basis of a premise that banks will be paying out all the interest earned on deposits to their depositors and similarly would be charging for all the services provided to their depositors by taking imputed values for each of the services rendered to them. Income earned is obtained after these adjustments are split into final and intermediate services in accordance with the ratio of personal deposits to business deposits. Hence, earnings from the services rendered by banks to households become part of final services and are included in national output. Whereas, earning from the services given to business enterprises are considered intermediate services and, therefore, not included in national accounts.

Similarly, adjustments have also to be made while calculating the contribution of insurance companies to national output. To identify how much contribution has been made by insurance companies, they are treated as associations of policy holders. Receipts from premium paid by policy holders and payments made against claims of policy holders are regarded as transfer of funds amongst policy holders. Any investment earning which is not distributed to policy holders is imputed as an additional income to policy holders accounts. The total of such incomes, which are actually imputed, are treated as current factor incomes of the policy holders and become part of national output.

Similarly, to identity the contribution of insurance companies from expenditure side of national accounting framework, incomes of insurance companies are also imputed by accounting for all the charges for services provided by insurance companies to the policy holders. This is obtained by aggregating all the operating expenses incurred by the insurance companies while providing their services. The operating expenses include the total amount of expenditure incurred on wages and salaries of the employees, commission paid to agents and employees, and services purchased from other organizations.

The most difficult part of estimating the contribution of services to national income is to evolve a system to accomodate the contribution of government services. It is quite difficult to resolve whether government services should be considered as final services or as intermediate services. Some economists believe that all the services provided by the government should be recognized as intermediate services, therefore, should not be considered as a part of current years, output. The reason given in support of this view is that the entire government machinery is needed to supply services like security, safety as well as civil services.These services do not produce values in addition to the flow of goods and services directly purchased by the households. Moreover, value of these services is already included in the value of final consumption of good and services. Therefore, inclusion of government services in national output will amount to double accounting [Studenski (1958) Part II p.36].

Some other economists take a contrary view and advocate that all the services provided by the government should be treated as final output and, therefore, should be added to the national output. These economists can be divided into two segments. One group advocates for the inclusion of government services in national output because it is difficult to partition the output of government services into final and intermediate services, therefore, they suggest, it is better to record the entire government services as final services [Hicks (1939) p. 150]. However, another group of economists split government services into final and intermediate categories and advocate for the inclusion of only final government services in national output. They have a theoretical basis for doing so [Colm (1954)]. These economists consider government services like education, health and general welfare as final services, whereas services like police and army are considered as intermediate services.

The contribution of government services to national income is accounted differently depending upon whether we are estimating it with output method, income method or expenditure method. In the output method, contribution of government services is represented by net output or value-added. This is measured in terms of compensation paid to government employees and interest paid on government debt. It is also represented by the same values in the income method. When we estimate the contribution of government services to national income with the help of expenditure method than it is estimated as total expenditure on the compensation of government employees, government purchases from other businesses, or as government expenditure on its various functions. Therefore, what is generally done to arrive at the contribution of government services to national product is that the expenditure incurred by the government on provisioning of government services is accepted as the criterion. The underlying assumption in following this practice is that these services are worth their costs.

The SNA 1993 includes two specific categories of services produced for self consumption of the household (i.e. own account services), whose contribution is included in the national output. One is the services of paid domestic servants, cooks, gardeners, chauffers etc. (i.e. paid domestic services). The contribution of these services to national income is equal to the compensation paid to the employees of the household [U.N.O. (1993) p. 134)]. Similarly, the services of own occupied house are also included in the estimation of national income. This is based on the understanding that the dwelling unit owned by the household produces housing services whereas households who do not own a dwelling unit obtain housing services through market determined rental for housing. Therefore, the value of the housing services obtained from the owner occupied house can be obtained from the rents prevailing in the market for similar housing facilities [U.N.O. (1993) p. 134].

To estimate the contribution of transportation, its output is estimated by the value of amount receivable from transporting goods or persons. In economic theory the nature of the good changes with its change of location and changing the space of the good is considered as an act of production (by creating utility of space). Therefore, the volume of transport services can be measured in terms of *ton-kilometres* and *passenger-kilometres*. Similarly, the role of *storage* is to make goods available at a later point of time. The product, at different points of time, is also treated as two different products. Therefore, storage also generates output by using time utility. In fact it amounts to transportations of a good over time. Some products become different over time because of physical or chemical changes, like storing of wine. The output of storage can be measured by *space-days* i.e. combining the volume of product stored with length of time over which the product is stored. The output of storage can also be measured by measuring the changes in the value of inventories. The prices of goods may alter while being stored because (a) quality of good may improve or deteriorate with time period of storage (b) the product might be subject to seasonal variation in prices, and (c) prices of the stored product may change due to general inflation or recession [U.N.O. (1993) pp. 136-137].

In System of National Accounting, the role of *wholesale* and *retail traders* is to buy and sell goods and they are not treated as *intermediate* products so long as these products are resold with minimum changes in the product (i.e. only graded, cleaned, packaged etc). Their output is also measurable in terms of total value of trade margins realized on the goods they have purchased for resale. Here, the trade margin is considered as difference between the actual inputed price realized by selling and the price which the distributor will pay to replace the goods. The replacement cost may also include losses due to wastage, theft or accidental damages.

To accomodate the contribution of Research & Development in the measurement of national output, it is treated as a separate establishment. In the case of R&D activities carried out by private sector commercial undertakings, its contribution is estimated on the basis of estimated basic prices that would have been paid if such research activity was outsourced, or total cost of production of R&D. The earnings are recorded in terms of receipts from sales, commissions and fees. In contrast, R&D activities of government financed undertakings and universities are valued at the total costs incurred in maintaining R&D activities because these services are not marketed.

Services provided by non-profit institutions are also included while estimating contribution of different services to national output. Since these institutions provide services to their members, therefore, subscriptions and membership fees are considered as a payment for such services. Hence, these services are valued equal to the amount of money received as subscriptions and contributions [U.N.O. (1993) p.146]. In the case of all other services like *education*, *health* and *entertainment*, the estimation of their contribution is not difficult because there always exist public as well as private service providers in each of these categories. Since these services are final services, they are included in the estimation of national output. In the case of private service providers, it is easy to know their incomes from providing these services, whereas in such cases where service provider is government, then its contribution can be estimated by annual expenses incurred by the government in providing these services.

III. Inter-temporal Comparison of Contribution of Services

The annual estimate of national output, generated by using different national accounting frameworks, gives time-series data on various economic aggregates. The inter-temporal variations in the value of these aggregates might be due to only variations in the prices of different services rather than due to actual increases in the supply of services. This is because changes in the monetary value of national output, contributed by services, may change due to two different reasons (a) inter-temporal variations in the prices of services, (b) inter-temporal changes in the real supply of services. The process of growth emerges when services record real increase in their availability. Therefore, it necessitates that the impact of variations of price changes be removed to obtain changes in the real output of services. To adjust the time series data, we estimate the contribution of services at constant prices to obtain real changes in the contribution of services. For this the prices are assumed to be constant i.e. prices prevailing in one time period are applied to the flow of services of another time period under consideration. The constant price estimates of contribution made by services provides information about real changes in the quantity of services, changes in productivity of inputs and also regarding economic fluctuations.

The value of services is expressed as a product of their respective prices and quantities. Therefore, the value of the ith service can be expressed as

$$P_i\, Q_i = \text{Value of the ith service}$$

Same services may be available at different prices in different locations and at different periods of time. In economic theory it is being considered that the same good, when delivered at different locations or at different times, should be treated as separate goods. The prices over time may vary due to variations in durability, storeability and preservability of the service. These involve additional costs. Similarly, spatial variations in prices may occur due to costs of transportation and variations in trade margins. Price variations over time and space may also occur due to inter-temporal and spatial variations in indirect taxes and also due to market imperfections of different types. However, for computing real changes in the output of services, what is needed is inter-temporal changes in prices. This can be adjusted by *price indices.* A price index is an average proportionate change in the prices of a specified set of goods and services between two points in time. On the other hand, a *volume index*, which is an average of proportionate changes in the quantities of specified services, can also be computed to analyse real changes in the output of services. To evolve price indices or quantity indices, the time period that is accepted as the reference year (i.e. the base year) is designated as period O and the period which is being compared with reference to the base year is described as terminal year or t. The ratios of prices or quantities of ith service in period t to prices or quantities of the reference year O are described as relative prices or relative quantities

Price relative of the ith service = P_it/P_io,
Quantity relative to ith service = Q_it/Q_io

Most of the different types of price and quantity indexes are obtained from weighted averages of these relatives. Various kinds of indices have been evolved by scholars by changing either the weights that they attach to individual prices and quantities or by using different measures of central tendency i.e. arithmetic, geometric or harmonic mean.

There are two most common indices which are used to arrive at the contribution of services at constant prices. These are Laspeyres and Paasche indices. Both are computed as weighted averages of price or quantity relatives; however, the weights can be values of the individual service in base year or current year. If we define the value of the ith service at point of time O as

$$V_io = P_io \cdot Q_io$$

than Laspeyres index can be described as a weighted arithmatic mean of price relatives, using the prices of base year as weight

$$Lp = \sum_{i=1}^{n} \frac{V_io . P_it / P_io}{\sum_{i=1}^{n} V_io} \qquad (1)$$

where $\sum_{i=1}^{n}$ stands for summation of all the services. Similarly, Laspeyres quantity index can also be described as

$$L_q = \sum_{i=1}^{n} \frac{V_i o . Q_i t / Q_i o}{\sum_{i=1}^{n} V_i o} \tag{2}$$

If we expand the price index of Laspeyres then it takes the form

$$L_p = \frac{\sum_{i=1}^{n} P_o \cdot Q_o (P_t / P_o)}{\sum P_o \cdot Q_o} \tag{3}$$

$$= \frac{\sum P_i Q_o}{\sum P_o Q_o} \tag{4}$$

Similarly, Laspeyres quantity index will be

$$L_q = \frac{\sum_{i=1}^{n} P_o \cdot Q_o (P_t / P_o)}{\sum P_o \cdot Q_o} \tag{5}$$

$$= \frac{\sum P_o \cdot Q_t}{\sum P_o \cdot Q_o} \tag{6}$$

Paasche Price Index (P_P) and Quantity index (P_q) are expressed reciprocally to Laspeyres indices. However, it uses current year values of prices and quantities as weights and is based on harmonic mean rather than arithmatic mean. Paasche Price Index is defined as

$$P_P = \frac{\sum V_i t}{\sum V_i t . P_o / P_t} \tag{7}$$

$$= \frac{\sum P_t Q_t}{\sum (P_t Q_t)(P_o / P_t)} 1 \tag{8}$$

$$= \frac{\sum P_t Q t}{\sum P_o Q_o} \tag{9}$$

Similarly Paasche's quantity index (p_q) is expressed as

$$p_q = \frac{\sum V_i t}{\sum V_i t \cdot (Q_o / Q_t)} \tag{10}$$

$$= \frac{\sum PtQt}{\sum (Pt \cdot Qt)(Q_o / Q_t)} \tag{11}$$

$$= \frac{\sum P_t Q_t}{\sum P_t Q_o} \tag{12}$$

Theoretically speaking, it has been established that the Paasche index is reciprocal of a 'backward working' Laspeyres index. Because of the existence of this reciprocity, there also exist important symmetries between these two indices: one is that the product of Laspeyres price or quantity index and corresponding Paasche's price or quantity index is identical with the proportionate change in total value of flow of services between the base and terminal year [U.N.O. (1993) p. 382]

$$L_p \, . \, P_p = \frac{\sum P_t Q_o}{\sum P_P O_o} \cdot \frac{\sum P_t \, Q_t}{\sum P_t \cdot Q_o} = \frac{\sum V_i t}{\sum V_i o} \tag{13}$$

$$L_q \cdot P_p = \frac{\sum P_o Q_b}{\sum P_o Q_o} \cdot \frac{\sum PtQt}{\sum P_o \, Q_t} = \frac{\sum V_i t}{\sum V_i o} \tag{14}$$

However, it is quite important to know that Laspeyres index shows larger increases over time in comparison to Paasche index, i.e.

$$L_p > p_p \text{ and } L_q > p_q$$

This relationship between the two indices emerges because of negative correlations between price and quantity relatives, therefore, Laspeyres index systematically shows higher increases than Paasche's index, and their gaps keep on increasing with time. It has also been observed by scholars that the Laspeyres and Paasche indices are upper and lower bounds respectively of the theoretical indices. Fisher's ideal index is quite close to the underlying theoretic index and is a geometric mean of Laspeyres and Paasche indices i.e. Fisher's price index (F_p) and quantity index (F_q) can be written as

$$F_p = [L_p \cdot p_p]1/2 \tag{15}$$

and

$$F_q = [L_q \cdot p_q]1/2 \tag{16}$$

The index of Fisher is considered to be an ideal index because it satisfies both the time reversal test and factor reversal test. The time reversal test is satisfied when the index for terminal year based on the base year is a reciprocal of index for base year based on terminal year. Similarly, factor reversal test is satisfied when the product of price index and quantity index is equal to proportionate changes in current values i.e. $\Sigma V_i t/\Sigma V_i O$.

In the context of evolving contribution of services at constant prices, it should be noted that price indices are more relevant than quantity indices because, in the case of most services, it is difficult to specify quantities. The conventional method which is used to estimate contribution of wholesale and retail trade (i.e. distributive services) is the difference between the amount received by the distributor and the amount that is paid to the producer or some other distributor. Moreover, it should also be noted that traders, while trading, also supply several other complementary services while distributing goods, like transporting, grading, efficient arrangement and display of goods. What is relevant for the purposes of calculating the contribution of distributive services is the trade margins at constant prices. This can be obtained by the following ratios

$$\text{Laspeyres quantity index } (L_q) = \frac{\sum P_s o \cdot Q_s t}{\sum P_s o \cdot Q_s o} \tag{17}$$

where P_s stands for price of distributive services and Q_s stands for quantity of distributive services; O stands for base year values and t stands for terms year values. Therefore, Laspeyres price index will be

$$L_p = \frac{\sum P_s t \cdot Q_s o}{\sum P_s o \cdot Q_s o} \tag{18}$$

Therefore, Paasche's price and quantity index can also specified as

$$P_q = \frac{\sum P_s t \cdot Q_s t}{\sum P_s t \cdot Q_s o} \text{ and} \tag{19}$$

$$P_p = \frac{\sum P_s t\, Q_s t}{\sum P_s o \cdot Q_s t} \tag{20}$$

To obtain the contribution of transport services at constant prices, we first compute all transport margins.The transport margin for a single product is calculated in the following manner

$$T_m = P_L - P_{EF}$$

i.e. transport margin per unit of output (T_m) is the difference between P_L i.e. price at location inclusive of transportation cost and P_{EF} which stands for exfactory price of the product i.e. price without transport cost. These trade margins can be calculated for all the products transported in an economy by summing the transport margins for each good transported

$$\Sigma TM \cdot Q = \Sigma(PL - PEF) = PLQ - PEF\ Q$$

Therefore, transport margins at constant prices can be computed by multiplying the goods sold in the current year (i.e. at time t) by their transport margins attached to different locations from where the goods were transported in the base year i.e.

$$\Sigma\ Tm\ Qt = \Sigma\ P_L{}^o\ Qt - P^o{}_{EF}\ Qt$$

Laspeyres and Paasche indices can be calculated as follows

$$L_q = \frac{\sum Tm^o Qt}{\sum Tm^o Qo} \tag{21}$$

$$L_p = \frac{\sum Tm^t \cdot Qo}{\sum Tm^t \cdot Qo} \tag{22}$$

and

$$p_q = \frac{\sum Tm^t \cdot Qt}{\sum Tm^t \cdot Qo} \tag{23}$$

$$p_p = \frac{\sum Tm^t \cdot Qt}{\sum Tm^t \cdot Qo} \tag{24}$$

Sometimes, instead of calculating trade margins, contribution of transportation services can be obtained directly from the data on price of transporting goods per unit of distance (*TP*), distance over which the good is being transported (*D*). Then income from transportation can be rewritten in the following manner, e.g. Here, m = TP.D.

$$L_q = \frac{\sum Tm^o Q^t}{\sum Tm^o Q^o} = \frac{\sum TP^o \cdot D^o \cdot Qt}{\sum TP^o \cdot D \cdot Q^o} \tag{25}$$

In the case of *financial institutions*, obtaining their contribution at constant prices becomes relatively difficult. The difficulty arises because it is difficult to get information on suitable measures on quantity of services rendered by them, because their output at current prices includes imputed values of several services which can be identified with specific type of bank output. To overcome this problem, it has been suggested to substitute input based measure for output measure. Input variations over time, in the case of financial institutions, consist of changes over time, the number of employees, hours worked, wages and salaries etc. These, when computed for base and terminal years, provide better estimates for the contribution of financial services.

Health services, as well as educational services, are quite heterogenous in nature. Some part of these services is marketed and some part is provided for with varying level of subsides. Therefore, it is suggested that quantities (or volumes) of each type of service should be obtained, e.g. in the case of health care, number of patients visited, number of consultations and, in the case of education, it can be computed with the help of enrolment of students in various educational programmes. By giving appropriate weight to each type of health care and level of education, volume index can be prepared. It may also require the generation of data regarding prices of each kind of health service and level of education either directly from the market on the basis of actual cost incurred in the supplying of that service or through some imputed prices.

Attempts have also been made to arrive at measures of output of government services and public enterprises also at constant prices. Conventionally economists measured the volume of government services and public sector services in terms of labour inputs used to provide them [Hill (1977)]. Justification of this system has (already been mentioned in Section II of this chapter) been that the value of the services given by them is at least equal to the costs of their production [Hicks (1940)]. This practice has been followed because it was difficult to generate output data for such services. In 1979, UNO prepared a Draft Manual on Public Sector Statistics (DMPSS). This draft evolved a new methodology for measuring output of public enterprises and government services. According to the methodology, data on quantities of these services will be combined with the extent of use of these services (i.e. utilization of these services) to obtain the measure of volume for these services. Information regarding the volume of such services can be obtained by recording transactions between producer of services (i.e. government) and their users. Therefore, for government services like health and education, which involve transactions between producers and users, gross output in constant prices should be estimated (DMPSS, p. 83). Whereas, for government services like public administration, judiciary, police and armed forces, such transactions between producers and consumers do not occur (these are collective public goods); the manual suggested that their contribution should be measured in terms of work performed (DMPSS, p. 85). However, some scholars have suggested substituting input measures for output measures.

The economic importance of output measures is that they are related to the concept of social welfare [Saunders (1977). However, some economists explicitly assume that productivity cannot be increased in services [Baumol

(1968) and Skolka (1977). These views have been discussed in greater detail in this book in Chapters 2 and 3. Attempts have also been made to evaluate the appropriateness of volume measures of government services in terms of their impact on measurement of contribution of government services to national income and its impact on the measurement of productivity of such services [Hjerppe (1980)].

However, there ae several theoretical questions associated with the use of volume measures [Sen (1979)]. One important question is whether the objective of measuring volume is to know about production possibilities of the economy or welfare of the citizen. The second issue is concerned with the assumptions regarding individual utility function and its relation with aggregate utility function.

IV. Spatial Variations in the Prices of Services and International Comparison

In real life situations, price may vary not only over time, but may also have spatial variations; the same product may be priced differently at different regions/countries at the same point in time. Therefore, when we intend to compare the contribution of services among different countries/regions, these spatial variations in the prices of services have to be adjusted to arrive at some meaningful international comparisons. The need for having appropriate adjustment for spatial variations in prices arises because, in the past, international comparisons were generally based on their *nominal values*, obtained by converting the values found in each country's national accounts to a common currency (usually the U.S. dollars) by means of exchange rates. However, it has been observed that these estimates generally provide erroneous comparisons. The errors emerge because exchange rates deviate from appropriate conversion factors to various purchasing power parities (PPP) of currencies.

It is quite logical to compare prices and quantities between countries using the same methodology for international comparisons. For this purpose, international quantity indices are essential to know spatial variations in productivity and standards of living, while price indices are necessary to measure spatial variations in the purchasing power parities among different economies. We have already mentioned about different indices which have been evolved to analyse inter-temporal variations. These indices cannot be used without modification for spatial analysis i.e. just by replacing the term for time by the term space. Moreover, in the time series estimates, the comparison over time is made in terms of time periods of same durations (generally a year). However, it is difficult to have unit of space of similar sizes. The comparisons between economies may involve different magnitudes i.e. economies of different *geographical sizes* and *economic sizes*. In the case of time series data on prices and quantities, there exists a continuity over time. Which does not exist amongst spatial data. Therefore, there does not exist any objective criterion either to identity a benchmark spatial unit (i.e. country) or to organize different economies in a particular order. Despite these problems, economists have evolved different methods for comparing spatial differences in the contribution of services to national output.

Some scholars have developed price and quantity indices between pairs of countries, using same kind of indices that have been described in Section III. They have developed a Laspeyres quantity index for a country B based on country A. The index is

$$\underset{ab}{L}q_i = \frac{\sum Va \cdot qb/qa}{\sum Va} = \frac{\sum paqb}{\sum paqa} \tag{26}$$

In this formulation, the advantage is that despite the fact that price can be expressed in terms of two currencies, this becomes immaterial as prices of country A are used. Therefore, exchange rate problems become irrelevant. This Laspeyres quantity index can be calculated for comparing goods as well as services among pairs of countries. It is also possible to construct a Passche type quantity index for country B on A as given below

$$\underset{ab}{pq} = \frac{\sum Vb}{\sum Vb \cdot Qa/ab} = \frac{\sum Pb\,Qb}{\sum Pb\,Qa} \tag{27}$$

Given the theoretical relationship between Laspeyres and Paasche indices, we can derive Paasche price index, for *B* based on *A*, as

$$\underset{ab}{P_p} = \frac{\sum Vb}{\sum Vb \cdot Pa/pb} = \frac{\sum PbQb}{\sum PaQb} \tag{28}$$

The price relative (*Pa/Pb*) that has been used in equation (28) is the expression of prices of the same product in country *A* and country *B*. The price relative can be correctly estimated between two countries because each economy collects information about prices for different goods and services for growth accounting as well as for measuring inflation.

The price relative can be interpreted as an estimate of the number of units of *B*'s currency that are required in *B* to buy the same quantity of an individual service as one unit of A's currency will purchase in *A*. This ratio is, in fact, known as purchasing power parity between two countries for a service. Therefore, a weighted harmonic average of the individual services *PPP* can be described as Paasche type *PPP* index rather than a price index.

Purchasing power parity is in the centre of monetarist theories of the determination of exchange rate. It is in fact the bilateral exchange rate to prices of each country. If the same good is available in both U.K. and U.S.A, then tariff transportation costs and other distortions aside, the two goods will sell for the same price after translation through the spot exchange rate. Thus let p denote the price in sterling, P^* price in dollar and S stand for exchange rate i.e. dollar price of sterling (S/L). Hence, the service which is being sold at P in U.K. will sell for Sp in the U.S.A. If $Sp < P^*$ than consumers in U.S.A. will not buy the service. If $Sp < P^*$ then people in U.S.A. will buy the service from U.K. Thus, for a single service, we will have the condition

$$Sp = P^* \text{ or } S = P^*/p$$

If this is true for all the services then

$$SP = P^* \text{ or } S = P^*/P$$

Hence, purchasing power purity is determined by price levels in two countries.

It has been observed that the purchasing power of the currencies of low-income economies in comparison to very high income economies is generally two to three times greater as exchange rates would show. A two or three fold overstatement of the number of currency units will lead to a corresponding large underestimation of the real income of low income economies. Not only this, for economies at any level of income levels, exchange rates do not reflect the true quantity relationship for GDP as whole. These distortions emerge because the purchasing power parity deviates from rates not in uniform fashion, for example capital goods are more expensive relative to consumer goods in low income economies. Therefore exchange rate conversions provide higher proportion of GDP that is contributed by capital goods [Kravis et al (1982) pp. 3-4]. In real life situations, PPP indices are useful to derive international quantity indices by using them as deflators or values in local currencies. However, as PPPs are related to domestic final expenditure, they are not able to explain international flows of goods and services.

Laspeyres and Paasche quantity index formulation given in equations (26) and (27) suggests that whereas in the case of Laspeyres method the value of quantity of each service is taken at the base country's prices, in Paasche index the quantities are valued at partner country's own prices. Since inter-temporal price and quantity comparisons remained confined to adjacent time periods, whereas spatial variations in prices may involve countries far away from each other, therefore, the differences between relative prices and quantities for two different time periods for the same country will be smaller in comparison to spatial variation in prices and quantities between two countries. The negative correlation, when accompanied with substantial differences in relative price between countries, may generate a large spread between the Laspeyres and Paasche indices both for quantity and price indices. For country *B* the use of its own price weights in Paasche formula is likely to produce a lower quantity index relative to base country A's price level in Laspeyres index. This emerges because of negative correlation that exists between price ratios and quantity ratios. This suggests that compared with the base country, a country will usually absorb relatively larger quantities of goods and services that are cheaper and relatively smaller quantities of goods and services which are expensive. This observation that Paasche quantity indexes are lower than Laspeyres indexes is referred to as *own-weight effect* by Kravis et al (1982), and is similar to Gershenkron effect in inter-temporal series [Kravis et al (1978) Table 5.31, Kravis et al (1982) p. 74]. It has also been observed that neither Laspeyres index nor Paasche index satisfy the *country reversal test.* However, geometric mean of these two indexes, i.e. Fisher's index can satisfy the country reversal test.

The necessity for international comparisons may require knowledge of the relative size of GDP and its various components for all countries. Aggregation methods that produce a unique quantifiable scaling for more than two countries simultaneously requires multilateral methods of comparison which should have at least one basic characteristic—that while comparing different countries, every country's prices and quantities enter into comparison of all pairs of countries. Most multilateral methods of comparison emerged in late 1960s and 1970s. There are three group of methods which have been used for multilateral comparisons (a) selective set of binary comparisons (b) multilateral comparisons based on binary comparisons and (c) multilateral methods not based on binary comparisons.

Selective set of binary comparisons are based on binary comparisons for inferring the comparisons of other pairs. The simplest procedure followed in this category is the *star system of binary comparisons*. In this system, each country, a point of star, is compared with the base country (centre of the star). Comparisons between point country and base country are expressed as ratios of corresponding point-to-centre comparison. This method can provide matrix consistency and transitivity, provided prices of the centre (i.e. base economy) are used to value quantities for all the point economies. Only this procedure fulfills the base-country-invariatic condition.

If there are n number of countries and binary comparisons of prices and quantities are needed for each pair of countries, then, to make complete comparability among any pair of countries the possible binary comparisons required will be equal to $n(n-1)/2$. Under these conditions, transitivity can be explained with the help of the following example.

If price or volume index number of country *b* based on country *a* be written as *a*/*b*, the set of indices can be described as transitive when

$$a/b \cdot b/c = a/c$$

This condition suggests that the direct binary index for country *c* based on country *a* should be equal to indirect index obtained by multiplying the direct binary index for country *b* on country *a* by the direct binary index for country *c* on country *b*.

Moreover, in all multilateral methods of comparison, the choice of base can be more important in international comparisons because relative prices and quantities show greater spatial variation than inter-temporal variations. The use of single country as base country may not be acceptable to serious scholars because results of such indices are highly sensitive to the choice of the base country.

In order to obtain multilateral measures that give transitive set of prices and quantity measures, and also provide equal weight to all countries or to all economic activities irrespective of their location, two different approaches have been evolved. One such approach tries to achieve transitivity by using average prices within a block to calculate multilateral measures; whereas in the other approach, all possible binary comparisons between all possible pairs of countries are transformed to achieve transitivity. The most common block method is *Geary Khamis method* and the other method which also provides transitive comparisons has been evolved by Eleteo, Koves and Szule (EKS) [Geary (1958), Khamis (1967); and Drechsler (1975) pp. 17-34]. However, it should be noted that EKS method utilizes binary comparisons whereas Geary Khamis's is not dependent on binary comparisons.

One of the landmark approaches to evolve meaningful international comparisons has been developed by the United Nations International Comparison Project (ICP) which was established in 1960 to develop methods for plausible international comparisons to answer questions like: What is the role of tastes in making cardinal comparisons of the bundles of goods and services consumed by citizens of different countries in the world? What is the possibility that people located in different countries, and embedded in different histories, values and cultures, may have similar tastes? If their tastes differ, is there any justification for comparing the welfare values of the bundles of goods and services consumed by consumers of different countries?

The role of tastes appears more significant in spatial variations than in inter-temporal comparison of the same unit of space. One can see in real life the differences in the physical form of things that people consume, for example, French wines, Italian pasta, Japanese sake, German beer and American cola can be indicative of differences in tastes. These diversities in tastes make comparison between countries irrelevant and of limited economic value. However, when looked at alternatively, one can regard basic needs and desires of man as being fundamentally same. Therefore, what varies with space is not what people desire but what different economies are able to afford, and means by which their needs are satisfied. The obvious fact on which this premise, that there exists a similarity of goods found in all major cities of the world, is based is that as economic levels increase there emerges convergence in tastes in different parts of the world. This view has been endorsed by the ICP itself which observed that consumption patterns were not affected by differences in tastes but due to spatial variations in relative prices and level of per capita income [Kravis et al (1975), Kravis et al (1978) and Kravis et al (1982)].

The basic methodological approach of ICP is to derive quantity comparisons through price and expenditure comparisons. Here Q stands for quantities, E for expenditure and P for prices. These variables are linked to each other in the familiar identity $E = P \cdot Q$. Therefore, for any pair of countries, j and k, with respect to commodity i

$$\frac{Eij}{Eik} = \frac{Pij}{Pik} \cdot \frac{Qij}{Qik} \text{ in such a way}$$

that

$$\frac{Qij}{Qik} = \frac{Eij}{Eik} \div \frac{Pij}{Pik}$$

Thus, the quantity ratio between countries can be estimated either directly or indirectly through ratio of Eij/Eik to Pij/Pik.

The ICP project has shown a great deal of attention in evolving methods of comparisons for the services component of final expenditure of GDP. The attention was specially focused on those services for which output data are difficult to obtain such as medical care, education and government services. Therefore, it will be interesting for us to know how *ICP treated services* while making international comparisons. The most important problem posed by services is how to record their real products. This problem is not serious in the case of final product services like barber shops, laundry services, which are rendered by individual producers to individual customers in exchange of a price. Therefore, for the purposes of international comparison, ICP divided services into two well defined segments.

Segment one consists of those services where there exists, well defined unit of services, output. Services such as repairs to variety of consumer owned products, drycleaning and laundering, transportation, entertainment and cultural services, barber shops, services of restaurants, cafes, hotels, space rental services, are included in this category; ICP defines these services as priced services. Indirectly ICP also defines them as *comparable services* [Kravis et al (182) p. 131]. In the case of such services, ICP constructed price and quantity indexes in Phase I and Phase II of their project similar to indices computed for goods. This was done by developing purchasing power parity for each of these services and quantity ratios were obtained by dividing PPP into the expenditure Ratio. ICP observed that the expenditure on these services accounted for 58 per cent of all the services and 16 per cent of GDP per capita (in own prices) for the aggregate of 16 countries in Phase II of the project (i.e. in 1978).

The other segment consisted of those services where clearly defined units of output were not available. These were three problem services—health care, education and government services—for which it is difficult to obtain a reasonably accurate measure of output. They were referred to as *comparison-resistant services* [Kravis (1970) and Kravis (1982) p. 131]. These services constituted 42 per cent of all service expenditure and 11 per cent of GDP per capita [Kravis (1978), Kravis (1982) Table 5.2]. This category of services includes the services of physicians, dentists, hospitals, nurses and government employees (in medical care, education and government services). In Phase I and Phase II of the project, it was assumed that output of these services were proportional to their inputs. This implicitly assumes that productivity of each input is equal in all the countries. Based on this assumption, output comparisons were made directly from quantities of relatively homogeneous inputs or indirectly by price comparisons of such inputs.

In the case of healthcare, the important inputs are physicians, dentists, nurses, physiotherapist, midwives etc. To evolve quantity comparisons, the number of health care personnel in each category were used. In the case of hospitals, the number of bed-days or number of beds was used for output comparisons. The ICP recognised that output of health care personnel depends significantly on the availability of complementary medical equipment (i.e. capital stock). Therefore, they adjusted the output data with a crude measure based on limited information; this adjustment reduced the quantity ratio of France/USA by 4 per cent, while it reduced by 14 per cent the Kenya/USA ratio.

In education, the basic input is teacher, therefore, ICP took into consideration teachers of students at first, second and third levels and converted them into standardized persons engaged in providing services. To calculate standardized persons for first and second levels of education, quantity was based on the number of teachers who have completed two years of college/ university studies. This necessitated the adjustment of raw-quantity ratios relative to United States by 16 per cent for Colombia and India, and 33 per cent for Kenya. Quantity comparisons for third level of education were simply based on the number of teachers. The project computed *PPP* indirectly by dividing expenditure ratios by quantity ratios.

For the purposes of international comparisons of government services, ICP obtained relevant measures from the data on government expenditure. Governments inccur expenditure on (a) compensation of employees, and (b) purchases of commodities. Commodity inputs were compared among countries in Phase I and Phase II of the project by means of price comparisons and were treated as commodity categories. The other part of government expenditure on employee's compensation was segmented into four categories of government employment based on level of skills and their education (a) unskilled blue-collar (b) skilled-blue collar (c) white collar and (d) professional. For each of these categories, *PPP* were computed relative to U.S.A. based on compensation per employee for each category of occupations.

In the final phase of the project, i.e. Phase III, several new experiments were made to make international comparisons more plausible and meaningful. These experiments, though enriching, could not be used because of non-availability of data or feasibility of the estimates [Kravis et al (1982) pp. 135–162]. Therefore, it was observed that there is not much scope for improvement in methodology of international quantity comparisons. Despite this fact, Phase III estimates did incorporate some new changes like adjustment for complementary capital stock used in health care. The ICP Phase III observed a linkage between amount of medical care capital and level of real income of the countries. Therefore, direct quantity indicators were divided by 1.30 for low-income countries, and 1.15 for middle-income countries. Similar adjustments for complementary capital stock were not made for educational services.

One of the important finding of the ICP project was that services are much cheaper in developing economies than in rich countries. Kravis et al (1982) provides explanation for this phenomenon. According to them this happens because the prices of traded goods (mainly commodities) are the same in different countries. This means that wages in industries producing traded goods will vary in accordance with productivity differences in different countries. They also believe that the wage level achieved in the traded goods sector will determine the wage rates in industries producing non-traded goods, essentially services. Therefore, low wages prevailing in the traded goods producing industries in poor countries with comparable low productivity will determine wages in industries producing non-traded services. The consequence will be the prevalence of low prices in services in low-income economies. This finding has been elaborated Bhagwati (1984). He explains the prevalence of low prices of services in developing countries without resorting to a particular specification of comparative-productivity ranking between countries in their traded (goods producing) and *non-traded* (services producing) sector, while also explaining the labour productivity rankings [Bhagwati (1984) p. 282]. He explain this with help of an alternative general equilibrium explanation which focuses on differences amongst countries in terms of comparative endowment, instead of differences in terms of productivity used by Kravis et al (1982)].

The analysis given above clearly shows that national accounting frameworks have been evolving over time and, in the process of their evolution, they have developed a new perception towards recording the contribution of services in national income. It also shows how innovations have been made to include the contribution of services. The analysis also demonstrated the kind of problems that arise when attempts are made to study inter-temporal and spatial variations in the contribution of services.

CHAPTER 7

GLOBAL TRADE IN SERVICES—THEORETICAL ISSUES

For a considerable period in the history of economic analysis, it was believed that services cannot be traded over time and space. This belief emanated from the understanding of economists regarding characteristics of services. They believed that services are intangible and need *simultaneity* in the producer and the consumer of the service and *instantaneity* in their production and consumption. They also believed that service products cannot be alienated or separated from their producers. These characteristics of services led to the mistaken belief that they cannot be traded globally. The acceptance of intangibility axiom suggests that services also cannot be stored. The belief in the simultaneity axiom makes it obvious that the location of producer and consumer of the service should be the same for its delivery: this means that the service provider and user of service cannot be separated in space. Therefore, trade in services over space is impossible. The instantaneity axiom suggests that production and consumption of service occurs instantaneously i.e. at the same time, therefore, the two activities cannot be separated in time i.e. they cannot be stored. The axiom of non-separability between service product and service producer also makes us believe that service products cannot be traded, because they cannot be alienated from their producer. Acceptance of these characteristics of services made the term 'trade in services' an oxymoron—a term that contains an internal contradiction [Feketekuty (1988) pp. 2 and 68].

Despite the understanding of economists regarding trade in services, it continues to occur; in fact it is as old as trade in goods. Economists did not realize that migration and immigration result in trade in services that are embodied in persons, like skills and education. Similarly, so may services are being traded through trade in goods because some of them are embodied in goods. Rapid developments in the technology of information and communication have significantly altered the context in which some services are traded globally in the contemporary world. Services like entertainment, information and knowledge can be stored in magnetic tapes and are traded globally.

Economists remained oblivious to this fact for quite a considerable period, therefore, attention of the world's trade policy makers has remained focused on trade in goods. Trade in services is a complex phenomenon which consists of heterogenous service products which are subject to complex regulations whose nature is also changing over time. Hence, in the present chapter, an attempt has been made to understand the complexity of trade in services; for this purpose, we will first try to understand its increasing importance. An attempt has also been made to analyse the differences between trade in goods and trade in services, and how far the theories evolved by economists to understand the trade in goods can provide appropriate knowledge about the trade in services. Hence, we will be indirectly exploring whether there is a need for separate theories for trade in services. We will also make an attempt to study the nature of barriers to trade in services and their differences, or similarities, with barriers to trade in goods. Here we will also try to learn the methods that are being used to measure the extent of barriers to trade in services.

The chapter has been organized in two different sections, where each section deals with a specific aspect of trade in services. Therefore, in Section I we will deal with broad differences that exist between the trade in goods and services, and how far these differences have been accomodated in international trade theories evolved by economists to analyse trade in goods. In section II, we will study different kinds of trade barriers that exist in the trade in services and will also try to understand different methods that are being used to know the magnitude of trade barriers.

I. Characteristics of Trade in Services

There exists a long debate regarding the differentiation between goods and services. This debate has been described in detail in an earlier chapter dealing with the conceptualization of services. Despite several technological improvements that have been experienced in the means of information and communication, trade in services is still guided by two distinct characteristics that are inherent in them and continue to influence their trade. The first characteristic is based on the initial understanding of services that they are intangible and a precondition for their trade is simultaneity in the producer and consumer and instantaneity in their production and consumption. This characteristic is still very important because even now there exist some services which have retained this characteristic, viz. haircut, live music concert, health care etc. The second characteristic of services is that some of them are embodied in goods. These services can be traded with same facility as trade in goods [Sampson and Snape (1980) and Melvin (1987)]. However Bhagwati (1984) has further classified services that possess the first characteristic, i.e. they need simultaneity and instantaneity in their delivery, into three sub-categories. These sub-categories depend on who makes the attempt, consumer or producer, to achieve proximity to the other. Based on this criterion he divides these categories into (a) mobile supplier of services and immobile user of service. This occurs through the mobility of service provider to the country of service users. Several services belong to this category, viz. migration of teachers, doctors, consultants to serve their customers in the host country (b) mobile user of service and immobile service provider. In this case consumers travel abroad to consume services. This category includes travels by students, patients, tourists to foreign countries to consume services, and (c) mobile service provider and mobile consumers. Services that belong to this category are cultural events, sports competitions etc. However, due to complexity in the international transaction in services, trade in services consists of international transactions in services between the residents of one country and the residents of another country, irrespective of location where the transaction is taking place.

A close examination of these characteristics of trade in services suggests that whereas in the case of goods, factor mobility occurs through trade because goods embody the factors that are used while manufacturing them (i.e. factor intensities). Therefore, trade in goods is proxy for mobility of factors. However, in the case of services, factor mobility is intrinsically related to the trade in services. Due to this reason, most of the research on trade in services interprets it as trade in service factors. These services factors, when traded, combine with local factors to produce a non-tradable service [Deardorft (1985), Melvin (1989), Burgess (1990) and Jones and Ruane (1990)]. Services trade amounts to trade in factor services because some of the services are embodied in persons. It is due to this reason that mobility of natural persons is essential for the delivery of services, across borders. Therefore, it should be noted that some services encourage trade in goods, some others discourage trade in goods, while certain other do not affect trade in goods. This depends on whether services are substitutes, complementary or independent of trade in goods. Complexity in the trade in services also arises because services can be embodied in products as well as in persons. Therefore, free trade in services necessitates not only free trade in goods but also free mobility of persons across borders of different countries.

Because of the existence of these complexities in the trade in services, it takes place through diverse kinds of transactions. These transactions have been classified into four broad categories. This typology, which distinguishes the nature of trade among different services, helps in the identification of different kinds of barriers that hinder the trade in services and help in evaluating the role of technology in their trade [Sampson and Snape (1985)]. These four categories are (a) movement of consumers to another country to consume services (e.g. tourism, to receive education and health care) (b) movement of service providers to another country to supply services (e.g. software experts, consultants, doctors, teachers etc) (c) commercial presence of service provider by starting an establishment (like banking, insurance, retail stores, management consultancy firms etc) and (d) cross-border trade, exactly like merchandize trade which occurs in the services which are embodied in goods (e.g. floppy disc containing entertainment, data base, software or business report, telephonic talks, computer to computer transfer etc).

The categorization of services, based on the nature of international transactions, led to the standardization of these transactions, classified by Sampson and Snape (1985) and Sapir and Winter (1994). This categorization of transactions to facilitate the trade in services has also been adopted by General Agreement on Trade in Services (GATS), on January 1, 1995. These four categories have also been adopted as four modes of global transaction in services and have been given standardized meaning. These four modes are

Mode I : Cross-border trade, which is similar to merchandize trade.

Mode II : Consumption abroad, which necessitates the movement of consumers to the country which supplies services.

Mode III : Commercial presence, movement of capital for establishing service enterprises in the country of consumption.

Mode IV : Movement of natural persons leading to temporary migration of citizens of service providing country to the service consuming country.

The relative importance of each mode of service transaction is determined by the regulatory environment prevalent among the trading countries regarding trade in goods and services, movement of persons and technological capabilities of these countries. These factors determine the options available to service providing and service using countries; they also result in the requirement of market access or right to establishment and acceptability of academic standards across countries. This also depends on the ease with which visa regimes are working in different countries to facilitate global travel of natural persons.

Apart from the typology of services used in their classification into different modes of international transaction in services, there also exist a variety of classifications evolved by different economists. These classifications have been discussed in greater detail in the chapter on categorization of services. However, the classification of service products, developed by the United Nations, known as Central Product Classification (CPC), which helps in identification of service products (includes 600 service products at present) is also being used by GATS for the purposes of trade in services. The same classification is also used to measure balance of payment, in different service segments, evolved by IMF's Balance of Payment Manual [IMF (1993)].

As has already been mentioned that despite the fact that trade in services has been occuring since a considerable period of time, economists remained preoccupied with the conceptualization and theorizing of trade in goods. Most theories of international trade that occupy valuable space in most books on International Economics deal with trade in goods. Economists did not pay attention to evolve theories of international trade specifically to explain trade in services, perhaps due to certain obvious reasons (a) they believed that trade in goods and services are not significantly different from each other, therefore, trade in services does not require a separate theoretical construct to analyse it and (b) their misunderstanding that services cannot be traded, therefore, there is no need for evolving separate theories of trade in services.

It is well known that the theories of international trade are based on a well defined conceptual and analytical framework, and that this framework does not impose any limitation on using it for the understanding of trade in services, one can conclude *a priori* that there is no need for evolving separate theories for trade in services. Moreover, it is also quite obvious that the theories of international trade do not specify the characteristics of goods for which they have evolved their analysis. It seems that the use of the word 'good' is a matter of tradition, not deliberately designed to exclude services. "Had Ricardo, in his classic example, specified wine and insurance policies instead of wine and cloth, his demonstration of gains from trade would have still succeeded.... Nothing in the logical structure of his proof *ipso facto* excludes international transactions in services" [Hindley and Smith (1984) p. 374]. However, questions raised by another scholar raise doubts in the mind of policy makers regarding the appropriateness of trade theories to explain the trade in services. These questions are: Where in economic literature on comparative advantage can a discussion on service sector be found? Can even one example using a service product to illustrate comparative advantage be recalled? [Shelp (1981) p. 85].

These questions are based on the premise that goods and services are two distinct categories of products and, therefore, need separate theories to analyse their trade. The distinction between trade in goods and trade in services emerges because some services are subject to regulations, and in the case of some other services the seller needs to acquire requisite licenses or qualifications to enter into trade. Moreover, services can be traded in different modes, which have been described above in detail. This happens in the case of services because some of them better served by permanent presence in the market while in the case of some other services, trade may involve travel by natural person either as a consumer or as a producer. These distinctions suggest that in the case of services, investment flows can substitute for trade as also mobility of persons. These distinctions may pose problems for mainstream international trade theories because, in the case of services, it becomes difficult to identify whether comparative advantage should be understood in terms of trade flows, investment flows or labour flows. Even if we believe that goods and services are two distinct "logical categories" [Hill (1977)], this does not lead us to think that they need different theoretical frameworks for their analysis.

Feketekuty (1988) provides two instances where international trade theories evolved for analysing trade in goods were used to explain trade in services. The first instance, which he mentions, is related to Adam Smith who championed the argument of free trade in goods based on his concept of absolute advantage. He applied the same principle to argue against the Navigation Act which imposed restrictions on the right of foreign ships to bring foreign goods in Britain. Smith argued that "the act of navigation is not favourable to foreign commerce, or to the growth of that opulence which can arise from it. The interest of a nation in its commercial relations to foreign nations is like that of merchant with regard to the different people with whom he deals, to buy as cheaper and sell as dear as possible" [Smith (1776) p. 431 and Feketekuty (1988) p. 93]. The argument given by Smith against the Navigation Act clearly suggests that restricting the right of foreign ships to carry British imports is equivalent to import tax (i.e. tariff) and he rejects it on the same ground as he rejected restricted trade in goods. By adopting such an argument, Smith shows that the same criterion can be used for trade in services.

Another instance, which has been mentioned by Feketekuty (1988), is when the same argument was used by a French economist, Fredric Bastiat, while construction of railroad between Paris and Madrid was being discussed in the French assembly. It was in response to a suggestion made by one of the members of the assembly (Simiot) that the railway line should have a gap at Bordeaux. The member believed that such a gap would increase the income of the porters, commissionaires, hotel keepers and bargemen at Bordeaux, which will help in increasing the wealth in France. To demonstrate the illogicality implicit in this argument, Bestiat used the same principle which Adam Smith used to argue against the Navigation Act. He reasoned "If Bordeaux has a right to profit by a gap ... than Angoulema, Poitier, Tours, Orleans should also demand gaps being of general interest ... In this way we will succeed in having a railroad denominated by Negative Railway" [Heilbroner (1961) pp. 151-152 and Feketekuty (1988) p. 94].

On similar lines, there are some other economists who also believe that there does not exist any difficulty in using theories of international trade to explain trade in services. They argue: "But a bunch of flowers, a ton of coal and jet airline are very different things as well. It may be true no economist has discussed international trade in brussell sprouts, so that somebody does not raise any substantial question as to whether... the theory of comparative advantage is applicable to brussell sprouts" [Feketekuty (1988) p. 369]. Therefore, there is no "*a priori* reason to believe that the theory does not apply" [Hindley and Smith (1984) p. 370]. Some economists have established that with slight modifications, the general applicability of the law of comparative advantage can be accepted in explaining the pattern of trade [Deardorft (1980) and (1985)]. The same preposition is also common to the theory of Heckscher-Ohlin's factor endowments. Some economists have explored the possibility of using mainstream theories of international trade to explain the trade in producer services and to evaluate the relevance of trade theories in explaining the trade in services [Melvin (1989), Francois (1990) and Francois (1990a)]. The increasing role of producer services, as a bond that holds together diverse specialized functions in modern economies, has been analyzed in greater details by several economists [Greenfield (1966), Katouzian (1970) and (1989)]. It has been envisaged that these services are likely to grow rapidly with the increasing use of roundabout production methods and integration of fragmented local markets into a national market. There are some studies that have analyzed the role of non-traded producer services on gains from foreign investment, but have ignored the role of international returns to scale in the intermediate services (i.e. producer services) [Markusen (1989)]. Some scholars have expanded the analysis of the relationship between producer services, scale and specialization. To take into account these factors, they have incorporated in their analysis the role of internal market expansion and increases in the size of market of producer services due to emerging opportunities thrown open by international trade. They argue that the post-war expansion in producer services sector might have been as a consequence of expanded opportunities of international trade in producer services. This expansion may have occured due to post-war trade liberalization [Francois (1990) and Francois (1990a)]. Francois (1990a) has developed a model to explain these relationships. The integration of markets through trade liberalization leads to effective integration of markets and it provides appropriate conditions for the expansion of market of producer services. The elimination of trade restriction and barriers, and emergence of free trade, facilitates the process of consolidation among existing firms. This reduces the total number of firms because some firms become larger in size in comparison to their pre-trade size; however, it provides more choices to consumers, because variety of services increases due to the presence of domestic as well as foreign firms [Francois (1990a) p. 727].

Melvin (1989) suggests that when producer services are incorporated into the standard Heckscher-Ohlin framework, contrary to the conclusion arrived at by Hindley and Smith (1984), it does require modifications; this necessitates the reformulation of the law of comparative advantage because, in the context of services, it is difficult to know what is exactly being traded. He illustrates this problem with the help of an example: If there is a productive activity with a production function $Q=f(x_1, x_2)$, where Q stands for output, x_1 and x_2 are inputs one of which is producer service. If production of the product is being organized in Canada and x_1 is supplied by U.S.A., the product here is automobile, x_2 represents Canadian labour and x_1 capital from U.S.A., then x_1 represents foreign direct investment by U.S.A. in Canada, but not trade. If, instead, x_1 represents foreign know-how or management service then x_1 represents trade in services. On the contrary, if Q represents haircut, x_1 represents barbers who commute between U.S.A. and Canada and x_2 represents rented barber shops. We can interpret Q as U.S. exports of haircut, despite the fact that production of this service is located in Canada. If we take another example where x_1 stands for Japanese cars; x_2 for Canadian car dealership and Q stands for number of Japanese cars sold in Canada. Here, Q will stand for imports of car from Japan, though a part of value has been added by the services rendered by the Canadian car dealer.

The examples given above illustrate the fact that even though the structure of production is the same in the production of Q, it leads to different consequences depending on what is being imported. To avoid the complexity of these situations, if we just pay attention to international payments and accept x_1 as an import, when international payments are made for x_1, ignoring whether it stands for capital, a service or as an intermediate commodity. Following this logic leads us to believe that x_1 is always an import and Q stands for domestic production. Hence, in the haircut example, the import is barber's services not haircut. This distinction is quite crucial to avoid logical inconsistencies.

To extend the Heckscher-Ohlin framework, to analyse trade in services, he begins his study with a situation where trade is a pure commodity trade or a pure factor trade. He establishes that, as predicted by Heckscher-Ohlin model and the analysis of Mundell (1957), factor flows are perfect substitutes of commodity flows i.e. same final equilibrium can be reached if service factors are traded in the right amount. His model of trade in services is the same except that in the case of services trade occurs neither alone in the form of commodity flows or pure factor flows, but in the form where both the flows occur in tendem. Therefore, he extends the model of trade in services in two different contextual situations (a) where one of the products is non-tradable, and (b) where both the commodities are tradable. With the help of these two extensions of the model, he shows that principle of comparative advantage and Hecksher-Ohlin theorem need different interpretation than the standard explanations given in textbooks. He shows that the export of factor services in exchange for a good when both goods continue to be produced in both countries, will result in the same kind of equilibrium given by either commodity flows or factor flows. However, trade pattern will differ, especially in a situation where mobile services are used intensively in the production of mobile commodities. In this situation the economy which is better endowed with capital will import capital intensive commodities. He also describes, with the help of his model, that one of the implications of the service trade model is that the service exporting country will have merchandize trade deficit which he thinks reflects that the country has advantage in service sector exports. However, according to Hindley (1990), the global integration of markets of services is quite different from global integration of markets of goods. Due to the differences in the nature of integration of markets in goods and services, price equalization, as a consequence of trade, as predicted by Heckscher-Ohlin theory, may not occur in services. This happens because services remain embedded in local economic and regulatory environment, and also because trade in services involves the use of local as well as imported factors.

Unlike the work of Melvin (1989), which has analysed the relevance of international trade theories in the context of producer services, Jones and Ruane (1990) have explored the relevance of trade theory in the context of a range of services which provide possibility of separation between the locations of their production and consumption in space as well as in time which facilitates the emergence of trade in these services. In the case of these services, more than one option exists in selecting the mode in which they can be traded among different countries. These services can be traded as *service factors*, where imported service factors combine with local factors to produce non-tradable services, or they can also be traded in the form of *service products* itself, needing no further production in foreign countries. Such services are management consultancy, accounting services, data processing, telecommunication services, financial and insurance services.

Since there exist alternative ways of trading in them, either as factor services or as a service product, it provides options to the service exporting nation in terms of either to expose its service sector to global market forces by trading in service factors by giving, in the process, to foreign companies, the right to establish service enterprises, while seeking reciprocal agreement for its own companies. The other alternative is to trade in service products by negotiating a right to do business or market access. These two options have important consequences for an economy while trading in services [Aronson and Cowley (1984) and Neu (1988)]. For a considerable period, due to regulations, trade was highly restricted in these services. However, process of liberalization and globalization and improvements in the technology of information and communication have now made it possible to trade in these services at longer distances. For example, in the banking sector, new technological improvements have facilitated the possibility of trading in several banking products for longer distances from the location of supplier. In such cases, the trade in banking services will be significantly influenced by domestic regulations; in the absence of such possibilities it will depend largely on the banks right to establish branches and subsidiaries in host countries. Under such circumstances foreign banks generally operate under restrictions imposed by the regulatory environment prevalent in the host country to protect the interest of local banks [Caves (1983), Neu (1988)]. In the context of these alternative ways of trading banking services, Jones and Ruane (1990) explain the consequences of each option of trading exercised by an economy on its own trade in services and on the host country.

For instance, say there is an economy which has high prices of banking services and gives high rate of return to banking factors, and is selecting an option to open its banking sector for international trade with banking products or banking factors. In this regard, the pertinent question being asked is whether this economy should allow foreign banks to establish businesses and operate under the same regulations as domestic banks in the same range of service activities, or whether, it should allow the foreign banks the right to do business in banking products from abroad more cheaply. They suggest that if this economy takes the first option (i.e. allows the foreign banks to establish businesses), initially it would increase the supply of domestic production of banking services because establishment of businesses by foreign banks will require combining of local factors to produce more locally traded non-tradable services. However, afterwards, domestic production will fall because domestic customers will shift their demand to cheaper service products supplied by foreign banks. Similar will be the consequences for insurance companies, stockbroking, data processing and telecommunication services. To evaluate the implication of each of these options Jones and Ruane (1990) have developed a simple model.

Their model is based on the assumption that service factors as well as service products are completely protected by the economy from global competition. All production processes of goods as well as services make use of a factor which is used only in that process and another input (labour) which is used by all the sectors. Labour is assumed to be the globally immobile factor, whereas the other factor is fully mobile. There exists free trade in all the products, other than service products. The economy is assumed to be a price taker in the international factor and product market. The model is Ricardian two sector model where economy produces only one non-service product, which is manufacturing (M). The production in manufacturing earns highest available return on labour, where the rental of specific factor is deducted from the total revenue and the rentals of factors are determined by world markets. Under these assumptions, the income of the economy depends on earnings of the specific factor sent abroad. Trade occurs only in the specific factor used in goods manufacturing and manufactured products are exported to get in exchange variety of consumer goods which are not produced locally. Economy is producing service products which are consumed locally, therefore, the prices of factors used in production of services and service products are determined by domestic supply and demand conditions. Since labour is immobile across the national boundary, the domestic wage rate is determined by the extent of openness prevalent in the non-service specific factor and products. However, the authors state that this wage rate is not exactly the rate observed in the rest of the world. The difference exists because of the differences in the level of technology being used in the domestic economy in comparison to the technology being used in other economies. Under these assumptions, competitive forces will determine the wage rate (W) as given below

$$W = \frac{P_M^* - aKM^{r^*} M}{aLM} \qquad \text{(i)}$$

Here P_M^* and r_M^* are world product price and return on the specific factor in the manufacturing sector (i.e. non-service sector) in which the economy has greater comparative advantage, and aKM and aLM are capital and labour input-output coefficients in the manufacturing sector. Once wage rate is determined in this way, the competitive profit equation of change in service sector takes the following form

$$\text{Ø}ks\ \hat{r}s = \hat{p}s \tag{ii}$$

Here a circumflex over a variable refers to a relative change (i.e. $\hat{X} = \Delta x/x$), Ø*ks* is distributive share of specific factor in the services sector, *rs* is local return on service factor and *ps* is the domestic price of the service product [Jones and Ruane (1990) p. 666]. The equation (ii) indicates that any increase in the price of service product (*ps*) will lead to more than proportionate change in the return on service factor.

Given these relationships, technological comparative advantage of services sector and the influence of domestic factor endowments on supply and demand curves are shown in Figure 7.1. The figure consists of two panels, where *left-hand panel* shows presumed technological advantage of service sector of the home country; and the *right-hand panel* shows impact of factor endowments on demand and supply of service products.

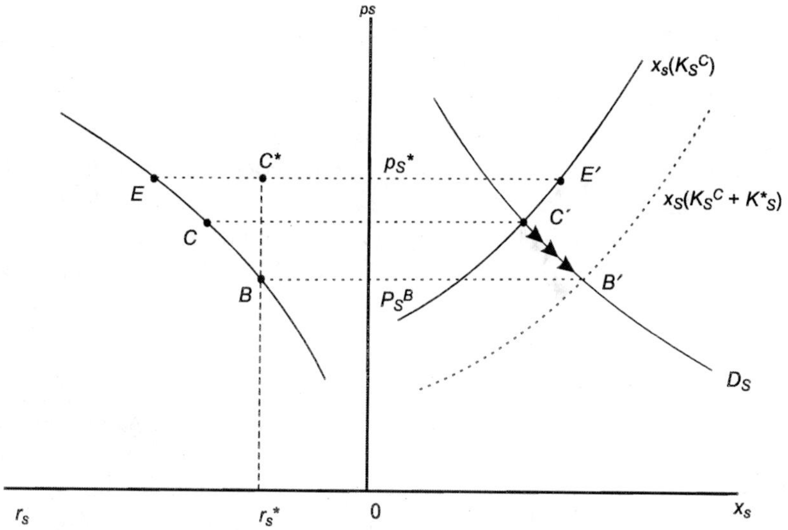

Fig. 7.1 Jones and Ruane Model of Trade in Services.

(*Source*: Jones and Ruane (1990) p. 676)

The relationship between returns to services factor (r_s) and the price of home service product (p_s), which has been described in equation (ii), is depicted by the locus in the left-hand panel of Figure 7.1. As has been mentioned above, the world values of r_s and p_s differ from the domestic values due to difference in level of technology and factor endowment between domestic economy and the rest of the world, therefore, these values do not lie on this locus. Authors have taken C^* in Figure 7.1 to denote the given value of r^*_s and p^*_s. Comparing $r^*_s\, p^*_s$ with r_s and p_s shows the presumed technological advantage of the service sector of $r^*_s p^*_s$ on the economy. This can be obtained by knowing how the home and world returns to the service factor would compare if the service product is traded at the world price of service product (P^*_s). Here the distance EC^* shows the higher return to service factor in the domestic economy. However, it should be noted that the pattern of trade will be determined by not only differences in the level of technology but also by the relative factor endowments which help in determining pre-trade values of r_s and p_s in the left hand panel.

The home factor endowment, which has influence on demand and supply curves of service products, is shown in the right-hand panel of Figure 7.1. In the present context, the demand and supply curves are intersecting at point C. This point determines the initial values of r_s and p_s on the r_s–p_s locus in the left hand panel. The Figure 7.1 shows presumed technological advantage of the domestic economy in terms of low cost of service products ($p_s\,(C) < p^*_s$) and in terms of relatively higher returns to the service factor ($r_s\,(c) > r^*_s$). These facts establish that the domestic economy could gain from trade by either trading in service factor or service product.

After evolving these initial conditions for the domestic economy with regard to services in the absence of trade, Jones and Ruane (1990) explain what happens to this economy when it begins exporting service products, or service factors, to know be the consequences for the domestic economy when it exposes its service factor or its service product to global trade. If the economy selects the option regarding trade in service products, when home prices of service products are lower than the prices prevailing abroad, at C or C¢, the price advantage will motivate domestic producers to enter in the production of the service product. This will increase the output of service product along the supply curve. Given the prevailing world price of service product p_s*, output of the domestic service product will expand upto the point E'. With the expansion of output of service product, the gains to the domestic economy from the export of service product will be equal to the integral overall increments in output from C' to E', of the gap between foreign price p^*_s (given at C^*) and ever increasing costs, $p_s\,(x_s)$ along the supply curve.

On the contrary, the domestic economy can follow the second option and allow the entry of foreign service factors into the home economy with service product remaining non-traded. This will facilitate the inflow of foreign specific factor K_s* which will be used in combination with local labour at wage rate determined by trading activity in manufacturing. This will shift the supply curve in Figure 7.1 rightwards until local price of service product becomes equal to price (P_s*). At this lower price, the total return to the service factor is equated to r_s*. During this entire process, each increment in foreign service factor inflow dk_s* increases the welfare in the domestic economy. The magnitude of the welfare gain is proportional to the gap between $r_s(p_s)$ and r_s*. Thus this model shows that whichever option is exercised by the economy to expose its service sector to global market forces, each option will result in expansion of service output in the domestic economy. The authors have extended this model to different initial conditions of the economy to know under what conditions which one of the option will be better for the economy. These conditions are (a) extreme factor endowments, and (b) complete free trade.

The authors conclude, from various extensions of their basic model, that in the context of simple competitive model, opening of trade in services through any of the alternative options, i.e. opening-up trade in only factor services or service products, will improve economic welfare in the domestic economy. This improvement in welfare will occur irrespective of relative factor endowment or technological comparative advantage. They also suggest that the extent of gains in welfare will depend on which trading option has been exercised by the economy, when technological levels differ between home economy and rest of the world. Under the conditions when domestic economy gradually opens up its service sector for trade, i.e. opening the service trade with one of the options followed by the second option and finally adopting completely free trade in services, if technological levels differ, differences in the factor endowment will determine the pattern of trade. They observe that the economy which has superior technology employed in the production of services will adopt complete specialization in trading services and the economy which uses inferior technology in the production of services will follow complete specialization in manufacturing sector.

In comparison to the approach of Jones and Ruane (1990), who have studied the trade in services when there exists an option with the economy either to trade in factor service or service product, Rymes (1990) explores the competitiveness and direction of flows of international banking services when banks of different economies operate in different economic and monetary environment. The variations in the monetary environment among different economies is largely determined by the instruments that the central bank of the economy follows with respect to cash reserve requirements. After exploring the neo-classical and Keynesian theories of banking, it becomes apparent that there theoretical frameworks have different implications for the trade in banking services. It is because where one of the approaches treats the central bank of the economy as some sort of unnecessary distortion in competitive banking, the other approach envisages a central role for central bank or monetary authority in the direct provisioning of transactions and portfolio services of competitive banks.

In the context of the new monetary theory of banking, the international competitiveness of banking services will depend on monetary policy reflected in the form of tax restriction imposed on the banks. Therefore, the traditional hypothesis, like the factor endowment argument propounded by Heckscher-Ohlin Theorem, will not be able to predict which country will be the net exporter of banking services and may have limited empirical validity [Steedam and Metacalfe (1985)]. Hence, it seems plausible to state that international production and distribution of banking services will be determined by the regulatory environment in which banking sector operates in an economy. Similar conclusions have also been obtained by other studies [Tucker and Sandberg (1988)].

On the other hand, the Keynesian approach to banking suggests that countries will export banking services when the central bank of the country has performed its 'lender of the last resort' functions successfully which has created confidence in the banks amongst domestic as well as international borrowers and depositors. Therefore, this approach suggests that only those economies which have a well-developed and efficient central bank, acting to stabilize the real value of bank deposits, will be able to export banking services [Rymes (1990) pp. 408-409].

The analysis of Rymes (1990), when extended to other services, suggests that establishments in different economies will work under the local policy regimes and regulatory environment. These variations across different economies are likely to influence costs of production. Moreover, trade in services may involve combining of imported factors with local factors, which may create difficulty in reproducing the services across national boundaries in same price-quality combination. The analysis given above clearly shows that there are possibilities of explaining the trade in services with the help of existing theories of trade. However, there is a need for a theory, specific to explaining trade in services, which is all encompassing and has the capacity to predict the pattern of global trade in services.

II. Barriers to Trade in Services and Methods to Measure Them

Barriers to trade stands for government regulations which impose additional costs or create bottlenecks for the movement of goods and services across countries. The word barrier, in the context of trade policy, can be viewed as unnecessary burden on foreign producer of goods and services which may not necessarily help in achieving non-protectionist, domestic policy objectives. When barriers to trade are analysed in the context of public debates, they are seen as government measures, which are undesirable, unjustified and illegitimate. However, it is generally believed that the movement of services across nations remains invisible, therefore, it is difficult to impose barrier on trade in services at the borders. The fact is that, as mentioned above, trade in services occurs in different modes (four modes mentioned above) as compared to trade in goods. These variety of transactions, which occur while trading services, makes it impossible to comprehend different ways in which barriers can be erected for trade in services. The barriers to trade in services are created at diverse places where diverse kind of transactions take place. This suggests that barriers to international trade in services are quite distinct from barriers on trade in goods.

Each mode of international transaction of services, which has been described above, can be subject to regulations; because it is possible to impose barriers on each of the modes. Barriers to trade in services can be erected by (i) sale of services produced abroad in the domestic economy can be regulated by the government when government regulates sale of such services whether produced by domestic or a foreign enterprise (ii) consumption of foreign produced services in the domestic economy can also be regulated when government regulates the consumption of these services produced by domestic or foreign supplier (iii) when government regulates the purchase of foreign exchange for the purposes of payment to foreigners because it controls all transactions in foreign trade (iv) by regulating the movement of goods that embody services and (v) by regulating movement of persons that embody services [Feketekuty (1988) Ch. 7].

A comprehensive list of barriers to trade in services was prepared by the services committee of the U.S. Chamber of Commerce in cooperation with the office of U.S. Trade Representative. This is now popularly known as USTR Inventory of Barriers to Trade in Services. This document appeared in 1979 and represents the first such attempt to identify barriers to trade in services. This effort was followed by attempts made by a private consultancy firm, Price Water House, to identify such barriers through two separate surveys. The first survey report was published in December 1983, and the second report in February 1985 [Price Water House (1983) and (1985)]. These two surveys were complemented by a detailed exercise conducted by another consultancy firm Peat, Marwick and Mitchell for the European Community Commission in 1986. Thereafter, several attempts have been made after the establishment of WTO to identify and analyse these barriers in the context of GATS [Hoekman, Mattoo and English (2002) and Mattoo and Sauvi (2003)].

The existing information regarding barriers to trade in services suggests that most services are regulated industries by national governments. Therefore, non-tariff barriers are more significant in the case of services and are often designed to exclude foreign competition. Sometimes entry costs are imposed or quota's are fixed on the foreign supplier of services. These measures are complemented by complementary local content restrictions, subsidies, taxes, technical and knowledge standards, licensing and procurement policies. Some of the services are also subject to price regulations, like financial services [Hoekman *et al* (1997)]. Hoekman and Sauva (1994) and Hoekman *et al* (1997) have categorized these trade barriers into five categories which are used in isolation or in different combinations to restrict the trade in different modes in which services are traded (a) quantitative restriction (b) price regulations (c) barriers to the right to establishment to restrict physical presence of foreign supplier in the domestic industry (d) barriers imposed through imposition of standards, certification, licensing and service industry specific restrictions; and (e) barriers created by government's procurement policies: subsidies and taxations.

With the establishment of the WTO and multilateral trade agreement, and General Agreement of Trade in Services (GATS), recurring rounds of trade negotiations have helped in achieving the removal of these barriers to liberalize trade in services. Attempts have also been made to restrict the use of non-tariff barriers also. However, there still exists inertia among different countries to remove institutional barriers to trade in services. Therefore, a great deal needs to be accomplished to achieve greater degree of liberalization of trade in services. There is vast scope for making institutional changes to increase the extent of global competition for trade in services. Traditionally the belief in the non-tradability of services created an impression that there are no gains in liberalising their trade. However, because of the fact that a very large part of service industries play an intermediate role, it is now being realized that liberalization of trade in services creates enormous gains through its linkages with other sectors of the economy. It has been estimated that the potential gains from the liberalization of trade in intermediate services (i.e. producer services) are significantly higher than liberalization of trade in final goods (i.e. consumer goods) [Markusen (1989)], and gains from liberalization of trade in services, in general, are approximately equal to the gains from trade obtained from the liberalization of trade in both agricultural and manufactured goods [Dee and Hanslow (2001) and Hodge (2002)].

Most economies, ignoring the gains from liberalization of trade in services, continue to protect trade in services due to various political and economic reasons and they generally protect uncompetitive service industries [Warren (1997) and (1998)]. Therefore, it is quite difficult to remove such barriers on trade in services. Hence, without complete information regarding impediments on trade in services and their consequences on the rest of the economy, it becomes difficult for policy makers to argue for liberalization of trade in services. To overcome this problem, there is a need to measure the extent of barriers to trade in services and also to know the impact of these barriers on the economy. There exist two broad categories of barriers to trade in services (a) market access and (b) derogations from national treatment [Hoekman (1995) and Snape (1998)]. GATS article on market access has broadened the meaning of market access by conceptualizing it as encompassing all policies that restrict access to the market.

In its broader conceptualizations, market access means nondiscrimination between incumbents in a particular market and also for possible other entrants. Hence, legislated monopoly is considered as a market access limitation [Warren and Finally (2000) p. 59]. Similarly *national treatment* means nondiscrimination between domestic and foreign service suppliers. Hence, policies that create barriers for foreign direct investment are considered as a breach of national treatment [Warren and Findlay (2000) p. 60]. As has been mentioned above, trade in services has distinct characteristics, which necessitates the imposition of several non-tariff barriers (NTBs). The existence of NTBs makes it difficult to identify and quantity the barriers to trade in services. Due to these reasons, there does not exist a comprehensive data base on NTBs regarding services, like the one that has been evolved by the United Nations Conference on Trade and Development (UNCTAD), although it is trying to evolve Measures Affecting Service Trade (MAST).

In the absence of suitable data on non-tariff barriers on trade in services, it was difficult to measure the extent of impediment on trade in services. This problem of availability of data has been solved, to a large extent, by GATS rules which make it mandatory on the part of member countries to specify their individual GATS schedule regarding the sector for which they are prepared to make commitments and specify barriers they want to retain. This data has facilitated the quantification of GATS schedules and helped in the evolution of methods that are being used to measure barriers to trade in services. These measures are (a) frequency measures (b) quantity-based measures (c) price based measures (d) partial impact measures (e) computable general equilibrium based modeling.

II(a) Frequency Measures

Frequency measures of services have been developed by PECC (1995) and Hoekman [(1995) and (1996)]. Their method is based on qualitative information available in the country schedules of the General Agreement on Trade in Services, which refers to all the four modes of trade in services described above in Section I. Frequency ratios are arrived at on the basis of the number of commitments scheduled in the GATS by the member countries. Each country specifies sector or sub-sectors as unrestricted or partially restricted. There are a total of 155 sectors, including sub-sectors; four modes of trade in services and two categories of commitments. Therefore, it yields a total of 1240 commitments on market access and national treatment [Hoekman (1996)]. If a member country gives a firm commitment without any condition a weight of 1 is allocated; weight 1 is also allocated to a member country if it declares that a particular mode of supply is unbound due to lack of certain technical feasibilities, provided other modes of trade in services are without any barriers. In case a member country agrees to a commitment but maintains certain specific restrictions than weight of 0.5 is allocated. When a member country makes explicit recording of entry 'unbound' or does not make any commitment, a weight of *O* is allocated.

The study of Hoekman (1996) uses a judgemental set of benchmark tariff equivalents for individual sectors to reflect the degree to which market access to the sectors is restricted. These benchmark tariff equivalents vary between 200 per cent (for highly restricted sectors like maritime trade, air transport and postal services) to 20–50 per cent (which have lesser trade barriers). Based on frequency ratios and benchmark tariff rates, he arrives at a value for each country. These values are called openness scores. Using these scores Hoekman arrives at Hoekman coverage indices of openness to trade which are proxy for the prevailing policy regime regarding trade in services. The Hoekman's openness indices can be converted into a measure of barriers to trade in service by a simple procedure (i.e. 1-Hoekman's indices). These measures have been given in Table 7.1 and 7.2. Some scholars prefer to use the inverted form of this approach and have examined the number of commitments not made by the member country (i.e. the extent of barriers maintained) which seems to be more appropriate because, the intention is to measure the magnitude of barriers rather than openness [Warrens and Findley (2000) p. 63].

Table 7.1 Sectoral Coverage of Specific Commitment in Services (%)

	High income countries	*Low and middle income countries*	*Large developing countries*
Market access			
Unweighted average count (sectors/modes as a share of maximum possible)	47.3	16.2	38.6
Average coverage (sectors/modes listed as a share of maximum possible, weighted by openness/ binding factors)	35.9	10.3	22.9
Coverage/count (average coverage as a share of the average count)	75.9	63.6	59.3
'No restrictions' as a share of total offer (unweighted count)	57.3	45.5	38.7
'No restrictions' as a share of maximum possible	27.1	7.3	14.9
National treatment			
Unweighted average count (sectors/modes as a share of maximum possible)	47.3	16.2	38.8
Average coverage (sectors/modes listed as a share of maximum possible, weighted by openness/ binding factors)	37.2	11.2	25.5
Coverage/count (average coverage as a share of the average count)	78.6	69.1	66.1
'No restrictions' as a share of total offer (unweighted count)	65.1	58.0	52.3
'No restrictions' as a share of maximum possible	30.8	9.4	20.2
Memo items			
No restrictions on MA and NT as a share of maximum possible	24.8	6.9	14.3

Source: Hoekman (1996). p.42

Table 7.2 Commitments by Services Sector

	No. of GATS sectors	*Av. no. of commitments*		*Commitments/GATS items per sector*	
		High income countries	*Low and middle income countries*	*High income countries*	*Low and middle income countries*
Construction	20	11.2	3.3	56.0	16.5
Motor vehicle repair	4	1.8	0.3	45.0	7.5
Wholesale trade	8	4.6	0.5	57.5	6.3
Retail trade	8	4.4	0.8	55.0	10.0
Hotels, restaurants	4	2.8	2.8	70.0	70.0
Land transport	40	9.4	2.3	23.5	5.8
Water transport	48	4.4	3.0	9.2	6.3
Air transport	20	3.7	1.5	18.5	7.5
Auxiliary transport	20	5.1	1.3	25.5	6.5
Postal services	4	1.3	0.6	32.5	15.0
Basic telecommunications	28	1.5	1.3	5.4	4.6
Value-added telecomms	28	18.7	5.0	66.8	7.8
Financial services	60	31.3	12.4	52.2	20.6
Real-estate services	8	3.5	0.3	43.8	3.8
Rental activities	20	9.5	1.3	47.5	6.5
Computer-related	20	15.5	4.2	77.5	21.0
R&D services	12	4.1	1./0	34.2	0.3
Business services	108	56.5	12.2	47.9	11.3
Refuse disposal	16	8.8	1.0	55.0	6.3
Education	20	4.7	1.3	23.5	6.5
Health & social	24	5.0	1.9	20.8	7.9
Recreation & culture	48	13.3	4.6	27.9	9.6

Source: Hoekman (1996). p. 43

The frequency measures of barriers to trade in services suffer from several limitations, one being that the weights assigned to different types of commitments are not based on their relative impact on the economy. Hoekman's measure provides relative magnitude of restrictions rather than absolute values of ad valorem tariff equivalent. The frequency weighting method has been used by several studies. Hordin and Holmes (1997) have used this method to estimate barriers to FDI in services. The method has also been used to analyse market access in financial services [Mattoo (1999) McGuire (1998) and McGuire and Schuela (2001)], telecommunication services [Marko (1998)] and maritime services [McGuire, Schuela and Smith (2001)]. The problem with these measures is that they generally assign equal weights to different kinds of restrictions and account for only those restrictions that restrict market access. However, these measures help in locating the variety of barriers and provide information on relative degree of protection given to a particular sector; they fail to inform policy makers regarding consequences of maintaining or eliminating trade barriers on services. Therefore, there is need for evolving measures which can help in evaluating the costs and benefits from reduction or increases in the barriers. Attempts have been made to evolve measures which are capable of estimating the impact of barriers to trade in services on prices and consumption. These attempts have led to the development of price and quantity based measures of barriers to trade in services.

II(b) Price Based Measures of Barriers to Trade in Service

The price based measures of barriers to trade in services measure these barriers from the price differentials that exist between domestic and world prices of different services [Deardorff's and Stern (1985)]. However, it is very difficult to use this method in the case of services because there is absence of world price data for many services since world prices are indeterminate. In the absence of world prices, scholars have to evolve benchmarks against which to compare actual prices. Studies have taken inspiration from the theoretical and empirical approach to measure market power of a firm i.e. the measurement of monopoly power, like the Learner index [Learner (1934)]. The basic motivation underlying this approach is to compare actual market outcome with a situation where competitive market conditions prevail. The theory underlying this approach is that in the absence of trade barriers (i.e. free entry), the competitive price will converge at the firm's long-run marginal costs. Therefore, in the presence of trade barriers, there will be a gap between price and marginal cost. Barriers to entry will also affect marginal costs because protected firms generally do not operate at the minimum point of marginal cost curve. Due to combined effect of all these possibilities; margin effect, the cost difference effect and cost reduction effect; price may exceed in the presence of barriers in comparison to a situation in which barriers are absent.

To evaluate how trade barriers influence prices, scholars compute price-cost margins. For instance, in the case of banking services, scholars have computed net interest rate margins, using two stage econometric technique to isolate the specific impact of trade restrictiveness index developed by Mc Guire and Schuele on interest margins. Their study revealed that these margins were smaller (between 9.30 to 4.75) in the case of developed economies, which have less trade restrictions; and higher values (60.61 per cent, highest for Malaysia; and 31.45 lowest for Singapore) for developing economies [Kalirajan et al (1999)]. Francois and Hoekman (1999) have suggested another method for computing price-cost margins, based on gross operating margins i.e. TR-TC/AC where TR stands for total revenue, TC for total costs and AC for average costs. Gross operating margins provide useful information about the effect of government policies regarding entry of firms and extent of competition prevailing in the market. It has also been suggested that one can use the difference between average margins of a benchmark country with relatively free trade, and margins of other countries which are being studied [Hoekman (2000)]. The data on operating margins gives useful information on relative profitability of services of different countries and therefore can be used as a measure of barrier to entry [Hoekman (2000) p. 37]. However, it is believed that in the case of those industries where international data are available regarding world's best practice cost functions, with the help of their own frontier cost functions it is possible to compute costs that the world's most efficient firm would incur. A comparison of this cost with actual prices will provide a better measure of rent (i.e. margin) being created by barriers [Warren and Findley (2000) p. 74]. Price based measures have been used in several studies [Kalira *et al* (2000), Kalirajan et al (2001), Kang (2001) and Nguyen-Hong (2000)]. In these studies, scholars have used price as a dependent variable and they identify several factors that determine variations in price. Among these independent variables, one of the variable is invariably a measure of trade restrictiveness index.

II(c) Quantity Based Measures of Barriers to Trade in Services

In market economies, prices of the product and their levels of output are determined simultaneously through the interaction of forces of demand and supply. It is anticipated that the demand for various services is likely to be higher under competitive conditions. At competitive equilibrium, the relative prices of services will be lower and quality better due to the pressure of competition. Low prices and better quality will increase the demand for the services. The expansion in the market due to pressure of demand and rivalary amongst firms in investment will also increase supply. Therefore, some scholars have evolved an alternative approach to estimate barriers to trade in services which uses quantities rather than prices as a basis to estimate the barriers. Such a measure uses empirical methods by using the econometric models based on concepts and techniques used in the standard models of trade determination. Here the approach is to estimate volumes of trade in a situation when there are no barriers and then comparing them with actual trade volumes.

Different scholars have used different approaches of trade determination. Some have used the Heckscher-Ohlin model based on the principle of comparative advantage determined by factor endowments; some others have used Helman-Krugman model which incorporates the impact of product differentiation. There are also some who have used the gravity model, initially developed by regional economists. These gravity models account for relative size of the economy, distance separating trading countries and socio-cultural distances in terms of language and culture etc. These models are used to estimate anticipated level of output which is compared with actual level of output. Size of non-tariff trade barriers is obtained from the residual which emerges from the actual and estimated levels of output through econometric models [Warren (2001) and Deardorff and Stern (1998)].

Initially this methodology was used to understand the consequences of barriers to entry by examining the volume of mobile telecommunication services consumed within an economy in comparison to international standards (benchmark). Through this process they wanted to estimate the impact of entry barriers on consumption of telecommunication services with the help of number of mobile operators in each country [Ralph and Ludwig (1997) and Ergas, Ralph and Small (1998)]. These studies observed that the presence of more than two players in the market increased the market penetration of mobile services quite substantially [Ralph and Ludwig (1997)]. In other studies, scholars have extended this analysis by including fixed network services to also estimate the extent of competition in the market: instead of just counting the number of players in the market, they have attempted to account for the policy regime also. for this they used the International Telecommunication Union's (ITU) computed indices. On the set of data evolved, two different simulation exercises were conducted. These helped in knowing the impact of full liberalization on network penetration. By comparing these predicted values of network penetration with actual network penetration, one can estimate the magnitude of trade barriers. If these values are combined with estimates regarding elasticity of demand, one can also estimate tariff-equivalent trade barriers [Warren (1999) and (2001)].

Francois (1999) used the gravity model for estimating non-tariff barriers that existed between U.S.A. and its other trading partners, using Hong Kong and Singapore as a benchmark for barrier-free trade. He uses the difference between estimated and actual imports as indication of non-tariff barriers. The scholars have accepted the usefulness of gravity model based measures in computing relative levels of protection across sectors and countries. However, attributing all the differences between estimated and actual values of imports to non-tariff barriers is not acceptable to some of the scholars [Hartel (2000), Stern (2000) p. 252]. Despite its weaknesses, the gravity model based estimates have been attempted by various scholars [Bergstrand (1985), Harris and Matyas (1998) and Rehman (2003)]. Price and quantity based estimates leave the nature of anticipated decline in prices and increases in the quantity of output as unexplained. As it has been mentioned above, the shift from restricted trade to liberalized trade (i.e. from the conditions of entry barriers to competitive equilibrium) leads to several kinds of changes emerging from different influences, like reduction in market power, improved efficiency and decline in the prices of inputs. Therefore, it becomes difficult to assess whether liberalization increases consumer's surplus or producer's surplus or both gain in the process. Therefore, to incorporate improvements in the analysis that can answer these questions, economists have evolved complex modeling techniques—the Partial Equilibrium Models and General Equilibrium Models.

II(d) Partial Equilibrium Models

As has been mentioned above, a shift from restricted to liberalized trade regime influences prices and quantities due to the combined effect of three different effects (a) *competition effect* which reduces the market concentration due to entry of more firms in the market. This, in turn, reduces price-cost margins (b) *cost-reduction effect* which operates through two different processes. Initially, the leading firm starts operating at the point closer to the minimum point of long-run marginal costs. Thereafter, entry of new firms, which provide more choices, also forces firms to further reduce costs (c) *cost-difference effect* which arises due to input price differentials among firms located at different places. These input price differentials provide comparative advantage to firms in the supplying of services. The impact of these three effects can be isolated with the help of modeling [Elek *et al* (1999)].

Partial equilibrium models have been used in air transport markets to analyse the effect of liberalization. In the case of air transport, market imperfections are created by series of bilateral agreements; therefore liberalization can be achieved either by encouraging entry of more domestic players (without altering the conditions of market access and right to establishment to foreign suppliers), or by providing permission for the right to establishment as well as market access to foreign airlines also [Warren, Tamms and Findley (1999)]. Therefore, in the case of air transportation, to identity the three effects that have been mentioned above, scholars use estimates of cost functions. They also estimate the frontier function to assess which of the airlines lie off the frontier [Tamms (1999)]. These models also focus on supply and demand in the air transport market and include different forms of market imperfections to measure the price-cost margins (i.e. extent of markup over costs). They also try to estimate the improvements in consumer's welfare due to liberalization and its impact on gains to the service suppliers [Trewin (1999) Johnson *et al* (2001)].

These improvements made by the partial equilibrium models suggests that they are able to overcome some of the shortcomings that exist in the price and quantity based measures i.e. they help in computing the impact of liberalization of trade in services on consumer and producer surplus. However, these being partial models which focus on a particular sector, they are not able to analyse the inter-sectoral effects of liberalization. To overcome this weakness of economic analysis based on partial equilibrium models, economists use general equilibrium models which can simultaneously analyse the inter-sector effect also.

II(e) General Equilibrium Models

In the presence of inter-sectoral linkages, and especially when services enter as intermediate input in almost all the economic activities, it becomes obvious that the impact of liberalization of trade in services can be more appropriately analysed with the help of general equilibrium models. One such model is Modified Global Trade Analysis Project (GTAP) which helps in estimating the costs to the economy of maintaining a policy regime which restricts the entry of domestic and foreign suppliers of services in the market [Hertel (1997)]. Moreover, as it is known that intermediate inputs of services enter the different sectors of the economy, therefore, a service sector which is inefficient can increase costs for other sectors of the economy and encourage firms to provide these services inhouse. Therefore, an economy which liberalizes all other sectors of the economy without liberalizing trade in services may experience inefficient allocation of resources in the other sectors also [Hoekman and Braga (1997).

However, estimation of general equilibrium models has been difficult due to paucity of data. Some scholars have made attempts to use tariff equivalent measures of frequency methods to simulate the effect of liberalization on the economy. With the help of one of the general equilibrium models, authors have been able to estimate that the impact of cuts in industrial tariffs on gains in welfare work have been three times larger if services trade has also been given 25 per cent cuts in barriers [Brown *et al* (1996)].

In the general equilibrium models, the consequences of barriers to trade in services are computed by comparing the actual values with the values generated by simulated free trade equilibrium. Most of the studies have used computable general equilibrium (CGE) models. Amongst the models which have been invariably used by the scholars are various modified versions of Global Trade Analysis Project (GTAP) model and the Michigan Model of World Production and Trade. The variants of GTAP models have been used in the studies of Hartal et al (1999), Dee and Hanslow (2000) and Verikies and Zhang (2000). The study conducted by Australian Department of Foreign Affairs and Trade (1999) also uses a variant of GTAP model. Michigen CGE model has been used by Dee, Hardin and Holmes (1999), Chadha (2000), Chadha *et al* (2000), Brown and Stem (2000) and Brown *et al* (1996).

The analysis given above suggests that the measurement of barriers to trade in services began with frequency based measures where scholars assign exogenously determined weights to different types of barriers. The improvements in the empirical estimates have now made it possible to compute these weights endogenously. The single regression equation based methods to compute price and quantity impacts hide impacts of several effects which collectively determine market outcomes. These hidden effects can be explicitly estimated with the help of partial and general equilibrium models.

References

Abler R. (1977), The Telephone and Evolution of American Metropolitan System, in I de Sola Pool (ed), *Social Impact of Telephone*, M.I.T. Press Cambridge, pp. 318-341.

Abler, R., J.S. Adams, and P. Gould (1977), *Spatial Organization—the Geographers View of the World*, Prentice Hall, Englewood Cliff, N.J.

Abramovitz. M (1956), Resources and Output Trends in United States, *American Economic Review* Vol. 46, pp. 5-23.

Acemoglu, Daron and Fabrizio Zilibotti (1997), Was Prometheus Unbound by Chance? Risk Diversification and Growth, *Journal of Political Economy*, Vol. 105(4), pp. 709-751.

Alexander, N. (1997), Objects in the Rearview Mirror may Appear Closer than They are, *International Review of Retail Distribution and Consumer Research*, Vol. 7, pp. 390-399.

Alexander, Nicholas and Gary Akehurst (1998) (eds), The Emergence of Modern Retailing 1750-1950 in the special issue of *Business History*, Vol. 40(4) pp. 1–16.

Amin Ash (1995) (ed); *Post Fordism - A Reader*, Blackwell, U.K.

Amin Ash and Nigel Thrift (eds) (2004), *The Blackwell Cultural Economy Reader*, Blackwell Publishing (Mass) U.S.A.

Anderson, Odin W. (1990), *Health Services as a Growth Enterprise in the United States Since 1875*, Health Administration Press, Ann Arbor, 2nd ed.

Aoyama, Yuke and Manual Castells (2002), An Empricial Assessment of the Information Society: Employment and Occupational Structure of G-7 Countries 1920-2000, *International Labour Review*, Vol. 141 (1-2), pp. 123-139.

Appelbaum, Eillen and Ronald Schettkat (2001), Are Prices Unimportant? The Changing Structure of Industrialized Economies, in Thijs ten Raa and Ronald Schettkat (eds) *The Growth of Service Industries, the*

Paradox of Exploding Costs and Persistent Demand, Edward Elgar, U.S.A.

Aristotle [(345 B.C. (2004)], *The Nicomachean Ethics*, (translated by J.A.K. Thomson), Penguin Books, London, U.K.

Aronson, D.A. and P.F. Cowley (1984), Trade in Services—a Case for Open Market, American Institute of Public Policy Research, Washington D.C.

Ashton, T.S. (1948), *Industrial Revolution 1760-1800*, Oxford University Press, U.K.

Banga, Rashmi (2005), Trade and Foreign Direct Investment in Services: A Review, ICRIER, Working Paper 154, New Delhi.

Bauer, P.T. and B.S. Yamey (1931), Economic Progress and Occupational Distribution; *Economic Journal* Vol. 61, pp. 741-755.

Baumol, W.J. (1967), Macroeconomics of Unbalanced Growth; Anatomy of Urban Crisis, *American Economic Review*, Vol. 57, pp. 415-426.

Baumol W.J. (1985), Productivity Policy and the Service Sector, in Robert P. Inman (ed) *Managing the Service Economy—Prospects and Problems*, Cambridge University Press, Cambridge, N.Y., pp. 301-318.

Baumol, W.J. (2002), Services as Leaders and Leader of the Services, in Gadrey Jean and Faiz Gallonz (eds). *Productivity, Innovation and Knowledge in Services*, Edward Elgar, Cheltenhom and Northampton U.S.A. pp. 147-163.

Baumol, William J. *et al* (1985), Unbalanced Growth Revisited: Asymptotic Stagnancy and New Evidence, *American Economic Review*, Vol. 75 (4), pp. 806-817.

Baumol, W.J., S. Blackman and E.M. Wolff (1989), *Productivity and American Leadership—The Long View,* M.I.T. Press, Cambridge (Mass) U.S.

Bell, Daniel (1973), *Coming of Post-industrial Society—A venture in Social Forcasting*, Arnold Heineman, Publishers; U.S.A.

Bendix, Richard (1956), *Work and Authority in Industry*, John Wiley and Sons N.Y.

Bentham, Jeremy (1789 [1948], *An Introduction to the Principles of Morals and Legislation*, Hafner, N.Y.

Bergstrand, Jeffrey H. (1985), The Gravity Equations in International Trade—Some Microeconomic Foundations and Empirical Evidence, *Review of Economics and Statistics* Vol. 71(1), pp. 48-59.

Berle, A.A. and G.C. Means (1932), *Modern Corporation and Private Property*, Macmillan, N.Y.

Berman, Bruce (ed) (2002), *From Ideas to Assets—Investing wisely in Intellectual Property*, John Wiley and Sons Inc. N.Y.

Bernardi, Oliviers and Ricardo Galli (1993), Dematerialization, Long-term Trends in the Intensity of Use of Material and Energy, *Futures*, Vol. 24(3) pp. 431-448.

Beyer W. and M. Alvine (1985), Export Services in Post-industrial Society, Paper of the Thirty First North American Meeting of the *Regional Science Association*, Vol. 57, pp. 35-45.

Beyers, W.B. (1990), *Changing Business Practices and Growth of the Producer Services: Geographical Implications*, Paper Presented at the Annual Meeting of American Association of Geographers, Toronto.

Bhagwati J.N. (1984), Why are Services Cheaper in the Poor Countries, *Economic Journal*, Vol. 94(2), pp. 209-286.

Bhagwat, Jagdish (2004), *In Defence of Globalization*, Oxford University Press, New Delhi.

Bhagwati, J.N. (1984), Splintering and Disembodiment of Services and Developing Nations, *The World Economy*, Vol. 7(2), pp. 250-262.

Bhagwati J.N. (1991), Trade in Services and Multilateral Trade Negotiations, in Dauglas, A. Irwin (ed) *Political Economy and International Economics*, M.I.T. press, Cambridge (Mass) pp. 282-306.

Bhalla, A.S. (1970), The Role of Services in Employments Expansion, *International Labour Review*, Vol. 101. pp. 203–220.

Bhasin V.K. and Vijay K. Seth (1980), Non-production Workers, Technological Change and Factor Substitution—A Case Study of Indian Manufacturing Sector, *Indian Economic Journal*, Vol. 28(1), pp. 28-38.

Bhathacharya, B.B. and Arup Mitra (1997), Changing Composition of Employment in Tertiary Sector—A Cross-country Analysis, *Economic and Political Weekly*, Vol. 32(11), pp. 529-534.

Blackhurst R.J. Francois and E. Enders (1996), Market Access and Developing Countries, In Will Martin and L. Alan Winter (eds), *The Uruguay Round and Developing Economies*, Cambridge University Press, Cambridge (U.K.)

Blassa Bela (1965), Trade Liberalization and Revealed Comparative Advantage, *The Manchester School of Economics and Social Studies*, Vol. 33 pp. 99-123.

Blassa, Bela (1977), Revealed Comparative Advantage Revisited, An Analysis of Relative Export, Shares of Industrial Countries 1953-1971, *Manchester School of Economics and Social Studies*, Vol. 45(4), pp. 327-344.

Blaugh T. and P. Streeten (1963), The Coefficient of Ignorance, *Bulletin of Oxford University Institute of Statistics,* Vol. 25, pp. 135-166.

Blouin C. (2000), The WTO Agreement on Basic Telecommunications, A Revaluation, *Telecommunication Policy*, Vol. 24, pp. 212-222.

Boddewyn J., M. Holbrich and A. Perry (1986), Service Multinationals, Conceptualization Measurement, and Theory, *Journal of International Business Studies*, Vol. 17(3), pp. 41-37.

Boden, Mark and Ian Miles (2000), *Services and Knowledge Based Economy,* continum, London and New York.

Bosworth, Malcolm *et al* (1997), *Measuring Trade Impediments to Services within APEC: The Economic Implications of Liberalization of APEC Tariff and Non-Tariff Barriers to Trade*, U.S. International Trade Commission (USITC), Publication No. 3101, Washington D.C.

Boyer, Robert (2002), *Regulation Theory—The State of the Art*, Routledge, London.

Brenner, Y.S. (1966), *Theories of Economic Development and Growth*, Allen and Unwin, London.

Bronckers, Marco C.E.J. and Pirre Larenche (1997) Telecommunication Services and World Trade Organization, *Journal of World Trade*, Vol. 31(3), pp. 5-48.

Brown Drusilla K. Alan V. Deardorft and Robert M. Stern (2003), Multilateral, Regional and Bilaternal Trade Policy Options for the United States and Japan, *World Economy*, Vol. 26(6), 803-828.

Brown, Drusilla K. and Robert M. Stern (2001), Measurement and Modeling of the Economic Effects of Trade and Investment Barriers in Services, *Review of International Economics*, Vol. 9(2), pp. 282-286.

Brown, Drusilla, Alan Deardorff, Alan Fox and Robert Stern (1996), Computational Analysis of Goods and Services Liberalization in Uruguay Round, in W. Martin and A. Winters (eds), *Uruguay Round and Developing Economies*, Cambridge University Press (Mass) U.S.A.

Browning J (1986), Information Technology, *The Economist,* July 12.

Burgess, D.F. (1990), Services as Intermediate Goods: The Issues of Trade Liberalization, in R. Jones and A. Krueger (eds) *The Political Economy of International Trade*, Oxford Blackwell, pp. 122-139.

Burnham J.A. (1941), *The Managerial Revolution*, John Day and Co. N.Y.

Callon Michael, Cecile Meadel and Valolona Rabeharisoa (2004), The Economy of Qualities in Ash Amin and Nigel Thrift (eds); The *Blackwell Cultural Economy Reader*, Blackwell Publishers, M.A. U.S.A., pp. 58-79.

Cameron, *R. et al* (1967), Banking in the Early Stages of Industrialization, Oxford University Press, U.K.

Castells, Manual (1996), *The Rise of Network Society*, Blackwell, Cambridge (Mass), U.S.A.

Caves, R.E. (1982), *Multinational Enterprises and Economic Analysis*, Cambridge University Press, Cambridge (Mass).

Chadha, Rajesh *et al* (2000), Developing Countries and Next Round of W.T.O Negotiations, *World Economy*, Vol. 23(4), pp. 431-436.

Chadha, Rajesh (2003), Competitiveness of Services Sectors in South Asia—Role and Implication for GATS, CUTS Centre for Intonational Trade, Economics and Environment, Jaipur, India.

Chanda, Rupa (2002), *Globalization of Services—India's Opportunities and Constraints*, Oxford University Press, New Delhi.

Channon, A.F. (1978), *The Service Industries*, MacMillan, London.

Chenery H.B. and M. Syrquin (1975), *Patterns of Development 1950-1970,* Oxford University Press, London.

Chenery, H.B. and L. Taylor (1968), Development Patterns: Among Countries and Over Time, *Review of Economics and Stalishes,* Vol. 50, (4), pp. 391-416.

Chenery, Hollis B. (1960), Patterns of Industrial Growth, *American Economic Review,* Vol. 53, pp. 220–335.

Christopherson, S. (1989), Flexibility in the U.S. Service Economy and Emerging Spatial Division of Labour, *Transactions Institute of British Geographers*, Vol. 14, pp. 131-143.

Clairmonte, Fredrick F. and John H. Cavanagh (1984), Transnational Corporations and Services—The Final Frontier, *Trade and Development*, An UNCTAD Review Vol. 5 pp. 215-273.

Clark, Collin (1940), *The conditions of Economic Progress*, Macmillan, London.

Clark, Collin (1984), Development Economics—The Early Years in Meiers, G.M. and D. Seer (eds), *Pioneers in Development*, Oxford University Press. N.Y.

Coffey, William J. and Antoine S. Bailly (1992), Producer Services and Systems of Flexible Production, *Urban Studies*, Vol. 29(6), pp. 857-868.

Commander, Simon (1983), Jajmani System in North India, *Modern Asian Studies*, Vol. 17(2), pp. 283-311.

Contractor, Farok J. and Smit K. Kundu (2000), Globalization of Hotel Services–an Examination of Ownership and Alliance Pattern in Maturing Service

Sector, in Yair Abaroni and Lilach Nachum (eds), *Globalization of Services: Some Implications For Theory and Practice*, Routledge, London and New York pp. 296-319.

Cowan, Ruth Schwartz (1997), The industrial Revolution in the Home: Household Technology and Industrial Change in the 20th Century, in S.H. Cutcliff and T.S. Reynolds (eds) *Technology and American History*, Chicago University Press, Chicago U.S.A.

Daniel, G. (1943), *Three Ages*, Cambridge University Press, U.K.

Daniel, P.W. (1985), *Service Industries—A Geographical Appraisal*, Matheun, London.

Datla Chaudhri Mrinal (1990), Market Failure and Government Failure, *Journal of Economic Perspectives* Vol-4 (3) pp 25-35.

Deane, P. and W.A. Cole (1969), *British Economic Growth*, 2nd ed. Cambridge University Press, Cambridge, U.K.

Deardorf, Allan V. (1980), General Validity of Law of Comparative Advantage, *Journal of Political Economy*, Vol. 88, pp. 941-957.

Deardorff, A. (1985), Comparative Advantage and International Trade and Investment in Services in R.M. Stern (ed) *Trade and Investment in Services, Canada/US Perspectives*, Ontario Economic Council, Toronto, pp. 39-71.

Deardorff, Alan P. and Robert Stern (1985), *Methods of Measurement of Non-tariff Barriers*, UNCTAD, Geneva.

Deardorff, Alan V. and Robert M. Stern (1998), *Measurement of Non-tariff Barriers—Studies in International Economics*; University of Michigan Press, Ann Arbor.

Dee Philipa, Alexis Hardin and Leanne Holmes (2001), Issues in the Application of CGE Models to Service Trade Liberalization, in Christopher Findley and Tony Warren (eds) *Impediments to Trade in Servicers: Measurement* and Policy Implications, routledge, N.Y.

Dee, Phillippa and Kevin Hanslow (2001), Multilateral Liberalization of Services Trade, in Robert M. Stern (ed), *Services in International Economy*, University of Michigan Press Ann Arbor.

Delaunay, Jean Claude and Jean Gadrey (1992), *Services in Economic Thought—Three Countries of Debate* (translation from French by Aart Heesterman), Kluwer Academic Publishers, Boston, U.S.A.

Delhanty G.D. (1968), *Non-production Workers in the U.S. Manufacturing Industry*, North Holland Publishing Co. Amsterdam.

Denison, E.F. (1963), Measuring Contribution of Education to Economic Growth, in *Residual Factor in Economic Growth*, O.E.C.D. Paris.

Dhrymes, P.J. (1963), A Comparison of Productivity Behaviour in Manufacturing and Service Industries, *Review of Economic Studies*. Vol. 31, pp. 120-145.

Dornbusch, R. *et al* (1988), *The Case of Manufacturing in America's Future*, Eastman Kodak Company, Rochester.

Dowie, J.A. (1966), Productivity Growth in Goods and Services—Australia, U.S.A. and U.K., *Economic Records*, Vol. 42, pp. 436-454.

Dowie, J.A. (1970), The Service Ensemble in C. Froster (ed), *Australian Economic Development in the Twentieth Century*, Allan and Unwin, U.K.

Drechsler, L. (1975), Weighting of Index Numbers in Multilateral International Comparisons, *Review of Income and Wealth*, Vol. 21(1), pp. 18-32.

Driver, Ciaran (1984), Testing the Gershuny Hypothesis, *Futures*, Oct pp. 508-512.

Drucker, P.F. (1956) *The New Society*, Harper and Brothers, New York.

Du Gay P. and M. Pryke (eds) (1999), *Cultural Economy—Cultural Analysis of Commercial Life*, Sage, London.

Dunning John H. (1989), Multinational Enterprises and the Growth of Services: Some Conceptual and Theoretical Issues, *Service Industries Journal* Vol. 9(1) pp. 5-39.

Dunning, J.H. (1981), *International Production and Multinational Enterprise*, Allen and Unwin, London.

Dunning, J.H. (1988), The Eclectic Paradigm of International Production. A Restatement and Some Possible Extensions, *Journal of International Business Studies*, Vol. 19, pp. 312-328.

Economic Council of Canada (1991), Employment in the Service Sector, Ministry of Supply, Canada, Ottawa.

Elek et al (1999), Open Skies or Open Clubs? New Issues for Asia-pacific Economic Cooperation, *Journal of Air Transport Management*.

Elfring, Tom (1989), New Evidence on the Expansion of Service Employment in Advanced Economies, *Review of Income and Wealth*, Series 35, Number 4, pp. 409-440.

Enderwick, P.(1987), The Strategy and Structure of Service Sector Multinationals—Implication for Potential Hot Region, *Regional Studies*; Vol. 21, pp. 215-223.

Feketekuty, Geza (1988), *International Trade in Services—An Overview and Blue Print for Negotiations*, Bellinger Publication Co., Cambridge (Mass).

Findley C (2002), *Multilateral Liberalization of Service Trade and Investment in Globalising World—Scope and Limitations*, Asia Pacific School of Economics and Management, NECP, 55.

Fisher Allen G.B. (1945), *Economic Progress and Social Security*, Macmillan, London.

Fisher, A.G.B. (1933), Capital and Growth of Knowledge, *Economic Journal* Vol. 43 pp. 374-389.

Fisher, Allen G.B. (1935), *The Class of Progress and Security,* Macmillan, London.

Fisher, Irving (1939), The Concept of Income; A Rebuttal, *Econometrica,* Vol. 7, pp. 27-40.

Fisher, A.G.B. (1939), Production—Primary, Secondary and Tertiary, *Economic Record*, Vol. 15, pp. 24-38.

Fisher, A.G.B. (1946), Tertiary Production and Post-war International Economic Problem, *Review of Economics and Statistics* Vol. 28, pp. 146-151.

Fisher, A.G.B. (1952), A note on Tertiary Production, *Economic Journal,* Vol. 62, No. 248 pp. 820-834.

Fisher, A.G.B. (1954), Tertiary Production: A Post Script, *Economic Journal,* Vol. 62 pp. 820-834.

Fogel, R.W. (1964), *Railroads and American Growth; Essays in Economic History*, Baltimore.

Foote, Nelson, N. and Paul K. Hatt (1953), Social Mobility and Economic Advancement, *American Economic Review*, Vol. 63(2), pp. 364-378.

Fowler, Christina (1998), Changes in Provisional Retail Practices During the Eighteenth Century with Particular Reference to Central-South England, *Business History*, Vol. 40(4), pp. 37-54.

Francois, J.F. (1990), Trade in Producer Services and Returns Due to Specialization Under Monopolistic Competition, *Canadian Journal of Economics* Vol. 23, pp. 109-124.

Francois, J.F. (1990a), Producer Services, Scale and the Division of Labour, *Oxford Economic Papers*, Vol. 42, pp. 715-729.

Francois, Joseph (1999), *Estimation of Barriers to Trade in Services*, Erasmus University, Rottendam, Netherlands.

Frenderberg, Herman and Redlick Fritz (1984), Industrial Development of Europe—Reality, Symbols and Images, *Kyklos* Vol.17, pp. 372-402.

Fuchs, V.R. (1964), Productivity Trends in Goods and Services, Occasional Paper No. 89 N.B.E.R. N.Y.

Fuchs, V.R. (1965), The Growing Importance of Service Industries, Occasional Paper No. 96, N.B.E.R. N.Y.

Fuchs, V.R. (1968), *The Service Economy*, National Bureau of Economic Research, New York and London.

Fuchs, V.R. (ed) (1972), *Essays in Economics of Health and Medical Care*, N.B.E.R. New York.

Fukazawa, H.K. (1972), Rural Servants in Maharashtrian Village, Demiurgic or Jajmani System, *Hitotsubashi Journal of Economics*, Vol. 13, pp. 108-124.

Fuller C.J. (1989), Misconceiving the Grain Heap: A Critique of Concept of Indian Jajmani System in J. Parry and M. Bloch (eds), *Money and the Morality of Exchange*, Cambridge University, Press Cambridge pp. 50-62.

Gadrey, Jean (2000), The Characterization of Goods and Services—An Alternative Approach, *Review of Income and Wealth*, Series 46(3), pp. 369-387.

Galbraith J.K. (1967), *The New Industrial State*, Hamish Hamilton, Ltd. London.

Galbraith, J.K. (1967), *The New Industrial State*, Hamish Hamilton, Ltd. London.

Gallman, R. and T. Weiss (1970), The Service Industries in the 19th Century, *Studies in Income and Wealth,* Vol. 34, pp. 287-353.

Galor Oded and David Weil (2000), Population Technology and Growth, *American Economic Review*, Vol. 90(4), pp. 806-828.

Geary R.C. (1958), A Note on Comparisons of Exchange Rates and Purchasing Power Between Countries, *Journal of Royal Statistical Society*, Vol. 121 (1), pp. 20-57.

Gemmell, Norman (1981), Economic Development and Structural Changes—The Role of Service Sector, *Journel of Development Studies,* Vol. 19(1), pp. 37-66.

Gershuny, J. (1978), *After Industrial Society—The Self Serving Economy*, Macmillan, London.

Gershuny J.I and I.D. Miles (1983), *The New Services Economy—The Transformation of Employment in Industrial Societies*, Francis Pinter, London.

Gill, B. (1973), Banking and Industrialization in Europe, 1730-1914, In Carlo M. Cipolla (ed) *Fontana Economic History of Europe—Industrial Revolution*, Fontana Collins.

Gini, Corrado (1948), The Content and Use of Estimates of the National Income, *Banka Nazionale de Lovaro Quarterly Review*, Vol. 5, pp. 282-307.

Girard, L. (1965), Transport, in H.J. Habakkuk and M. Postan (eds), Industrial Revolution and After, *Cambridge Economic History of Europe*, Vol. VI, Cambridge University Press, Cambridge, England.

Goe, W. Richards (1991), Producer Services and Flexible production—An Exploratory Study, *Growth and Change*, Vol. 22(4), pp. 95-117.

Goffman, Erving (1961), *Asylums*, Anchor Books, Doubleday Co. N.Y.

Goffman Erving (1983), The International Order; Presidential Address to American Sociological Association, *American Sociological Review,* Vol. 48(1) pp.1-18.

Goldar, B.N. and Vijay K. Seth (1975), Some Economic Aspects of Non-production Workers in Indian Manufacturing Sector, *Indian Journal of Industrial Relations*, Vol. 22(2), pp. 271-285.

Gottmann J. (1961), *Megalopolis*, Twentieth Country Fund, N.Y.

Greenfield, H.I. (1966), *Manpower and Growth of Producer Services*, Columbia University Press, London.

Grossman, Michel (1972), *The Demand for Health*: *A Theoretical and Empirical Investigation*, N.B.E.R. N.Y.

Greenfield, Harry I. (1966), *Manpower and Growth of Producer Services*, Columbia University Press, N.Y.

Grossman Michel (1972a), On the Concept of Health Capital and the Demand for Health, *Journal of Political Economy*, Vol. 80, pp. 223-255.

Grossman, Michael (2003), Human Capital Model, in Anthony J. Culyer and, Joseph P. Newhouse (eds), *Handbook of Health Economics*, Elsevier, North Holland, Vol. 1 A, pp. 347-408.

Guha, Sumit (2004), Civilization, Markets and Services—Village Servants in India From Seventeenth and Twentieth Centuries, *Indian Economic and Social History Review* Vol. 41(1), pp. 79-101.

Guir Ofer (1967), *Service Industries in a Developing Economy*, MacMillan New York, 1967.

Gurley J.G and E.S. Shaw (1955), Financial Aspect of Economic Development, *American Economic Review*, Vol. 47, pp. 201-242.

Haig, B.D. (1975), An Analysis of Changes in Distribution of Employment Between Services and Manufacturing 1960-1970, *Review of Economics and Statistics*, Vol.57 pp. 35-42.

Harbinson, Fredrick and Charles A. Myers (1964), *Education Manpower and Economic Growth*, McGraw Hill, N.Y.

Hardin, Alexis and Lenne Holmes (1997), Service Trade and Foreign Direct Investment, Staff Research Paper, Industry Commission Canberra, Australia.

Harris, Mark N. and Lázlo Mátyis (1998), The Econometrics of Gravity Models, Working Paper No. 5/98, Melbourne Institute of Applied Economics and Social Research.

Hartwell, R.M (1973), "The Services Revolution: The Growth of Services in Modern Economy" in C.M. Cipolla (ed) *Fontana Economic History of Europe—Industrial Revolution*, Fontana Collins pp. 358-396.

Harvey, Daniel (1989), *The Conditions Post Modernity—An Enquiry into the Nature of Cultural Change*, Basic Blackwell, Oxford.

Harvey, David (1989), *The Urban Experience*, Oxford, London, U.K.

Harvey, David (1989a), *Condition of Postmodernity—An Enquiry into the Origin of Cultural Change*, Basil Blackwell, Cambridge (Mass).

Hepworth, M. (1990), *Geography of the Information Economy*, Guilford N.Y.

Hertel T. (ed) (1997), *Global Trade Analysis: Modeling and Applications*, Cambridge University Press (Mass) U.S.A.

Hertog, Pim Den, Rob Bilderbeek and Meltha Sven (1997), Intangibles—The Soft Side of Innovation, *Futures*, Vol. 29(1) pp. 33-45.

Heston A. and Robert Summers (1992), Measuring Final Product Services for International Comparisons, in Z. Giriliches (ed) *Output Measurement in Services*, NBER Studies in Income and Wealth, Vol. 56, University of Chicago Press, Chicago.

Hicks J.R. (1940), The Valuation of Social Income, *Economica* Vol. 10, pp. 22-32.

Hill, T.P. (1977), On Goods and Services, *Review of Income and Wealth* Vol. 23, pp. 315-338.

Hill, T.P. (1977a), Price and Volume Measures for Non-market Services, (Mimeographed).

Hill, T.P. (1999), Tangibles, Intangibles and Services, A New Taxonomy for the Classification of Output, *Canadian Journal of Economics*, Vol. 32(2) pp. 426-446.

Hindley, Brain and Alasdair Smith (1984), Comparative Advantage and Trade in Services, *World Economy*, Vol. 20(5), pp. 369-389.

Hindley, Brian and Abasdair Smith (1984), Comparative Advantage and Trade in Services, *World Economy*, Vol. 7, pp. 369-389.

Hjerppe, Reino T. (1980), The Measurement of Real Outputs of Public Sector Services, *Review of Income and Wealth*, Vol. 26(3), pp. 237-250.

Hobsbawn, E.J. (1954), General Crises of European Economy in the Seventeenth Century, *Past and Present*, Vol. 5, pp. 33-53.

Hodge, James (2002), Liberalization of Trade in Services in Developing Countries, In Hoekman *et al* (eds), *Development Trade and WTO—A Handbook*, World Bank, Washington, D.C.

Hoekman, Barnard M. (1995), Tentative First Step—an Assessment of the Urguay Round Agreement on Services, World Bank Policy Research Working Paper 1455, Washington D.C.

Hoekman, Bernard M. (1996), Assessing General Agreement on Trade in Services, in Will Martin and L. Alan Winters (eds), *The Urguay Round and Developing Economies*, Cambridge University Press, Cambridge U.K.

Hoekman, Bernard (2000), Towards a More Balanced and Comprehensive Services Agreement, in Scott Jeffrey J. (ed) *The WTO After Seattle*, Institute of International Economics, Washington D.C., pp. 119-135.

Hoekman, Bernard and Aditya Mattoo (2000), Services, Economic Development and Next Round of Negotiations on Services, *Journal of International Development*, Vol. 12(2), pp. 283-296.

Hoekman, Bernard, Aditya Mattoo and Philip English (2002), *Development Trade and the WTO—A Hand book*, World Bank, Washington D.C.

Hoekman, Bernard and P. Sauve (1994), Liberalizing Trade in Services, World Bank Discussion Paper No. 243 Washington D.C.

Hoekman, Bernard *et al* (1996), Trade in Services—the GATS and Asia, *Asia Pacific Economic Review*, Vol. 2(1), pp. 5-20.

Hoekman, Bernard, A Carlos and Primo Braga (1997), Protection and Trade in Services—A Survey, *Open Economies Review*, Vol. 8 pp. 285-308.

Hoppit, Julin and E.A. Wrigley (1994), *The Industrial Revolution in Britain*, Vol. I to III, Economic History Society and Blackwell Publishers, Oxford U.K.

Hoselitz, B.F. (1960), Stages of Economic Growth, in B.F. Hoselitz (ed) *Theories of Economic Growth*, Free press of Glencoe, U.S.A.

Houthakker, H.S. (1957), An International Comparison of Household Expenditure Patterns Commemorating the century of Engle's Law, *Econometrica*. Vol. 25, pp. 25–48.

Howells, J. (1990), The Internationalization of R&D and the Development of Global Research Networks, *Regional Studies*, Vol. 24(6), pp. 495-512.

Hull, C.H. (ed) (1899), *The Economic Writings of Sir William Petty*, Cambridge University Press.

Hume David (1740) [1958], *A Treatise of Human Nature* (Edited by L.A. Selby-Bigge) Clarendon Press, Oxford.

Hutchins, E. (1995), *Cognition in the Wild*, MIT Press, Mass, U.S.A.

Illeris, S. (1989), *Services and Regions in Europe*, Gower, Aldershot.

IMF (2003), *Balance of Payment Statistics Year Book*, Washington, D.C.

International Labour Organization (1996), *World Employment 1996-97—National Policies in Global Context*, Bookwell, Delhi.

Jeffreys, J. (1954), *Retail Trading in Britain 1858-1950*, Cambridge, U.K.

Jeffreys, J.B. and D. Knee (1962), *Retailing in Europe*, *Present Structure and Future Trends*, Cambridge, London.

Jevons, W. Stanley (1871) [1963], *The Theory of Political Economy*, Longman, London.

Johnson, M. *et al* (2001), Modeling the Impact of Regulatory Reforms, in Christopher Findley and Tony Warren (eds) *Impediment To Trade in Services: Measurement and Policy Implications*, Routledge, N.Y.

Jones, Ronald W. and Frances Raune (1990), Appraising the Option for International Trade in Services, *Oxford Economic Papers*, Vol. 42, pp. 672-687.

Jones, Ronald W. and Frances Ruane (1990), Appraising the Options for International Trade in Services, Oxford *Economic Papers*, Vol. 42, pp. 672-687.

Kalirajan K. *et al* (2001), The Price Impact of Restrictions on Banking Services, in Christopher Findley and Tony Warren (eds), *Impediments to Trade in Services: Measurement and Policy Implications*, Routledge, New York.

Kalirajan, K. (2000), Restriction on Trade in Distribution Services, Staff Research Paper, Productivity Commissioner Canberra, Australia.

Kang (2001), Price Impact of Restrictions on Maritime Transport Services, in Christopher Findley and Tony Warren (eds), *Impediments to Trade in Services*: *Measurement and Policy Implications*, Routledge, New York.

Karmaker, Uday Kumar (2004), Will you Survive the Services Revolution, *Harvard and Business Review*, June, pp. 101-107.

Katouzian, M.A. (1970), The Development of the Service Sector—a New Approach, *Oxford Economic Papers*, Vol. 22, pp. 362-381.

Kenny M. and R. Florida (1993), *Beyond Mass Production*, Oxford University Press, London.

Khamis, S.H. (1967), Some Problems Relating to International Comparability and Fluctuating Production Volumes Indicators, *Bulletin of International Statistical Institute*, Vol. 42, pp. 52-65.

Kindleberger, C.P. (1958), *Economic Development*, McGraw Hill. N.Y.

Kirn, T. R Couway and W. Beyers (1990), Producer Services Development and the Role of Telecommunication, A case study of rural Washington, *Growth and Change* Vol. 21(4), pp. 33-50.

Koekkoek, K.A. (1988), Trade in Services, the Developing Countries and Uruguay Round, *World Economy*, Vol. 11(1), pp. 151-155.

Kravis, I.B., Alan Heston, Robert Summers (1982), *World Production and Income—International Comparisons of Real Gross Output*, John Hopkin's Press, Baltimore and London.

Kravis, Irvin B, *et al* (1978), *International Comparisons of Real Products and Purchasing Power*, John Hopkins University Press, Baltimore.

Kravis, Irving B. Zoltan Kenessey, Alan Heston and Robert Summers (1975), *A System of International Comparison of Gross Products and Purchasing Power*, John Hopkins University Press, Baltimore.

Kumar Shailendra (2005), *Trade in Services—Advantage India*, Bookwell, New Delhi.

Kutcher, R.E. (1988), Growth, of Service Employment in United States, in B.R. Guile and J.B. Quinn (eds) *Technology in Services: Policies for Growth Trade and Employment*, National Academy Press, Washington.

Kuznets, Simon (1948), National Income: A New Version, *Review of Economics and Statistics*, Vol. 30, pp. 152-152.

Kuznets, Simon (1951), Government Products and National Income and Wealth, *Income and Wealth Series II*, Cambridge.

Kuznets, Simon (1958), Quantitative Aspect of Economic Growth of Nations, Industrial Distribution of National Product and Labour Force, II *Economic Development and Cultural Change*, Vol. 15, Supplementary.

Kuznets, Simon (1966), *Modern Economic Growth; Rate, Structure and Spread*, Yale University Press, U.S.

Lall, Sanjay (1986), The Third World and Comparative Advantage in Trade in Services, in Sanjay Lall and Frances Stewart (eds), *Theory and Reality in Development*, Macmillan Press, London, pp. 122-138.

Landes, David S. (1969), *The Unbound Prometheus: Technological Change and Industrial Development in Western Europe from 1750 to the Present*, Cambridge University Press, Cambridge, U. K.

Leibenstein, Harvey (1962), *Economic Backwardness and Economic Growth*, Joh Wiley and Sons.

Lengelle, M. (1966), *Manpower Problems in Service Sector, Supplement to the Report*, O.E.C.D. Paris.

Lengelle, Maurice (1966), *The Grawing Importance of the Service Sector in Member Countries*, O.E.C.D. Paris.

Lerner A. (1934), The Concept of Monopoly and the Measurement of Monopoly Power, *Review of Economic Studies*, Vol. 1, pp. 157-169.

Leveson, Irving (1985), Services in U.S. Economy, in Robert P. Inman (ed), *Managing the Service Economy—Prospects and Problems,* Cambridge University Press, (Mass) U.S.

Levitt, Theodre (1972), Production Line Approach to Service, *Harvard Business Review*, Sep-Oct 1972, pp. 38-41.

Levitt, Theodre (1976), The Industrialization of Services, *Harvard Business Review*, Sep-Oct pp. 63-74.

Low, L. (2000), *Economics of Information Technology and the Media*, Singapore, University Press, Singapore.

Lowe, Alfred (1952), A Structural Model of Production, *Social Research*, Vol. 19; pp. 125-146.

Lucas, Robert E (2002), *Lecture in Economic Growth*, Harvard University Press, Cambridge (Mass).

Machlup, F. (1962), *The Production and Distribution of Knowledge in the United States*, Princeton University Press, Princeton, U.S.A.

Maddison, Angus (1971), *Class Structure and Economic Growth: India and Pakistan*, Allen and Unwin, London.

Maddison, Angus (2003), *The World Economy*—A *Millennial Perspective*, Overseas Press (India) Pvt. Ltd. New Delhi.

Markusen, James, R.(1983), Factor Movement and Commodity Trade as Complements, *Journal of International Economics*, Vol. 13, pp. 341-356.

Markusen, James R. (1989), Trade in producer Services and Other Specialized Intermediate Input, *American Economic Review*, Vol. 79 (1), pp. 85-95.

Marshall J., P. Wood, P.W. Daniels, A. McKinnon, J. Bechlor, P. Damesick, N. Thrift, A Gillespie, A. Green and A. Leyshon (1988), *Services and Uneven Development*, Oxford University Press, N.Y.

Marshall, Alfred (1879) [1929], *Economics of Industry*, Orient Longman, London.

Marx, Karl (1954), *Capital*, P.P.H. Moscow.

Marx, Karl (1956), *Theories of Surplus Value*, Foreign Language Publishing Home, Moscow.

Maslow, A. (1953), *Motivation and Personality*, Harper and Row, N.Y.

Mattoo Aditya (1999), Financial Services in the WTO: Liberalization Commitments of Developing and Transition Economies, Policy Research Working Paper Series 2184 World Bank, Washington D.C.

Mattoo Aditya (2001), Shaping Future Rules for Trade in Services, Lessons from GATS, in Takatoshi Ito and Anne Krueger (eds), *Trade in Services*, N.B.E.R. Cambridge Mass.

Mc Guire, Greg and Michael Schuela (2001), Restrictiveness of International Trade in Banking Services, in Christopher Findley and Tony Warren (eds) *Impediment to Trade in Services: Measurement and Policy Implications*, Routledge, N.Y.

Mc Guire, Greg, Michel Schuele and Tina Smith (2001), Restrictiveness of Trade in Maritime Services, in Christopher Findley and Tony Warren (eds) *Impediment to Trade in Services: Measurement and Policy Implications*, Routledge, N.Y.

McCrackin, B. (1985), Why are Business and Professional Services Growing so Rapidly? *Federal Reserve Bank of Atlanta Economic Review*, August 14-28.

McRae, J.J. (1985), Can Growth in Service Sector Rescue Western Canada? *Canadian Public Policy*, Vol. 11, pp. 351-53.

Meek, Ronald (1962), *The Economics of Physiocracy*, George Allen and Unwin. N.Y.

Meier, G. (1970), Development with Employment—Note, in G. Meier (ed) *Leading Issues in Economic Development*, Oxford University Press.

Melvin, James R. (1989), Trade in Producer Services—A Heckscher-Ohlin Approach, *Journal of Political Economy*, Vol. 97(5), pp. 1180-1196.

Melvin, James R. (1989), *Trade in Services, A Theoretical Analysis*, Institute of Research in Public Policy; Hali fax.

Melvin, James R. (1990), Time and Space in Economic Analysis, *Canadian Journal of Economics*, Vol. 23, pp. 725-747.

Melvin, James, R. (1995), History and Measurement in the Service Sector, *Review of Income and Wealth Series, 41(4)*, pp. 481-494.

Mendels, Franklin F. (1972), Proto-Industrialization—The First Phase of Industrialization Process, *Journal of Economic History*, Vol. 32 pp. 241-261.

Meyer, Peter (1993), Inventing Village Tradition—the Late 19th Century Origins of the North Indian Jajmani System, *Modern Asian Studies*, Vol. 27(2), pp. 378-86.

Mills, J.S. (1861 [1957]), *Utilitarianism*, Bobbs-Merril, Indianapolis, Indiana.

Mills, John Stuart (1852), (1920), *Principles of Political Economy*, John W. Parker & Sons, London.

Minks, A.L. (1955), Statistical Evidence and Concept of Tertiary Industry, *Economic Development and Cultural Change*, Vol. 13, pp. 366-373.

Mukerjee, Neela (2000), *World Trade Organization and India's Trade Policy in Services*, Vikas Publishing Ltd, New Delhi.

Mundell, Robert A (1957), International Trade and Factor Mobility, *American Economic Review*, Vol. 47, pp. 321-335.

Murray, Roman (1978), *Telephone Marketing; How To Build Your Business by Telephone*, McGraw Hill, N.Y.

Nau H. (1987), Bargaining in the Uruguay Round, in J. Michel Finger and Andrzej Olechowski (eds), *The uruguay Round: A Handbook for Multilateral Trade Negotiation*, World Bank, Washington D.C., pp. 75-80.

Nayyar, Deepak (1988), The Political Economy of International Trade in Services, *Cambridge Journal of Economics*, Vol. 12, pp. 279-298.

Neff, J.U (1943), Industrial Revolution Reconsidered, *Journal of Economic History*, Vol. 3, pp. 2-29.

Neu, C.R. (1988), International Trade in Banking Services, in R.E. Baldwin, C. Hamilton and A. Sapir (eds) *Issues in U.S.-E.C. Trade Relations*, N.B.E.R. and University of Chicago Press pp. 245-276.

Nguyen, Hong-Duc (2000), Restrictions on Trade in Professional Services, Staff Research Paper, Australian Productivity Commission, Melbourne Australia.

Nicholas, Georgescu-Roegen (1968), *Utility* in David Sills (ed) International Encyclopaedia of social Sciences, Vol. 16, pp. 236-267, Macmillan Company and Free Press. N.Y.

Nystorm, P. (1930), *Economics of Retailing*, N.Y.

O.E.C.D. (1984), *Employment Outlook*, Paris.

Oshima, Harry T. (1971), Labour Force 'Explosion' and Labour Intensive Sector in Asian Growth, *Economic Development and Cultural Change*, Vol. 19, pp. 161-183.

Pacific Economic Cooperation Council (PEEC) (1995), Survey of Impediments on Trade and Investment in the APES Region, APEC Secretariat Singapore.

Panchmukhi, V.R. *et al* (1986), Structural change and Economic Growth in Developing Economies, Annual Congress, International Economic Association, Dec.

Parker E. (1975), *Social Implications of Computer/Telecommunications Systems*, Standford University Press, Palo Alto, U.S.A.

Parsons, Talcott (1968), *Professions* in David Sills (ed), *International Encyclopaedia of Social Sciences*, Vol. 12, MacMillan Company and Free Press, N.Y., pp. 525-540.

Paulin, Gunter A. (1987), *Services—The Driving Force of the Economy*, Waterflow Publishers, London, U.K.

Petit, P. (1986), *Slow Growth and Service Economy*, Frances Pinter, London.

Piore M.J. and C.F. Sabel (1984), *The Second Industrial Divide,* Basic Books, N.Y.

Prescott, William H. (1847), *History of the Conquest of Mexico and History of Conquest of Peru*, Random House, N.Y.

Price Waterhouse (1983), Business Views on International Trade in Services: The Result of Survey of Fortune's Directory of Service Companies, December Mimeo.

Price Waterhouse (1985), Business Views on Public Policy and International Trade in Services—The Result of Fortune's Directory of Service Companies, Feb. Mimeo.

Quinn, J.B. (1988), Technology in Services—Past Myths and Future Challenges, *Technological Forcasting and Social Change*, Vol. 34(4), pp. 340-362.

Quinn, J.B. T.L. Doorely and P.C. Pacquette (1990), Beyond Products—Service Based Strategy, *Harvard Business Review* March, 55-65.

Rajan A. and C. Cook (1986), The Impact of Information Technology on Employment in Financial Services, *The National Westminster Bank Quarterly*, Vol. 21 (August), pp. 35-42.

Ramaswamy R. and R. Rawthorn (1997), Deindustrialization: Causes and Implications, I.M.F. Working Paper, Washington D.C. (April).

Ramfield, Joshua (1998), Consumer-owned Community Flour and Bread Societies in the Eighteenth and Early Nineteenth Century, *Business History*, Vol. 40(4), pp. 16-36.

Reddaway, W.B. *et al* (1973), *Effect of Selective Employment Tax—Final Report*, Cambridge University Press, Cambridge.

Rehman, M.M. (2003), *A Panel Data Analysis of Bangladesh's Trade—The Gravity Model Approach*, University of Sydney, Australia.

Reich, R. (1991), The Real Economy; *The Atlantic Monthly* No. 267(2) pp. 35-72.

Richta, R. (1969), *Civilization at the Crossroads: Social and Human Implications of Scientific and Technical Revolution*, International Art and Science Press, White Plains, N.Y.

Rostow, W.W. (1960), *The Process of Economic Growth*, Oxford University Press, New York and London.

Rostow, W.W. (1960), *The Stages of Economic Growth—A Non-Communist Manifesto*, Cambridge University Press, Cambridge (Mass).

Rowthorn, R.E. (1992), Productivity and American Leadership: A Review, *Review of Income and Wealth*, Vol. 38, pp. 475-496.

Rubin, Issac Ilych (1979), *A History of Economic Thought*, Ink-Link Ltd. London.

Russels, R.Sn. and Murdick (2003), *Service Management and Operations*, Pearson Education, first Indian Print, Delhi.

Rymes, Thomas K. (1990), On International Trade in Banking Services, *Review of Income and Wealth*, Series 36, No. 4.

S.S.S.R. Institute of Economics (1962), Politicheskia Economiia (translated in English), *Political Economy*, P.P.H. Moscow.

Sabel, F. Charles and Jonathan Zeitlein (1997), *World Possibilities—Flexible and Mass Production in Western Industrialization*, Cambridge University Press, Cambridge.

Sampson, G.P. and R.M. Snape (1985), Identifying Issues in Trade in Services, *World Economy*, Vol. 8(2), pp. 171-181.

Sampson, G.P. and Snape, R.H. (1985), Identifying the Issues in Trade in Services, *The World Economy*, Vol. 8(2), pp. 302-313.

Sapir, A. and C. Winter (1994), Services Trade, in D. Greenway and L. Winters (eds), *Survey's in International Trade*, Princeton University Press, Princeton.

Saunders C.T. (1977), Welfare and GNP, in Essays in Honour of Prof. P.J. Verdoorn, Martinus Nijhof Social Science Division, Leiden.

Sauve, Pierre and Robert Stern (eds) (2000), GATS 2000, New Directions in Services Trade Liberalization, Booking Institute Press, Washington, D.C.

Savitt, R. (1984), The Wheel of Retailing and Retail Product Management, *European Journal of Marketing*, Vol. 18, pp. 342-350.

Saxonhouse, Gary R. (1985), Services in Japanese Economy, in Robert P. Inman (ed) *Managing the Service Economy—Prospects and Problems*, Cambridge University Press, Cambridge (Mass) U.S.A., pp. 53-83.

Sayer Andew and Richard Walker (1992), *New Social Economy-Reworking Division of Labor*, Blackwell, U.S.A.

Schmid, G. (1988), Manufacturing—Key to Future Jobs; *Challenge*, Nov-Dec.

Schultz, T.W. (1961), Education and Economic Growth in National Society for the Study of Education (ed), *Social Forces Influencing American Education*, Chicago.

Schultzs, Theodore, W. (1964), *Transforming Traditional Agriculture*, Yale University Press, New Haven, Conn.

Scott A.J. (1988), *New Industrial Spaces*, Pion, London.

Scott, A.J. (2000), *The Cultural Economy of City*, Sage, London.

Sen. Amartya (1979), The Welfare Basis of Real Income Comparisons—A Survey, *Journal of Economic Literature*, Vol. 17, pp. 425-440.

Seth, Vijay K. (1986), State and Spatial Aspect of Industrialization in Post-independence India, *Political Geography Quarterly*, Vol. 5, pp. 331-350.

Seth, Vijay K. (1987), Industrialization in India—Spatial Perspective, Commonwealth Publishers, Delhi, India.

Seth Vijay K. (1989), *Themes On Spatial Perspective*, Commonwealth Publishers, Delhi India.

Seth, Vijay K. (2000), Technology and Labour in Retrospect and Prospect, *Management and Change*, Vol. 4(1), pp. 61-90.

Seth, Vijay K(2001), Flexibility Paradigm and Restructuring of Labour Market in Developed Market Economies, *Journal of Management Research*, Vol. 1(3), pp. 223-248.

Seth Vijay K. (2002), Primitive Flexible to Modern Flexible Manufacturing and The Process of Skilling and Deskilling of Labour, *Indian Journal of Labour Economics*, Vol. 45(4) pp. 1175-1194.

Seth, Vijay K. (2003), The Beginning and End of Primitive Flexible Manufacturing System, *Journal of Management Research*, Vol. 3(2), pp. 73-86.

Seth, Vijay K. (2005), Changing Composition of Employment in Services in Developing Economies, Faculty of Management Studies, Delhi University, (Mimeo)

Seth, Vijay K. and Ashok Seth (1994), *Dynamics of Labour Absorption in Industry*, Deep and Deep Publishers, New Delhi.

Seth Vijay K. and Suresh Chand Aggarwal (2003), Shifts in Policy Regime and Inter-industry and Inter-regional changes in Industrial Workforce

Structure, *Indian Journal of Labour Economies*, Vol. 46(4), pp. 971-982.

Seth, Vijay K. and Suresh Chand Aggarwal (2004), *The Economics of Labour Markets–Policy Regime Changes and the Process of Adjustment in the Organized Industry in India*, Ane Book India, Delhi.

Seth, Vijay K. and V.K. Bhasin (1975), Economics of Non-production Workers in Indian Manufacturing Industries, *Review of Commerce Studies*, Vol. 7, pp. 32-55.

Shelp, Ronald K. (1981), *Beyond Industrialization: Ascedency of Global Service Economy*, Praeger, New York.

Shoup, Carl S. (1947), *Principles of National Income Analysis*, Cambridge.

Singlemann J. (1978), *From Agriculture to Services*, Sage, Beverly Hill, U.K.

Singlemann Joachin (1978), The Sectoral Transformation of Labour Force in Seven Industrialized Countries, *American Journal of Sociology*, Vol. 83(5), pp. 1224-1234.

Singlemann, Joachim (1978), The Sectoral Transformation of Labour Force in Seven Industrialized Countries, 1920-70, *American Journal of Sociology*, Vol. 83(5) pp. 1224-1234.

Skolka. J.V. (1976), The Substitution of Marketed Services for Self-service Activities, *Review of Income and Wealth*, Vol. 22 pp. 297-304.

Smith, Adam (1961), *An Enquiry into the Nature and Causes of the Wealth of Nations,* Methuen, London.

Snape, Richard (1998), Reaching Effective Agreements Covering Services, in Anne O. Krueger (ed) *WTO as An International Organization*, Oxford University Press.

Solow, R.M. (1957), Technological Change and Aggregate Production Function, *Review of Economic and Statistics*, Vol. 34, pp. 312-330.

Stanbeck, T.M. (1979), *Understanding the Service Economy*, John Hopkins University Press, Baltimore

Steedam I and J.S. Metcalfe (1985), Capital Goods and Pure Theory of Trade, in D. Greenway (ed) *Current Issues in International Trade Theory and Policy*, Macmillan, London.

Stern, Robert M. (ed) (2001), *Services in International Economy*, University of Michigan Press, Ann Arbor.

Stigler, G.J. (1946), *Domestic Servants in the United States 1900-1940*, National Bureau of Economic Research, Occasional paper No. 3.

Stigler, George J. (1956), *Trends in Employment in the Service Industries*, Princeton University Press, for N.B.E.R. N.Y.

Storper, Michel (1994), The Transition to Flexible Sepcialization in U.S. Film Industry—External Economies, the Division of Labour and Crossing Industrial Divide, in Ash Amin (ed) *Post-Fordism—A Reader*, Blackwell, Cambridge, U.S.A. pp. 195-226.

Studenski, Paul (1958), *The Income of Nations—Theory Measurement and Analysis: Past and Present*, New York University Press, N.Y.

Suant K. (1986), *International Transactions in Services—The Politics of Transborder Trade Flows*, Westview, Boulder.

Summer, Robert, Irving B. Kravis and Alan Heston (1980), International Comparisons of Real Product and its Composition 1950-1977, *Review of Income and Wealth*, Vol. 26(1), pp. 19-66.

Summers, Robert (1985), Services in the International Economy, in Robert P. Inman (ed) *Managing the Service Economy—Prospects and Problems*, Cambridge University Press, Cambridge (Mass) U.S., pp. 27-48.

Tamms Vanessa (2001), Frontier Cost Estimates of the Impact of Restriction of Trade in Air Transport Services, in Christopher Findly and Tony Warren (eds), *Impediments To Trade in Services: Measurement and Policy Implications*, Routledge N.Y.

Tawney, R.H. (1958), *Social History and Literature,* Leicenster, U.K.

Thalheim, Karl C. (1973), *Services* in C.D. Kernig (ed) Marxism, Communism and Western Society—A Comparative Encyclopedia, Vol. VII, Herder and Herder pp. 324-327.

Thomas, D.R.E. (1978), Strategy is Different in Service Business, *Harvard Business Review*, Vol. 56(4), pp. 156-165.

Traintis, S.G. (1953), Economic Progress, Occupational Redistribution and International Trade, *Economic Journal* Vol. 63, pp. 627-637.

Trewin, Ray (2001), A Price Impact Measure of Impediments to Trade in Telecommunication Services, in Christopher Findlay and Tony Warren (eds), *Impediments to Trade in Services: Measurement and Policy Implications*, Routledge, New York, pp. 101-118.

Triantes, S.G. (1953), Economic Progress, Occupational Redistribution and International Terms of Trade, *Economic Journal*, Vol. 63, pp. 627-637.

Tucker, Ken and Mark Sundberg (1988), *International Trade in Services*, Routledgfe, New York.

U.N.O. (1968), *A System of National Accounts Studies in Methods*, Series F.No. 2 Rev. 3.

U.N.O. (1970), *Basic Principles of System of Balances of National Economy*, Series F. No. 17 Rev. 1.

U.N.O. (1993), *System of National Accounts*, Washington, U.S.A.

Udall, A.T. (1976), The Effects of Rapid Increases in Labour Supply on Service Employments in Developing Countries, *Economic Development and Culture Charge*, Vol. 24(4), pp. 611–625.

United Nations (1971), *Basic Principles of the System of Balance of the National Economy—Studies in Methods*, Series F. No. 17, United Nations, New York.

United Nations Conferences on Trade and Development (2004), *World Investment Report. The Shift Towards Services*, United Nations, NY and Geneva.

UNO (1979), *Draft Manual on Public Sector Statistics*, ST/ESA/STAT.85/ Rev.1.

Urquhart, M. (1988), The Service Industry: Is it Recession-proof, *Monthly Labour Review*, Oct, 12-18.

Vance, J. (1986), *Capturing the Horizon: The Historical Geography of Transportation Since the Revolution of Sixteenth Century*, Harper and Row, New York.

Veblen Thorstein (1961), Industrial and Pecuniary Employment, in *The Place of Science in Modern Civilization*, Rousell and Rousell, New York, pp. 279-323.

Viner Jacob (1949), Bentham and J.S. Mills, The Utilitarian Background, *American Economic Review*, Vol. 42, pp. 360-382.

Vogel, Harold L. (2001), *Entertainment Industry Economics*, Cambridge University Press, U.S.A. Fifth Edition.

Walker, R. (1985), "Technological Determination and Determinism" in M.Castells (ed) *High Technology, Space and Society*, Sage Bevely Hill, pp 226-64.

Walker, R. and D. Greenberg (1982), Post-industrialism and Political Reforms in City—A Critique, *Antipode* Vol. 14(1), pp. 17-32.

Warf, Barney (1989), Telecommunication and the Globalization of Financial Services, *Professional Geographer*, Vol. 41(3), pp. 257-271.

Warren, Tony (1997), The Political Economy of Reforms of Japanese Service Industries, Pacific Economic Papers 270, Australian National University, Canberra.

Warren Tony (1998), The Political Economy of Telecommunications Trade and Investment Policy, in S. Macdonald and G. Madden (eds), *Telecommunications and Socio-Economic Development*, Elsvier, Amsterdam.

Warren, Tony (2001), The Application of the Frequency Approach to Trade in Telecommunication Services, in Christopher, Findley and Tony Warren (eds), *To Trade in Services Measurements and Policy Implication*, Routledge N.Y.

Warren, Tony and Christopher Findley (2000) Measuring Impediments to Trade in Services, in Pierre Sauve and Robert M. Stern (eds) *GATS 2000, New Directions in Services Trade and Liberalization*, Brookings Institution Press, Washington D.C.

Weitzman, Martin, L. (1971), On the Welfare Significance of National Products in a Dynamic Economy, *Quarterly Journal of Economics*, Vol. 90, pp. 156-162.

Williamson, O.E. (1970), *Corporate Control and Business Behaviour*, Prentice Hall, Engleword Cliffs N.J.

Wiser, William Heridrick (1936), *Hindu Jajmani System*, Lucknow Publishing House, Lucknow.

Womack J.P. *et al* (1990), *Machines that Changed the World—The Story of Lean production*, Rawson Association, U.S.A.

Womack, J.P. and D.J. Jones (1996), *Lean Thinking—Banish Waste in Your Corporation*, Simon and Schuster, New York.

Wood, P.A. (1991), Flexible Accumulation and the Rise of Business Services, *Transactions, Institute of British Geographers*, Vol. 16, pp. 160-172.

Woronoff, J. (1983), *Japan's Wasted Workers*, Allen held and Osmun, Totowa, N.J.

Worton, David A. (1969), Service Industries in Canada 1946-66, in V.R. Fuchs (ed) (1969), *Production and Productivity in Service Industries*, N.B.E.R. N.Y., pp. 237-281.

Wright, Ronald (2000), *Stolen Continents—A Conquest and Resistence in the Americas*, Phoenix Press, London.

INDEX

D

E

F

J

K

L

M

N

T

U

V